RAISING
YOUR CHILD
ASTROLOGICALLY

MARIA COMFORT

EMPOWER
P   R   E   S   S

GracePoint Matrix, LLC
322 N Tejon St. #207
Colorado Springs CO 80903
www.GracePointMatrix.com
Email: Admin@GracePointMatrix.com
SAN # 991-6032

Library of Congress Control Number: 2021900374

ISBN-13: (Paperback) #978-0-9976035-9-0
eISBN: (eBook) #978-1-951694-21-0

Books may be purchased for educational, business, or sales promotional use.
For bulk order requests and price schedule contact:
Orders@GracePointPublishing.com

Printed in the United States of America

TABLE OF CONTENTS

PART ONE

Part Two

Part Three

Part Four

ACKNOWLEDGMENTS

I'd like to take this opportunity to thank Michelle Vandepas and the entire staff at GracePoint Publishing for making this book available. With her undaunted encouragement and no nagging, we were able to get this book to print in record time.

I would also like to thank my wonderful son, David Comfort, for all the graphic work he has contributed to this book. Without his help, the dynamic would be missing.

During the years, I have had the pleasure of being astrologer to many people throughout the world. I wish to thank them for their amazing insight and help in understanding the ups and downs of their individual lives.

There are many astrologers throughout the world, and it has been my privilege to study with some of the greatest ones.

I would also like to mention my many amazing and interesting clients. From them, I have learned much.

There are many different elements and circumstances that make an astrological chart poignant. From my dear friends in this field of study and from the many clients who have come along the way, my understanding has been greater.

I hope you, the reader, enjoy this book as much as I have enjoyed writing it. It may not have your idea of what you may expect, but it definitely is a good place to start and a guideline as to understanding that youngster.

Good luck and God Bless.
Maria Comfort
mariacom@pacbell.net

"It is easier to build strong children than it is to repair broken adults." Frederick Douglass

INTRODUCTION

I've never seen a smiling child look ugly. By nature, all children are beautiful and pure. After we get hold of their little psyches, however. . . there are a few changes. If you worry about your child, remember most of his/her deeds come naturally. You can guide with love and teach this wonderful gift of life to smile. It is simple and the joy it brings increases everywhere you go!

Over five thousand years ago, the Sudanese charted the skies and Astrology as we know it today was born. It is quite possible that for thousands of years before the charts were recorded the study was in practice. Ancient Alien Theorists believe the study was brought to the earth by Aliens. However it got here, the study is one of the oldest on Earth!

We know the Egyptians used Astrology and made beautiful charts of the skies. The Greeks and the Romans gave the constellations, as we know them: myths, gods, and titles. The Aztecs and the Mayans made their famous calendars and in India, Astrology has been used for thousands of years. The one thing about all of these exercises is that they had a common theme or denominator. Thus, we have Astrology - the study of the stars and how they affect our lives and personalities.

The Chinese assign animals to each of twelve years and their prediction phases are for periods of up to ten years. Their system is different from the rest of the world in that they use annual signs and then proceed from date, etc. They also use and give signs and titles to the hours and months. The months are counted in Moons (i.e., the fifth Moon after the Chinese New Year). The date for the Chinese New Year changes each year. It always falls between January 21 and February 20 and is determined by the Chinese lunar calendar.

In the northern hemisphere, the spring, or vernal, equinox happens around March 21 when the sun seems to move north across the celestial equator (in actuality, it is the Earth moving). The autumnal equinox occurs around September 22nd when the sun (as we see it) crosses the celestial equator going south. That is when the beginning of spring occurs in the Southern Hemisphere and the beginning of Autumn happens in the Northern Hemisphere.

In Tropical Astrology, the constellations were the guidelines giving us signs designated most popularly by the Romans and Greeks. Each sign has the name of either a Roman God (adopted from the Greek) and/or an Animal outlined by the star formation. Each planet has been designated to one of the constellations. As an example, Aries the constellation (and the Greek god of War), is ruled by Mars, the Roman god of War. What that means astrologically is that the Aries sign is designated as warrior-like, assertive and one with initiative.

As we look at these constellations and blinking stars, we may see a constant light. That light is usually a planet. Depending on its distance from the Sun, it has a slow or faster orbit. Mercury and Venus are closer to the Sun than Earth is. Therefore, their orbits are faster. Venus is close to the Earth and therefore is very bright in the sky. However, Jupiter is also very bright and is a greater distance from the Sun and the Earth. It is so large that its reflection is also quite bright in the evening sky. The planet Mercury, closest to the Sun, is a smaller planet and not as bright to our eyes. Mars, on the other hand, has a reddish hue to it.

Recent discoveries on the planet Mars show us that it is indeed a "red" planet.

The planets in our Solar System from the Sun are Mercury, Venus, Earth, Mars, Jupiter, Saturn, Neptune, Uranus, and Pluto, in that order. To date, life, such as ours, has not been discovered on any other planet of our Solar System. All these names (with the exception of Earth) are names of Roman and Greek gods. As an example, Mercury, the Roman Messenger, is the Greek god Hermes.

It doesn't make sense that there are only twelve types of people in the world. Of course, there are not. But the commonality of sun signs is amazingly accurate. Where, though?

We will attempt to show you in this book about the beginnings. Little children are essentially developing egos. Initially, they are not emotional (they are born with pure love), and they are not seeking careers or life partners. Children are simply establishing their own personalities.

The Sun Sign in an astrological chart shows the initial identity of the young person. Before moving forward, the child displays the characteristics of the sun sign, the development of the ego.

Time of birth is also important because it gives some insight into where the emphasis is in the child's life. Where the Sun is in relationship to the time of day s/he was born tells the Rising Sign. The Rising Sign in a chart shows how one approaches life. Part of this book is dedicated to the twenty-four-hour clock and the baby's Sun Sign in conjunction with the Rising Sign.

Houses: In general, these rules apply: Born from midnight to 2 a.m., The sun is usually in the third house. From 2 a.m. to 4 a.m., it is in the second House. From 4 a.m. to 6 a.m., the first house. And so on around the wheel. The wheel looks like a clock in that it is round. The time of day or night in which the child is born follows accordingly. There are twelve houses in an astrological chart and each house has a significance.

THE HOUSES AND WHAT THEY SIGNIFY

House	Significance	Comment
First	Approach to Life/ Physical appearance	Me, Me, Me
(4 a.m. to 6 a.m.)		"It's all about me"
Second (2 a.m. to 4 a.m.)	Values/Possessions	I want, I have "What did you get me?"
Third House	Communications/ Short Trips	Talk to me, take me
(Midnight to 2 a.m.)		"Let's go!"
Fourth House (10 p.m. to Midnight)	Foundations in life	I need a home "I like it here."

Fifth House	Love/Romance/ children	Look at me!!
(8 p.m. to 10 p.m.)		"Let's have fun!
Sixth House	Service to others/ Health	I can do it!
(6 p.m. to 8 p.m.)		"It's okay. I'll fix it!"
Seventh House (4 p.m. to 6 p.m.)	Contracts/Partnership	You're mine, I'm yours "Be my partner!"
Eighth House	Death and Benefits	I'll take care of your money
(2 p.m. to 4 p.m.)		"You can trust me!"
Ninth House	Higher Learning/ Philosophy	I need to know more
(Noon to 2 p.m.)		"Teach me more!"
Tenth House	How the World Sees You/Career	It's my reputation
(10 a.m. to Noon)		"What will they say?"
Eleventh House	Hopes and Wishes/ Friends	I'll be your friend
(8 a.m. to 10 a.m.)		"When I grow up . . ."
Twelfth House (6 a.m. to 8 a.m.)	Secrets and Wisdom	I'll keep your secrets "Don't tell anyone . . ."

The times above are general times. More detailed times are given and could still be off depending on where the child is born. You will find included in this book times that are generalized. Daylight Savings Times are included for your convenience. In a few cases, there are no times listed as the rising sign may dominate a particular house. In that event, I still added additional information for other rising signs should your child be born in an area where it is possible.

Enjoy your read and remember that kindness and respect go a long way when raising your child–astrologically or not.

You can go online and get a copy of your child's chart (and your own, for that matter). That will give you the Rising sign, the Moon's placement, as well as all the other planets. In this book, we will discuss the Sun Sign and its relationship to the Rising Sign.

PART ONE

Astrology is an age-old study and recent reports reveal that more than one-third of our world believes in its use. Mind you, it is not a religion, it is a science. Astrology is uncanny in its accuracy but more often than not, the infallibility is learned in retrospect. The reason, of course, lies with the interpretation.

As an astrologer, I have found that there are many alternatives in every chart. How a person reacts to the planets today is best understood from the knowledge of the past. It is said that history repeats itself and this is true of human nature. Most often we repeat patterns to avoid venturing into the unknown. No matter how wretched a situation, we find a point of comfort in the familiar and bemoan our fate.

The use of Astrology as a tool and guideline is not against any lessons we learn in our Religious training. This book is not a book of prediction but is written to show personality strengths and weaknesses of character, which can be developed or overcome with good parenting.

Astrology tells us when we will have those opportunities to repeat certain patterns in our lives. It is at these times that we have the freedom to make the changes that will enhance the future.

Astrology can also give you the timing of events. As an example, your chart could show that this is a time to learn new lessons. You can choose to go to school and learn the lessons you want to learn, or you can let the Universe teach them to you. With the former, you elect your lessons. With the latter, the lessons come to you. In either case, you will learn new lessons.

Children are not clones of their parents but rather reflections of the reactions they have to the way they have been treated. Every parent who has more than one child knows that each child acts differently in given situations. Each parent who has a "problem" child, reacts differently to the child from the way a "good" child is handled. This is human nature.

And yet, we ask ourselves questions as to why "Suzi" can't be as well-behaved as "Eddie". Or why "David" doesn't have his father's interest in sports or "Tami" her mother's talent in music.

In astrology, the Sun sign represents the development of the ego. Most children behave within the realm of their Sun signs until they develop an individual personality. Children display the characteristics of their individual sun signs until they develop an identity, usually at puberty. In this book, we will explore the Sun signs, in conjunction with the times of birth. This will give more information about the developmental potential of the child. We will look at the needs, the strengths, the weaknesses, and most of all, the potential of the child as shown by the Sun sign. A good example would be Sarah and Emily. Born four minutes apart, these twin girls have different "rising signs." Until they were about nine, they were two apples from the same tree. By the time they turned eleven they were so different that in spite of the fact that they are "identical" twins, Sarah is taller than Emily who is more filled out than her twin.

There are times when boys and girls act unlike one another. However, if in the early years they are treated without prejudice to sex, they will still make their own identities and assume more masculine or feminine roles after their formative years. Therefore, I have chosen to keep this book in a *unisex* mode. From time to time, I will note a difference but for the most part, the impact will be the same.

Once we know more about the way a child's ego begins to develop, it gives a better handle on rearing the child and setting him/her on the right path. With knowledge, love, patience, and understanding, your child can grow with healthy self-esteem, kindness and respect. I mention with each sign the sensitive part of the body associated with that sign. If your child has frequent injuries to that part of the body, your little one is saying, "PAY ATTENTION!"

Please remember that this approach is strictly from the Sun sign and then the Rising Sign; there are many other facets that will alter the analyses. However, you can be assured that it's a very good place to start.

The calculations may be different where your child was born but these times were generally calculated from mid-United States.

When reading this, you may find that there are descriptions for the Rising Sign at a given time, you can go and learn more about your child's approach to life by reading about the sign your child has as a Rising Sign (or Ascendant). For example, if your child is a Taurus with Capricorn rising, go to Capricorn as well to learn more. There are also many astrology sites online that will give you the information in regard to the rising sign and house where the sun is located on a chart. Many sites will actually give you chart information for free. You can use these charts to know the exact house in which the sun sits and the true Rising Sign of your little one.

This book is based on Tropical Astrology. Tropical Astrology is based on the Earth's relationship to the Sun and the relationship of planets to the Earth and the Sun. That means the first day of spring is the first day of Aries even though the stars have shifted in the sky. The Galaxy moves at an approximate rate of 50 seconds per year and although that seems minimal, after 2000 years, we are currently in the "Age of Aquarius"! That means that the first day of Spring, the Sun is in line with Aquarius and not Aries. In spite of that, because the charts were first mapped over 4000+ years ago, we use Tropical Astrology, or calculations, according to our Sun and the planets' movement around this Star and the relationships to our planet, Earth.

For the sake of this book, the times may be off for the area of your child's chart. Therefore, you are encouraged to look at the descriptions before and after the one that is designated in the following pages. Although there is an attempt for accuracy, a child born in Australia will have a different rising time from a child born in the United States. These times were calculated from Chicago and San Francisco and may be a bit different from say, Los Angeles.

When interpretations were first made, they were learned observations. The more and more scientific we become, the more we return to the basics and those early interpretations and guidelines.

Children are usually born with good instincts and good morals. They are open to learning and can become clones so please do watch your manners!

As a rule, children who are born from sunset to sunrise are supportive of others. They are the directors and producers. They are the writers and the Atlases who hold up the other half of the population.

Those born between sunrise and sunset are the ones who are more noticed and who are held up by the others. If your child is going to be a star, chances are that s/he was born during the daylight hours.

There are many other factors to determine this "ruling," however, this is a general overall look.

One child I know has a tenth house Moon in Leo. This child was born to be a star, no matter where the sun. There are many exceptions in a chart and no one "rule" can be applied. However, in this book, we can give you the most common explanations of how your child can be guided best using just the sun sign and the rising sign (which comes from the time of birth!)

THE THREE TYPES
OF SIGNS

T here are three types of astrological signs: Cardinal, Fixed, and Mutable. We will discuss these three types and what they signify.

The Cardinal Signs

The Cardinal Signs are Aries, Cancer, Libra, and Capricorn. The Cardinal sign person is an initiator. They enjoy beginning new things, new projects. Although these endeavors don't necessarily see an end, the venture is begun. The Aries is usually the first to start something and then drop it. This is often something that can be sold. The Cancer may continue the project even after beginning it, even though interest was long lost. These projects are usually things which will bring creature comforts. The Libran begins something artistic but may be dissatisfied that it isn't lovely enough and drop the project for that reason. The Capricorn has the most tenacity and as long as s/he can be the boss, may see the project to the end.

The Fixed Signs

The Fixed Signs are Taurus, Leo, Scorpio and Aquarius. The Fixed sign personality is tenacious. Once they have found their niche, the fixed signs will usually hang in there. In early development, the Fixed sign child will hold on to an idea or an ideal and see it to its end. The Taurus personality usually needs to gather things and will have collections of sorts. The Leo will find a way to entertain you, either by performance or athletics. The Scorpio has a strong need to investigate things and will want many answers. This child is the "hound dog" of the zodiac. The Aquarius will take the rules you give to heart and carry them to adulthood; conversely, this same child will push barriers to the limit trying to stretch the same rules as far as possible.

The Mutable Signs

The Mutable Signs are Gemini, Virgo, Sagittarius and Pisces. The Mutable sign person usually wants to go with the flow. Flexible and inventive, mutable sign personalities do not develop stubbornness at an early age. The Gemini child can walk and chew gum at the same time. This child will seldom be absorbed in one thing at a time and usually needs to be listening to music or the television while pursuing another project. The Virgo child is very methodical and looks for all the details. This child will usually pull a toy apart upon receiving it to see how it works. The Sagittarius child is adventurous and usually wants to be set apart from the others. This is usually done in dress, wearing an unusual piece of clothing that stands out. The Pisces child is the most sensitive of them all. Taking in all that surrounds him/her, this child goes with the flow but keeps to heart everything s/he learns.

THE ELEMENTS

In Astrology, there are four elements. They are Fire, Earth, Air, and Water. Fire needs Air to keep the flame going, and Earth needs Water to keep it nourished. Air feeds fire, and water feeds the earth.

The Fire Signs

The Fire Signs are Aries, Leo and Sagittarius. Often thought of as "a pistol" or aggressive.

Your Fire Sign child will want to be first! Keeping you on your toes, this bundle of energy will often challenge you. The phrase, "Catch me if you can" likely came from a Fire-sign child. You will see signs of your little one at an early age kicking and calling out for more of anything and everything. They want attention.

The Earth Signs

The Earth Signs are Taurus, Virgo and Capricorn. You've heard the saying, "Down to earth." This applies to these signs.

These are the children who seem to be deep in thought most of the time. They are practical and pragmatic. They understand most things quite clearly and you need only tell them once and they will retain it.

The Air Signs

The Air Signs are Gemini, Libra and Aquarius—Sometimes thinking of things in faraway places, while you are trying hard to show them something else.

This child is already on to the next subject before you have finished talking about the matter at hand. They nod and nod while their little minds are churning away at the next subject and an opportunity to start. Once a subject is finished and understood, this child does not want to be nagged to death. *On to the next* is his/her motto!

The Water Signs

The Water Signs are: Cancer, Scorpio and Pisces. These sensitive souls are often intuitive.

Your water sign baby will sense the environment. If you have fear or anxiety, your little bundle of joy will feel your emotions and respond in kind. If you are happy and laughing, listen to the gurgling sound emanating from your precious child. This is especially true of the Water Sign child but can also be attributed in general to most children.

THE PLANETS AND
WHAT THEY SIGNIFY

Sun   Ego/describes the father
Moon   Emotion/describes the mother
Mercury   Conscious Mind/Short trips
Venus   Where the Heart is/balance and beauty
Mars   Energy/entertainment/athleticism
Jupiter   Expansion/makes things seems larger
Saturn   Discipline/teaching or learning
Uranus   Change–freedom /follows the rules
Neptune   Dreams/intuition
Pluto   Power/where there is the most

THE WHEEL

T he Wheel of the Chart looks like a Pie. It is round and is always divided into 12 houses. Each of these houses represents a part of one's life.

The First House

This house describes the appearance of the individual. It also tells of one's approach to life. The first thing you look for the sign on the cusp (the Ascendant) and you can describe that sign and give someone a description of the individual. Next, you look to see which planets are in that house and you use them further to describe the individual.

The Second House

This house describes the values of the individual. It also describes how one feels towards his/her possessions. Planets in this house further describe the disposition of valuables and values.

The Third House

How does one communicate? This house shows how someone is in early years in school. It also describes one's siblings. For example, if there is the planet Venus in that house, there is likely to be a sister. If the Moon is in the third house, your individual has usually been mothered by an older sibling or is more of a mother to younger siblings.

The Fourth House

One's basic Foundations in life. This describes the home and often describes home-life in early childhood. The Fourth house will also describe part of the end of life of the individual (as will the eighth and twelfth houses).

The Fifth House

This is the House of Entertainment and of Children. When a child, this house describes what entertains the individual. When an adult, this house describes the children of the individual.

The Sixth House

Work and Service to other people, also your health, are the markers of the chart. This can describe your job but not necessarily your career. Insofar as your health is concerned, it will show by the planets in that house. Certain planets denote disease, pain, suffering, etc. These can all be eliminated by using those planets in that house as tools in service to others. As an example, Neptune in the sixth house can denote the disease of Cancer or other mysterious diseases. However, if the person does metaphysical work or tends to someone who needs spiritual support and/or who may have a peculiar disease, they fulfill the aspect of the planet.

The Seventh House

Describes your partner, in marriage and/or business. Anyone you make a partner, even in crime, is described in the seventh house. It also describes you as a partner, should you have any planets in this house.

The Eighth House

Death, Taxes and Other People's Money. This doesn't speak just of your own death, but it speaks to your understanding of death. This is also the house where you find the propensity to receive money and gifts from others, whether or not you are a beneficiary. Those who receive scholarships usually have planets in this house or Sagittarius on the cusp.

The Ninth House

House of Higher Education and things Foreign. The house of judges, the house of Philosophy. Great Philosophers usually have a lot of action in this house. Professors and Judges have strong ninth houses. Travel to foreign countries is indicated by planets in this house. It is also a good indication when Mercury or Jupiter are located in the Ninth House that languages come easily.

The Tenth House

Your Reputation and how the world sees you is denoted by the Tenth House. In order to gain fame, one usually needs to have one or more of these in this house: Sun, Moon, Jupiter, Saturn. These are the charts that make people famous.

The Eleventh House

This is the house of Hopes and Wishes and of your friendship relationships. This describes the types of friends you seek out and who makes you most comfortable.

The Twelfth House

The house of Hidden Secrets. Often times, if someone has a Personal Planet in the 12th house that person is the keeper of secrets. If Venus is there, there was probably a secret love affair.

YOUR CHILD'S
APPEARANCE AND
PHYSICAL AILMENTS

A s mentioned before, the first house identifies your child's appearance. When born, most children look the same (wrinkled and red). As they begin to develop, one will see a resemblance to a parent or other close relative.

Aries rising children are usually fair. They oftentimes have a great deal of energy and go darting from spot to spot. They are usually easy to lose, as they are busy checking out new horizons and adventures. If unhappy with his/her approach to life, this child could get headaches or earaches.

Taurus rising children are usually lovely and their voices are easily distinguished. They may have a firm attitude (also known as stubborn), but this can also be considered determination, and your little one can do anything if his/her mind is set to it. You can sing to them all day long and they will love it and try to imitate you. They are excellent at mimic, especially using their voices. If unhappy with his/her approach to life, your Taurus-rising child could develop sore throats.

Gemini rising children are usually smiling. They are able to walk and chew gum at the same time and also love puzzles. If not satisfied with his/her approach to life, your Gemini child could develop chest colds and other lung-related problems like coughing.

Cancer rising children are often times moody and tender-hearted. They are champions for the underdog and for putting things right. Little Cancer-rising girls often develop early (reach puberty). If unhappy with the way things are going, your Cancer-rising child could get stomach-aches.

Leo rising children often have a widow's peak (that's hair shaped into a 'V' at the top of the forehead). These children love to be noticed and to entertain. When unhappy with his/her approach to life, they may complain that their hearts are racing or that they have chest pains. They could mention their racing hearts.

Virgo rising children love details. They sometimes hold back an opinion until they are certain that what they say is right. Digestive problems are usually an indication of a not-so-happy Virgo-rising child. If they throw up a lot or have problems digesting their food, there is usually a problem with how they are approaching life.

Libra rising children usually have even features. They are harmonious in nature and enjoy art and music. Should there be any organ (kidney, liver, pancreas) problem, your Libra-rising child is unhappy with his/her approach to life.

Scorpio rising children are often intense and have sensual features. They ask "why" a lot and can delve into the unknown quickly. Constipation or rectal disorders mean your child is not happy with the way things are going.

Sagittarius rising children love to dress up and embellish their appearance. Often, they have long legs. Many times, they will select an unusual piece of clothing as a signature piece and wear it often (could be daily!). My legs or hips hurt are usually an indication of an unhappy child with Sagittarius rising.

Capricorn rising children often have a firm jaw. They put themselves in charge of others around themselves. They can be bossy. If you are going to the dentist early with this child or his/her bones ache or knees hurt, s/he is unhappy with his/her approach to life.

Aquarius rising children want rules. It is what holds them together! They are often even featured and quite beautiful to look at. They insist that everything is "fair." Weak ankles are a good indication that your little one is not happy with the way things are going.

Pisces rising children often have long eyelashes and/or big eyes. There is a dreamy look about your Pisces-rising child, that makes him/her look as though s/he is in another world. Should your Pisces-rising child have sore feet or other problems with his/her feet, this child is not happy with his/her approach to life.

When using this book, please know that the calculations are approximate and done from Middle America. If you go online, you can usually find a site that will calculate your child's (or your own) chart and give you the Sun, Moon, and Rising signs.

For the sake of this book, we will use definitions of the sun's relationship to the Rising Sign from its house.

The section entitled "The Wheel" may give you more perspective if you are calculating the entire chart.

PART TWO

YOUR FIXED SIGN CHILD - TAURUS/ LEO/SCORPIO/ AQUARIUS

Stubborn? Willful? Surely these are words that have been applied to those born under the signs of Taurus, Leo, Scorpio, and Aquarius. If, instead, these words were changed into *determined, stalwart,* and *tenacious,* your child would have a more positive self-image. Fixed sign children seem to walk around with blinders on. If they do not learn to like themselves, they become adults with blinders on and could be fifty-six before they finally mellow.

A friend of mine has parents who are both fixed signs. Throughout their marriage they have had a silent relationship. Her mother would not speak to her father for months. They both continued on this path of punishment to one another over the years. Rather than communicate, they would clam up. My friend's father had learned that if he did not say anything, he couldn't cause any trouble. Her mother was of the opinion that when she was angry, the best way to treat it was with silence until the anger or the problem went away. By the time they would speak, the problem usually did go away, only because no one remembered the reason for the silence in the first place.

I am happy to report that after forty years of marriage, they have discovered that they like one another and have been enjoying each other's company a great deal. You could say that it was the tenacity that kept them together. Again, each was too stubborn to end the marriage and give the other the satisfaction. Or, the love was so deep and strong, they finally realized that it was there. But they were resolute. These fixed signs wasted many years in silence for the same reasons they were silent as children—no one taught them to communicate.

The time of your child's birth gives additional understanding into his/her needs and what area of your child's life is important to him/her.

It is a good idea to remember to deduct one hour for daylight-savings-time (i.e. if your child was born at 8:41 PDT, subtract one hour and use 7:41). On the other hand, this book includes DST (Daylight Savings Time) calculations. Therefore, if the birth certificate says 9:00 a.m. in August, it is usually Daylight Savings Time. You can take it from there. Calculations are done on a computer and still give the true rising sign.

If the time is close to the hour, it is possible that the definition prior to or following the one given will apply. Also, if your child is born in a very northerly area or in a very southern hemisphere, the same may apply. There are times when the Sun may be in the tenth house but the description for the Ninth House Sun may be more applicable. In that event, just read the other description.

Without further ado, let's explore the nature of your fixed sign child:

TAURUS

This child of beauty and love needs to touch and feel. You will find that your child will have a favorite blanket or furry animal toy to caress when in a state of contemplation or of frustration. These props will soothe their nerves.

These children also love sugar and sweets. If you want your little one to be healthy, you know what to do. When keeping the sweets as a reward, you actually benefit your Taurus child by teaching good habits.

These children are very passionate about their feelings toward one of their parents. They have a strong need to love and be loved by "Mommy" or "Daddy" and will try to gain acceptance in every way possible. The one thing this child needs is a great deal of affection from his/her parents. It may seem at first that your child rejects you and your attention but in fact, you are being tested to see if you can be trusted and if you will still be there. When your Taurus child trusts you, you will receive a lot of affection from him/her. However, it is up to you to give the affection first. They want it, they need it, they need to learn it.

"Please don't throw me away," may be a phrase you hear from your Taurus child. When your little one finds something no longer of use, s/he will get rid of it. If it seems you are angry, s/he will not want to be discarded in the same way. It is important to teach your Taurus that relationships can be forever and to be valued and that sins are to be forgiven or your child will live a lonely life for want of acceptance and a sense of unworthiness.

With strong moral principles, this child will defend the down-trodden to the death. Beth was five years old and in a department store with her mother. When another woman came rushing through the store dragging her small, screaming, two-year-old, Beth walked up to the woman and tugged at her sleeve. "Excuse me," she said to the mother, "but you shouldn't treat little children like that." The woman, of course, was embarrassed as she looked around. She then picked up the child and gently wiped his tears away. Beth's action is typically Taurus.

Your Taurus child believes what s/he is taught and has an especially high code of ethics. Values are a key word when raising this child. If you show your child that something is dear or precious, your child will cherish it.

Your Taurus child has the memory of an elephant. Don't make a promise you cannot keep, or you'll find *that* to be a part of his/her behavior. Your standards are their standards until they reach the age of seven. At that time, they will look around and see if their ideals meet yours.

They value their reputation and usually believe that their looks and wardrobe play an important part in how people see them. Oftentimes, the clothes they put together may seem unusual to you, but you will see pride in your child's eyes. They love to borrow your jewels or other decorative ornaments to wear and show to their friends. Sons will bring your most prized possession to school to proudly display. Don't be surprised by stray pets being brought home.

Money is very important to this child. If your child thinks you are poor, you child will be poor in spirit. If you allow your child to know that there is always enough and that more can be earned, your little one will be happy to earn and will have self-esteem. In this way, you can teach your child the value of money and also teach him/her how to earn and save money. If you tell this little "bull" that s/he can earn the new scooter, watch the work s/he will do. The scooter will then become very valuable and your child's self-image will grow.

Sometimes your Taurus child may seem selfish. This is only due to the fear that an item cannot or will not be replaced. If, however, they thought another item could be earned, you will witness a great deal of generosity. Conversely, your son or daughter may become overly benevolent and you have the other problem of replacing many things. It is up to you to determine a way to teach compromise.

Your Taurean has a good deal of common sense and an ability to reduce ideas to their logical denominator. Many times, you will be surprised at how astute and how much awareness exists in that little head.

Don't be surprised if you feel nagged to death by your Taurus child. They do believe that you can be worn down, and often times, parents can be pushed into making the easier decision. It is better to explain in full your reason for a denial at the beginning of the question than it is to say, "NO." This is a hard word for the Taurus to understand. Like the bull, s/he will stand there and snort, stare, and prepare for the attack. If you, however, take the time out in the beginning to explain that there is a perfectly good rationalization for your "no", then your child will go easier on you. There may be anger or hurt but at least there will be understanding.

This child responds very negatively to nagging. If you want to inspire your little one, say it once. What you say is heard. If you have to nag, you have lost control. Your Taurus child does pay attention and responds to nagging by ignoring you altogether. However, your Taurus is usually born with the "nagging" gene. It is up to you to teach this wonderful little one that you won't be broken down and that you heard the first time what was said!

Oftentimes, people accuse the Taurus of being a fighter. It is true that your child will be able to display anger like no one else you know. But listen and you will hear that the fury is usually indignation toward an injustice being done. If your Venus-ruled child believes that something is unfair, you will have an angry Bull on your hands.

Your youngster has a strong need to be noticed and usually will demand that attention in his/her voice. Either screams or bellows will call you to them. It is important to teach them early how to temper their volumes. Of course, your own example is the best. You cannot scream at a child to "quiet down". If your little one sees a good response and attention gained when speaking softly, then your eardrums will have less of a chance of being broken by his/her volume.

After the age of seven, you will see that your Taurus child will display keen intelligence, desire, and ambition to achieve the better things in life. With your encouragement, better grades can be earned, as well as a richer life in school. Your child will also want to bring home friends and a lovely home will be important. This doesn't mean you must live in a mansion. It does mean that your child should not have to be embarrassed when inviting friends home. A neat house and a private area for your young one to entertain is sufficient.

Taurus children love sweets and remember the person who brought them their last piece of candy, cake, etc. This is another moderation necessary early in your child's life or later on poor eating habits could become a problem and difficulties with weight control could lead to unhappiness and ridicule from peers. Again, this leads to a poor self-image.

Your Taurus child should be encouraged to sing and use his/her throat in a positive manner. You should keep their necks warm in cold weather, as this is a sensitive part of their bodies. Oftentimes, a sore throat is a sign that the ego is hurting. If your little one complains of a sore throat, take the time to find out if anything else if bothering him/her. Their feelings may have been hurt at school or by a sibling. Your child's health can be an indication to you of how his/her ego is developing.

Your child may seem like a slow starter in the beginning. It is only because s/he want to be sure of doing things the right way before forging ahead. Once confidence is gained, watch out as your young one repeats and perfects his/her new-found talents.

These children are usually born beautiful with even features. Colors are important to your Taurus child. Yellow-orange, turquoise, peaches, and bright blues are especially good colors on them.

TAURUS - *Midnight to 1 a.m.*
Fourth house–Capricorn rising

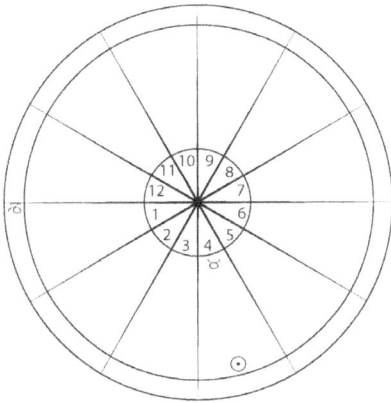

Control is the key word here. You may feel that your child is willing to assume countless responsibilities and you may feel inclined to give more responsibility to this strong little one. Be certain to introduce your child to play during the growing years or you may find a homebody who rules the roost. Ballet is a discipline that your Taurus can enjoy. Sporting activities such as horseback riding, and archery are also very welcome to your child. Any disciplined activity (even dancing) is a welcome activity.

Although the home is very important to him/her, as long as your child knows it's there, your little one may be absent often, busy with other activities. However, if required to stay at home, s/he will busy him/herself making the home comfortable and cozy. A warm environment is very important, and you may find this Taurean in the kitchen trying to cook the next meal.

In spite of the fact that you have a little homemaker on board, don't be surprised if your Taurus child doesn't also have other "important" things to do to occupy his/her time.

TAURUS - *1 a.m. to 2:30 a.m.*
Third house–Aquarius rising

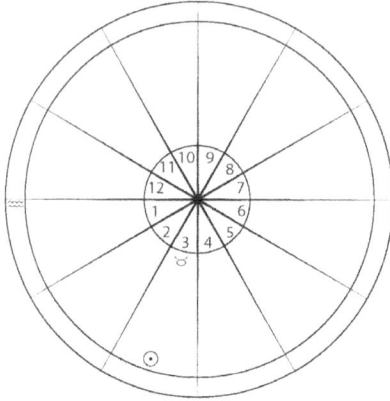

The most important thing you want your Taurus born at this time to know is how far s/he can go. Once you've given the parameters, know that your child is still going to push to see if they can't be a little wider. Rules are very important and once they are laid down, your little one will quote them–especially to his/her advantage. At the same time, if the rules are reasonable, you will find that you will have more cooperation from this child.

Talkative and intelligent, your child may be slow to start but once s/he gets going, nothing will stop him/her. New and unusual ideas interest your little one and at times you may wonder why there is such a fascination with the "bizarre". It is only a great curiosity about the world. Initially, it is the world around him/her but gradually it becomes a greater interest as your child's universe expands.

Your Taurus born at this time enjoys talking. It is important to teach him/her also how to listen. Only in listening will s/he be able to know what s/he is talking about. It is also a good idea to teach this child that a little bit of knowledge doesn't make him/her a college professor. Because they can conceptualize so well and have such great retentive skills, these children sometimes believe they have all the answers when they have only begun to hear the question.

Bob was born with Cerebral Palsy. One would think that it would be a great handicap in his life, but he used it to his own advantage. Rather than feel sorry for himself, he studied everything he could. He told me that he read the encyclopedia three times from cover to cover. (This happened after he beat everyone in a quiz game in two turns). I asked him why he had read it and he said that he didn't want to be lonely or feel sorry for himself when the other children were out playing so he did something constructive.

Bob's only drawback is that with his great intellect, he is easily bored in school. After a few sessions in a college class, he reads the test, doesn't bother to return to the lectures, and has eventually dropped out of most of his classes. It is difficult for him to be sooo verrrry intelligent because he bores easily.

Brothers and sisters are important to your child. An older brother or sister will be like parents to this little one and a younger brother or sister will receive parenting from this child. If your little one is an only child, a best friend will be called a brother or sister and will be treated that way.

The best way to teach this Taurus how to complete projects is to give him/her short projects to start and finish so that they know the satisfaction that comes with accomplishment. Gradually you can increase the projects. As an example, if you told your child to make an entire chess set, the project would not get done; but if you had him/her make one piece at a time, there would soon be an entire set.

TAURUS – *2:30 a.m. to 3 a.m.*
Third house–Pisces rising

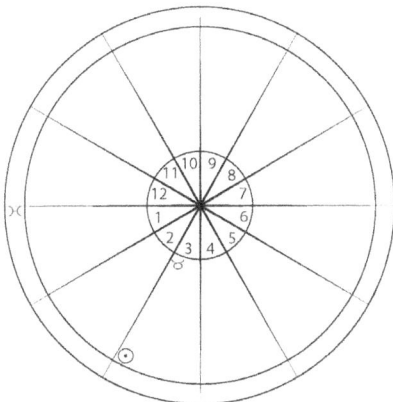

A good student and communicator, this child will ask many questions. This child doesn't want to be an only child and will assume responsibility for a brother or sister, no matter the age. Art and poetry play an important part of your child's creative side, and you can encourage him/her in sculpting and writing.

Your Taurus child born at this time should also want to join chorus classes in school and could also be encouraged to study a musical instrument. S/He should also be good in mathematics. A good traveler, your child will especially enjoy short expeditions.

You will discover that your child has a great deal of sensitivity and creativity. A strong spiritual side is noted here, and your child will want training in a spiritual ideal or endeavor. If you belong to a church or other place of worship, you will discover that this child will want to go, too.

Idealistic and dreamy, sometimes this practical child needs to be stimulated back into reality. It is especially important to teach everything in moderation at the earliest time possible so that your child will be able to see things as they are.

Encourage this Taurean to write. A scrapbook and/or journal will be very useful and help him/her to save memories. In moments of stillness, you may find your little one going through old family albums.

Good grammar goes a long way. Since your intelligent child doesn't want to be embarrassed while communicating, s/he will be grateful that you corrected his/her grammar early on. Communication is an important part of his/her growing up and if s/he doesn't speak well and is criticized for it, s/he will clam up and say nothing at all. This will be very frustrating.

Teach this Taurean to swim. S/he will enjoy the water and water activities all his/her life.

TAURUS - *3 a.m. to 4 a.m.*
Second house–Pisces rising

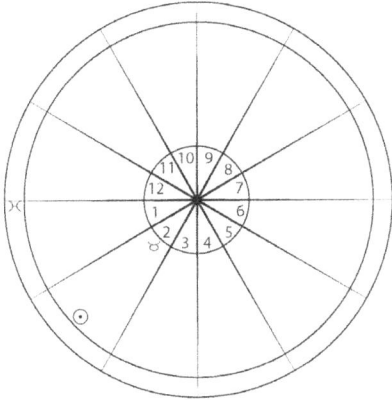

Your Taurean will look for creative ways to earn money and gain possessions. Usually they will want to make something artistic and then sell it. They place value on items that can sometimes seem unrealistic. And yet, their belief in this worth oftentimes pays off. You may be surprised.

Help guide your child to differentiate between the real and unreal aspects of worth. S/he can easily be hoodwinked into believing that a rag is an important piece of cloth. Your child is easily swayed and can be fooled by others who are cannier. They love the overall sense of getting something while doing nothing and must be taught to look at all the options when investing.

Your guileless child needs to be taught about swindling. Until that time, your child can be more the victim rather than the predator. With good moral sense, your little one is less likely to take advantage of others unless taught this trait.

Without a support system in place, this child could show insecurities by constantly looking for approval. It is up to you to let this little Taurus know s/he is valued.

TAURUS
Second House–Aries rising

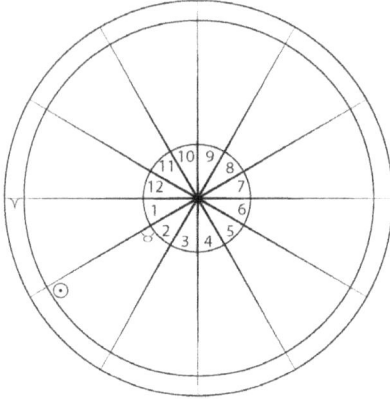

Your little bull is quite strong and a good athlete! You will find a good deal of resilience in your little Taurus and a good deal of introspection.

Your Taurus child wants to fit in and wants to be a part of the big picture. Therefore, it is good when around other peers s/he is a part of the group. S/He will endeavor to be important within his/her surroundings and among those s/he respects.

Tokens of appreciation are valued by your child and awards and certificates that are earned are also important.

It is not a good idea to praise this child for something that s/he did not do or earn. There are athletic events where all the children earn trophies. If your child is a part of one of these groups, the trophy may not be valued. Instead, it will usually be hidden because it was not an "earned reward." It is hard to fool this child.

Your child wants to be valued and rewarded for those accomplishments that took effort and that were well-deserved. Keep that in mind the next time you give a "trophy" for something that wasn't earned or deserved.

TAURUS - *4 a.m. to 5 a.m.*
First house–Aries rising

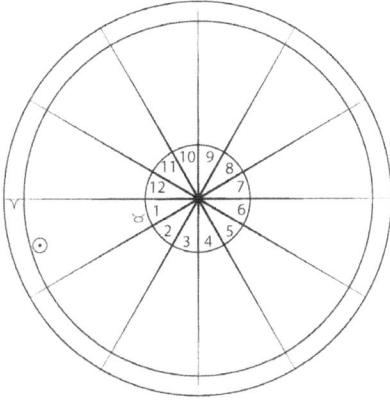

A self-starter, your Taurus child can be quite aggressive. Athletics and sports are wonderful outlets for him/her. A great competitor combined with tenacity will put many trophies on the shelf. The outdoors and fresh air are important to this child and you will find him/her wanting to run out and play at every given opportunity.

Although most Taurus children have persistence, your little one may get bored with projects after they have been started. S/he can be given short-term projects that have completion so that s/he can enjoy the feeling of finishing a project. This will help your child later in life with long-term projects.

Teach this child about following the rules and what is fair and what is not. A sense of team spirit can be instilled at an early age. Gymnastics, track and field, golfing, tennis, and other activities where a trophy is earned on one's own will be good activities for this child. S/he needs to excel and be a star. Techniques taught early in life will carry on to other endeavors for success later.

You can also find that this child is quite competitive.

TAURUS - *5 a.m. to 6 a.m.*
First house–Taurus rising

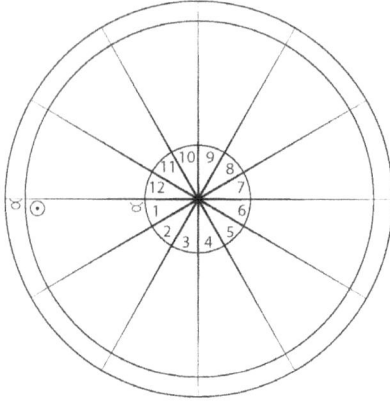

Now you know what the word "stubborn" means. But you will also understand "tenacity" and "determination" in its fullest detail. Give a project to your little one and watch him/her see it through. These children do not bore easily. With single-minded purpose, s/he will finish every task without boredom.

This is a Taurus who needs to sing. And I'm talking voice lessons, here. Control over the voice and a place to put it will help a great deal through life. Her voice won't be strident–his voice won't be booming. When your Taurean knows how to take hold of his/her voice s/he will also be able to temper the storm.

TAURUS - *6 a.m. to 7 a.m.*
Twelfth house–Taurus rising

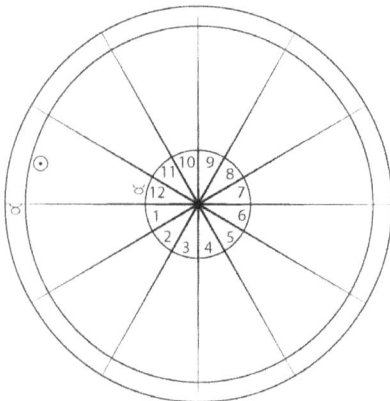

S/He isn't moody–more introspective. It will never be too early to teach your little one to pray or meditate. Your child needs to learn to trust and be trustworthy. Otherwise, you may feel secrets being kept from you. This Taurus child may ask you questions about him/herself. Answer as clearly as you can because your child is processing information.

This is a time when you understand what stubborn is. Your little one could easily clam up rather than tell you something about him/herself that could help you. Your little one could easily withhold information rather than make it easy for you. Do your best to teach this child to communicate and to open up. If that doesn't work, teach him/her to meditate and to journal. Some of these thoughts that are kept within can be put down on paper and it will be easier for this child to learn to communicate.

Sometimes you will notice a desire to open up. It takes a lot of patience and gentleness to get your little one to that point. Rather than badgering this child to tell you what is going on in that little head, encourage their confidence by letting them know that you are there for them when they decide they want to tell you what is going on. Once you have your child's confidence, you will be able to better understand his/her concerns and advise accordingly. This child needs your patience and trust. It will then be returned to you in many ways.

TAURUS - *7 a.m. to 8 a.m.*
Twelfth house–Gemini rising

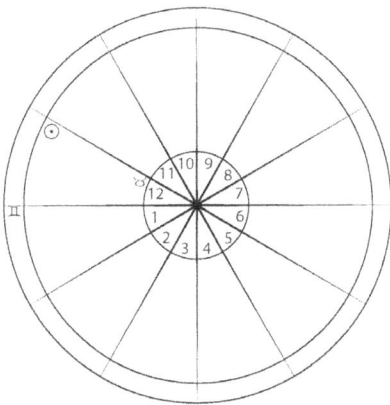

Needs to tell feelings. A need to communicate is essential and yet needs to be learned. Your little one may have a tendency to keep secrets. Although a good communicator, your little one needs to know s/he is being heard. S/he wants to connect with a higher power. S/he is intuitive and understanding and will tell you, "I know . . ." often. Because s/he does know.

Singing lessons will help a lot, especially if your child stutters. Eager to get things out, you may see that the stuttering is from being out of breath because s/he is in a hurry to share information with you. Teach your little one to slow down and that you will still be there.

If your child is quiet and stubbornly clams up, just give it time. S/he cannot stay still and perhaps a key word will open up your little Bull! It is sometimes easier to get this child to open up through laughter. Find that which triggers his/her funny bone and use it to lighten a mood. Your little one will grow healthier habits in later years!

TAURUS - *8 a.m. to 9 a.m.*
Eleventh house–Gemini rising

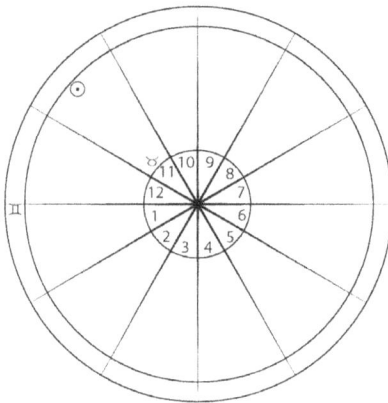

Needs to talk–needs to sing–needs to do it with a chorus. Singing is good for your Taurus and especially in groups. You will find that your Taurus child brings home new "friends." There will always be friends, as this child is very social. Some of these friends can last a lifetime. Others will be the "best friend" for a while, until the next bestie comes along.

Encourage your child to join social groups in school or church or other places where there are gatherings. A social butterfly, your little one will attract many. S/he can learn to discriminate and will likely ask your advice. It is a good idea to teach your little one to learn to tell the difference between real friends and those who have other motives. Encourage talking these things out so that ideas are shared and the ability to tell the difference becomes second nature!

TAURUS - *9 a.m. to 10 a.m.*
Eleventh house–Cancer rising

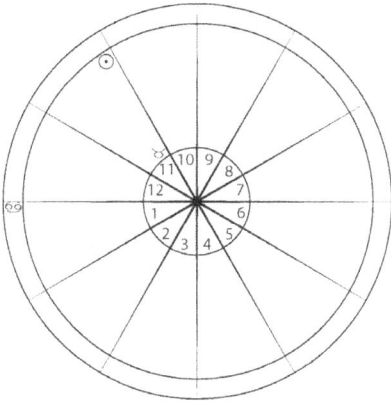

A true crusader, your Taurus child wants to belong to the group as the leader and is louder than everyone else. A self-starter and innovative, your little one will gather up everyone else to join in on a project that benefits all. Who knows, s/he could save a park or a tree!

A true influence in his/her crowd, your little Taurus will do his/her best to have everyone share his/her point of view. Therefore, equip your child with as much information as possible and let him/her choose the course of his/her cause! This will carry on throughout his/her life.

Your little Taurus will make a home, no matter where s/he is. This means that if you should go camping, you will find that your Taurus child will create an environment for him/herself using whatever belongings s/he brought on the trip. As long as it is set and just the way s/he wants it, your little one can abandon the space, knowing it will be there when s/he returns later.

TAURUS – *10 a.m. to 1 a.m.*
Tenth house–Cancer rising

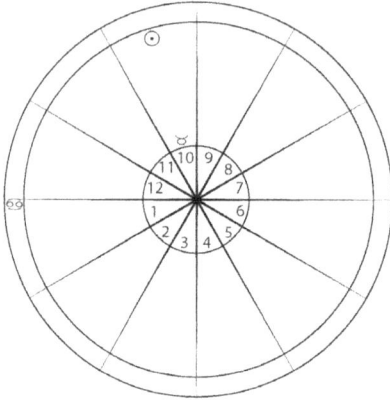

Wants to be the boss. Is louder than everyone else. Your Taurus knows the value of organizing everyone in his/her environment. A good business mind accompanies her/him, and you will be surprised to find how industrious s/he is.

It is a good idea to give projects to this child and allow him/her to make mistakes and learn from them. This will help him/her in later life. A good idea is to encourage your child to pick him/herself up and do it again until s/he gets it right. Don't worry about giving up because your little one has enough tenacity to see things through. They only need to be encouraged to complete a project and they will be on their way!

If your child is wishy-washy about a project or idea and decides to let it go, ask your little one to first determine what would make it a success and what would not. That way a lesson of value is still learned and can be used later in life.

TAURUS - *11 a.m. to 12:30 p.m.*
Tenth house–Leo rising

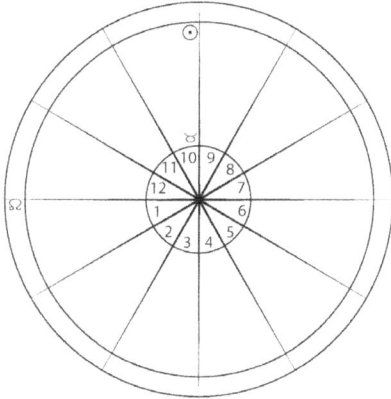

You cannot keep this little one off the stage. Filled with presence, you will find your child has an easy capacity for entertainment. Don't be surprised if the stage is not in the theatre. S/he will stand on a stage or in a classroom or in front of any crowd on the street! This child will be heard! Usually, a singer because Taurus rules the throat and Leo is an entertainer!

This child should also have great hair. May possibly have a widow's peak (a V on the forehead made by hair).

When she went on her first audition, Lisa looked around and asked who all the other kids were there. Her mother told her patiently that the others were also on the audition and that one would be selected. Lisa got up and said, "Let's go." Bewildered, her mother asked the problem. "You tell them when they want me to call me. I'm not going to sit here with a bunch of other kids waiting to be picked!" She chose not to be in show business but later in life became a star in her own right in another field where she stands in front of people and "performs" by teaching!

TAURUS – 12:30 p.m. to 1:30 p.m.
Ninth house–Leo rising

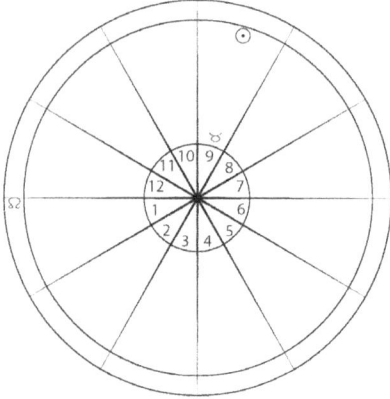

A great philosopher and orator, your Taurus child will be a wonderful teacher to others around him/her. When traveling, s/he will have a propensity for easy communication with those who are foreign to him/her. This child usually has a talent for languages and, if not, can still communicate with others who don't know his/her tongue with sign language. Your child is a good mimic and can easily entertain you with a description of a conversation, accent and all!

Education is very important for your little one. Learning comes easy and a lifetime of philosophy will be formed during the first seven years. It is good to introduce your child to many thoughts and ideas and let him/her form his/her own. You won't be sorry if you allow your child's spirit to grown on its own. Be there to guide and to teach the difference between right and wrong but let the ideas form by themselves.

TAURUS – *1:30 p.m. to 2:30 p.m.*
Ninth house–Virgo rising

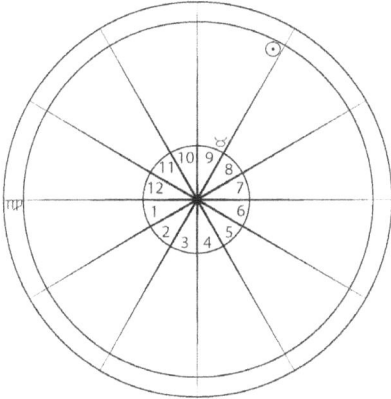

Perfection comes easily to this youngster. A need for organization and order, your child may initially seem messy. This seems contradictory, however, your little one will first see if someone else is going to do the cleaning up. Once it is determined that s/he is responsible for the appearance of his/her "spot," your little one will not want to be judged as messy and will come around to keeping things in an orderly fashion.

Reading is essential to this child. It is important to show your little one the importance of versatility so that s/he won't be boring or bored. Staying with one subject and being single-minded could end up being more of a curse than a blessing.

Higher education is important. Go along to get along is a mantra of this child. You will always want to take him/her with you when you travel, especially abroad. Your little Taurus has an uncanny ability to communicate with people no matter where s/he is.

TAURUS – *2:30 p.m. to 3:30 p.m.*
Eighth house–Virgo rising

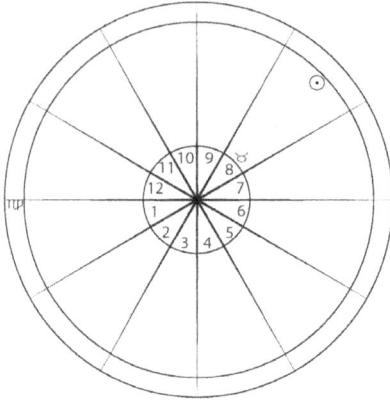

This child has a canny look at the "bizarre." Harmonious and down-to-earth, your child could be somewhat of a perfectionist. At an early age, don't be surprised if you are asked questions about death. Your little one will also enjoy "scary" movies and stories. It is alright to bring this child to a funeral at an early age.

With a memory tight as a drum, you can be sure that s/he has memorized favorite lines from a recent movie or show s/he has watched. You can also be assured that something you may have said in the past will come back to haunt you at an inappropriate time. Let it go and laugh with your child. This will dissuade him/her from doing it again, especially if you are unphased by it.

TAURUS – 3:30p.m. to 4:30 p.m.
Eighth house–Libra rising

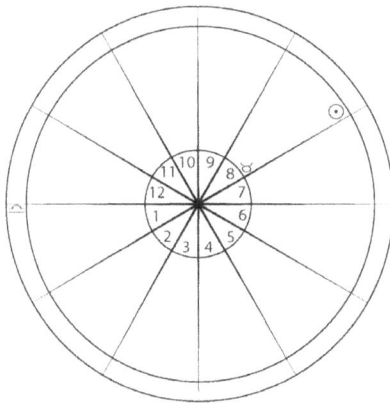

Your child has a need for harmony and beauty. S/he will also have a curiosity about life and death. Your child will feel naturally lucky and want to enter contests. This should be encouraged. There will be endowments and possibly scholarships available to your little one in later years. Encouragement to excel is necessary at an early age. Creating a beautiful environment is a goal of this lovely child. S/he will seek beauty everywhere and will want balance and fairness in all things.

You may want to ask him/her what motivated him/her to do a certain thing. Expect an "I don't know" type of response.

Art and beauty are important to your lovely child and an interest in creating his/her own "beauty salon" or "art studio" will be prevalent. The whole idea is to make things lovelier than they were. Enhancement is quite important.

Even if s/he seems messy, don't touch a thing unless you clean up together because this child is quite fussy about his/her things. Possessions are important.

TAURUS – 5:30 p.m. to 6:30 p.m.
Seventh house–Libra rising

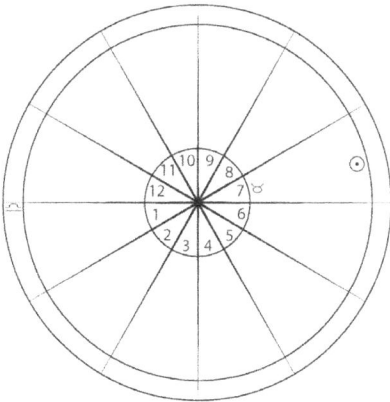

Industry and business combined with a sense of fairness dominate your child's consciousness. Everything must be lovely. Twice ruled by Venus, s/he will fight to the death for peace. Business endeavors and partnerships will be a constant goal of your little one. Don't be surprised when "partner-in-business" show up at your doorstep, even when quite young. Your little business entrepreneur will usually find a way to "earn." If the school or an organization is selling tickets or candy, your Taurus child is usually the first to score the big sales!

You may also witness mock weddings. A romantic at heart, your little one will want elaborate settings for this turning-of-life situation. Mocking your child during this time will only hurt him/her. As s/he grows into a teen, don't pester him/her about marriage. When the time comes, it will come, and your nagging will only delay the process. Don't forget, your child can be defiant.

Their sincerity is real, and every action is taken to heart. Should you criticize this child, you will get an argument back on why s/he is right and you are wrong. It is very hard for this child to take criticism and even if it is constructive or helpful, your child will not accept what you have to say, to the point of being "hurt." In these cases, you will have to go into great explanation to make your point. You will also have to be diplomatic at these times.

Your stubborn child will argue with you until s/he is blue in the face just to make you think his/her way. If you don't teach this child early on that his/her point of view is not the only point of view, s/he will make many enemies throughout his/her life.

TAURUS – 6:30 p.m. to 7:30 p.m.
Seventh house–Scorpio rising

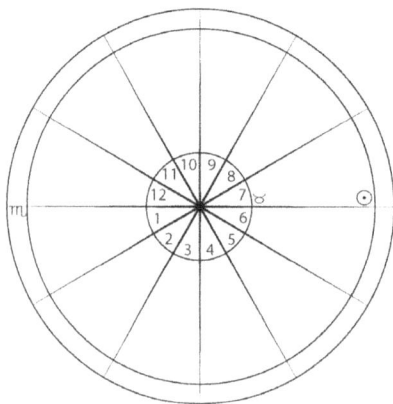

Partnership is sought by this beautiful child. In his/her first social situation (usually school) your child will come home and announce who his/her boy/girlfriend is. Embrace these relationships because they could be life-long-lasting. Betrayal does not sit well with this child and you can be assured that any hint of such may set your little one off in tears but once through, it is over! That includes relationships.

Your child will be a good student at whichever endeavor s/he takes on. S/He will be able to put everything together and with a plan! You can encourage this action, as it will help later in life and will also build confidence.

This Taurus child will move heaven and earth to prove a point. Also, self-education will be important so that s/he can function. If there is a legal matter, your Taurus child will do his/her own research and will astound the courts with his/her knowledge. Your child is not afraid to be right and will do as much research as it takes to get all the facts. In presentation, this child is quite powerful!

Constipation or other disorders of the bowel system is a sign of unhappiness and trouble with relationships.

What a hard worker your little bull is! S/He is not afraid of hard work at all and will amaze you with his/her accomplishments.!

TAURUS – *7:30 p.m. to 9 p.m.*
Sixth house–Scorpio rising

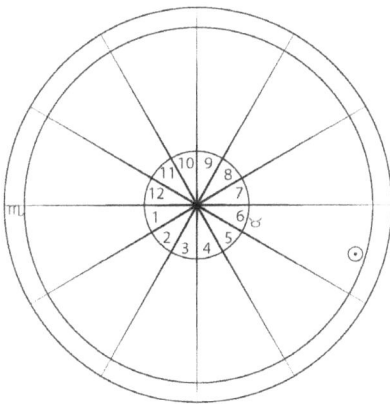

S/he will want to "fix" anyone or anything that is "broken." It may begin with a toy but will eventually move on to people. Your child has great instincts. You will find yourself referring to this child as the family psychologist. This Taurus has great nursing and healing skills and will move heaven and earth to repair anything or anyone broken.

"The Psychiatrist Is In" could be a sign you put on his/her door. Your Taurus child has an uncanny ability to solve the problems of others and understands beyond his/her age just what is going on in peoples' lives.

If your child has problems of constipation, s/he is holding too much in and it could be affecting his/her life and health. It is good to teach your stubborn child to communicate or at least to journal and keep a little diary where s/he can release all that pent-up frustration.

TAURUS - *9 p.m. to 10 p.m.*
Sixth house–Sagittarius rising

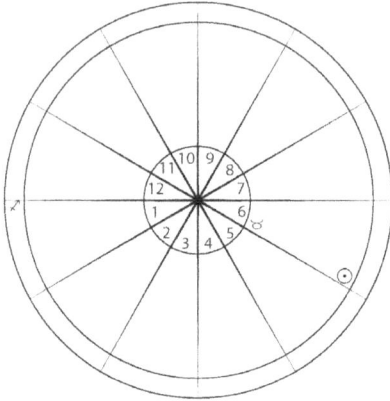

A natural healer and spiritual guide, your Taurus will appear a great philosopher at an early age. Much wisdom comes from the lips of this babe and it is good to keep a journal of all the things you learn. Later (in adulthood), you can give this book to your child and see how many of these words of wisdom still apply. In many cases, a lot will have the same meaning. Don't be surprised to see your little one playing doctor or nurse at an early age.

In spite of being such a caring soul, your little one is quite the adventurer. New places and new people are exciting to him/her and you can take him/her any place. Your child will not only shine but will feel quite good about being with others who share his/her penchant for adventure.

If your little Taurus is having problems with a sore hip or sore thighs, you can be assured that things are not going well. S/He could easily be troubled by something that can only be solved by him/her. You can ask but not pry. The truth will come out in time and when s/he is ready to confide. In the meantime, Mr./Ms. Fixit will take care of the problem his/herself!

TAURUS - *10 p.m. to 11 p.m.*
Fifth house–Sagittarius rising

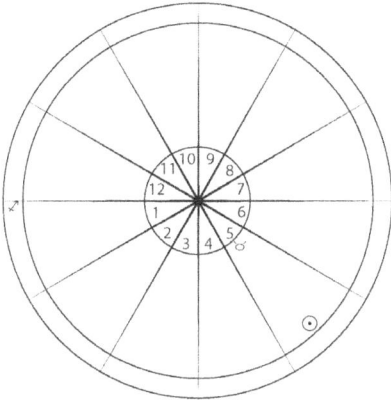

A strong need to entertain, your Taurus child will arrange parties at home. S/He also wants brothers and sisters. If you do not provide them, s/he will find some and bring them home.

Don't be surprised if your little Taurus is looking for a boy/girlfriend early on. An announcement will be made that s/he has found a new boy/girlfriend. This is the beginning of romance for your little one and s/he will always want to have someone to call his/her own.

This child will also want to dress in less-than-conservative outfits. Either the addition of a hat or colorful scarf will not only brighten this Taurus' day but will also brighten his/her mood.

TAURUS - *11 p.m. to 12 a.m.*
Fourth house–Sagittarius rising

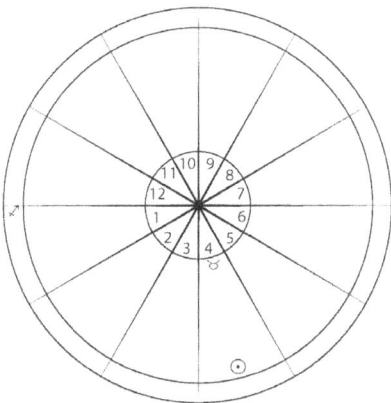

Stray pets may find their way into your home. Eventually, it will be stray people. Although your little one will love to travel, home is always import-ant. As long as s/he knows s/he has a home base, travel will be easy. Moving can be an emotional experience for this child. If your attitude is, "Guess where we get to go next . . ." your child will embrace the new experience. On the other hand, if you are unhappy about the move, don't expect joy to emanate from your little one. Your attitude will be reflected in the attitude of your child.

Judgmental at times, your prejudices will become his/her choices. It is good to teach this little one acceptance of all because s/he will make certain choices from experience, rather than from the opinions of others.

Chances are your child will have long legs and be tall.

LEO

The bold and beautiful Lion responds to praise best of all. S/He may learn from the school of hard knocks, but s/he will learn. Your child is a great student, especially of human nature, and is quite astute, learning as s/he goes along. If s/he didn't learn it in school, it is possible that on-the-job-training is where s/he learns but there are many lessons and a very eager learner.

Your little one will be quite entertaining with or without talent. Gary was seven when his grandfather told him he would pay him to sing. Gary sang his heart out and was paid. In spite of the fact that it took him many years to carry a tune, he sang for everyone in sight. After all, he was a paid entertainer.

Leo children are great students. They want to know more and will study hard when necessary. They are usually quite bright and perceptive. There are times when an underachieving gifted child is a Leo. Without encouragement, there can be a lack of enthusiasm. One Leo child I knew barely made it through high school. After he served four years in the Marines, he returned and went to college where he graduated Magna Cum Laude! He told me that he never felt appreciated at home and it affected his entire life. Once free and on his own, he blossomed.

Your Leo child will put his/her best foot forward. They need to be noticed. If, for any reason, they receive a negative response to their behavior, they will continue to behave accordingly for that negativity, such as a spanking, bullying, or anything that will draw attention. Praise when your child does something well will elevate your Leo's sense of self-esteem and will give you an enjoyable, funny, fun-loving companion.

Leos love to laugh. That is why they tend to play practical jokes. Early-on, they should learn the difference of a joke that might do harm or one that might generate mirth.

Remember that Leo has pride. It is good to teach your Leo to say "thank you" when complimented. One little girl I know (at age 5) was wearing a "label" outfit. She was at a gathering when someone commented on her lovely designer outfit. She brought herself up with such pride, lifted her head and chest and uttered, "Why, thank you!" She wore the biggest smile as she strutted around the rest of the day!

Leos are loyal!!! It is important to know that you can trust your Leo child to be true and faithful to you. When you are the most important person in this child's life, it is up to you to live up to what you have created that eventually become expectations.

In physical appearance, your Leo usually has a mane of beautiful hair. Sometimes, you can find a "widow's peak" on the forehead. (A "widow's peak" is a shape from the hairline to the forehead–like a 'V').

Leos are beguiling children and often fun. They will sometimes be the class clown or the class scholar. Once in a while, they are both but usually one or the other. If they are really funny, look for the pain underneath.

Leo children need to know their worth and that they have value.

Gold and Red are two colors that are most attractive to your Leo.

LEO - *1 a.m. to 1:45 a.m.*
Fourth House - Gemini Rising

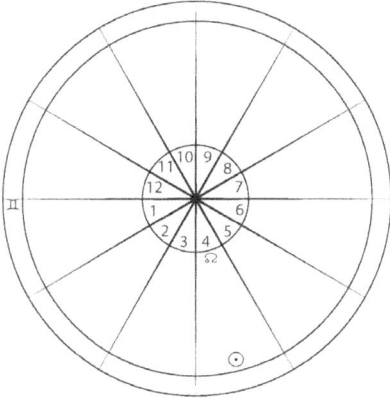

Your Leo wants lots of gold embellishments in his/her environment. A place for people to visit is also important and s/he wants to get in on the conversation. It is good to teach your child early on how to speak with others and not interrupt but wait his/her turn.

Your little one may have a great sense of humor and can easily entertain any guests you may have in your home. They easily can relate a story or lesson learned and if you have secrets you don't want shared, keep them to yourself.

It is a good idea to teach your little Lion to not dominate the conversation but to join in the conversation. This child will want a lot of attention and may find a voice to be noticed. They will have a much better time communicating with others when they learn to listen first. This is taught by you!

LEO – *1:45 a.m. to 2:15 a.m.*
Third House - Gemini Rising

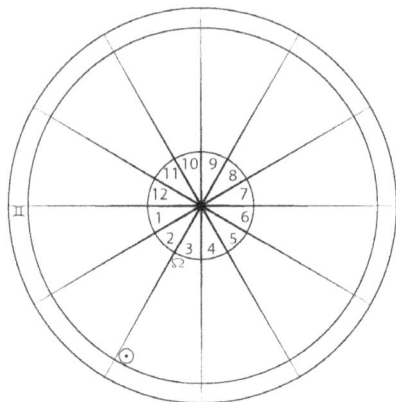

What a great student your Leo Child is. Not only will your Little Lion retain all that s/he has learned but s/he will also be delighted to pass on the knowledge to you. Should you have dinner around the table, your little one will be able to repeat all that were in his/her lessons of the day.

This child will also be able to relate events that happened almost verbatim. Pay attention and you may learn a few things. Math and music are good studies for this child.

Your little one doesn't enjoy being an only child and likes to have siblings around for playtimes. If there are no other children, you may want to get your child a pet.

Your Leo should be a good musician and entertainer.

LEO - *2:15 to 3:15 a.m.*
Third House - Cancer Rising

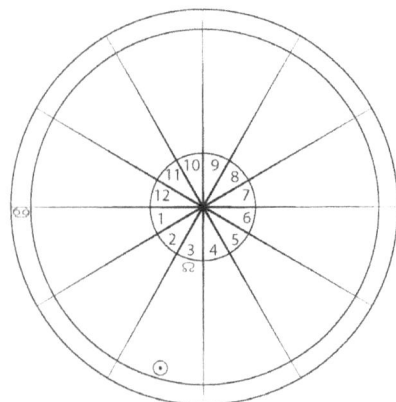

Your delightful child may tend to have mood swings. Brothers and sisters are important to this intelligent child. If you do not give one to him/her, perhaps a pet can help. You may find strangers in your home who are treated as siblings by your friendly little one.

A good student, in general, you want your child to connect with his/her teacher. Encourage good study habits even through moods. Lessons in meditation can be very helpful.

As long as s/he knows s/he can come home, your Leo will look for a way out of the home. You may sense in this child a feeling of not belonging and it is up to you to include him/her in activities and in your life so that s/he can feel wanted and a part of the family dynamic.

Seldom is this child an only child; however, if that is the case, a pet is recommended to help your little one maintain a sense of balance.

LEO – *3:15 to 4 a.m.*
Second House - Cancer Rising

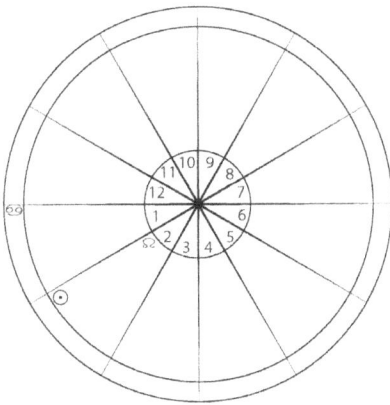

Filled with determination and purpose, your Leo child will amaze you with his/her strong values. S/he may find ways to leave home at an early age to go off and study or to leave an unhappy situation. As long as your little one knows there is home *somewhere* s/he may find another place to live at least temporarily.

You may find this little Leo a bit moody but that is just a reaction to surroundings that do not suit him/her. Once corrections are made, you may find him/her singing.

Your Leo child may want to sing on any occasion and if not given music lessons, s/he will learn on his/her own.

This child will always find a way to have enough. Usually, s/he will find coins or bills in his/her pocket. Always generous, your Leo child is willing to share the wealth!

Often an optimist, your Leo can surprise you with observations that are "off-the-wall," and yet, realistic. Do not underestimate this child! You will be surprised at how s/he can pull a rabbit out of a hat!

Gary was five when he left home to follow a rainbow. It took his family hours to find him after he got lost, literally chasing a rainbow so that he could get the pot of gold at the end!

LEO
Second House - Leo Rising

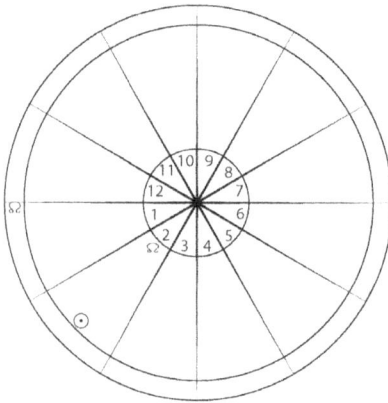

Convinced that s/he is not vulnerable, your Leo always feels lucky and may tend to gamble on his/her perceived good fortune. It is a good idea to allow a few losses so that this little lion can see that not all things come so easily, and money does not grow on trees!

A good idea is to give an allowance for recreation and to allow that when money runs out that there is no reprieve. This way, your child will learn early that budgeting is a part of his/her life and that financial responsibility is a necessity for successes in life.

S/He can also learn from this that not everything is FREE!

Your child has great determination and is willing to see something through. Although seemingly stubborn, you will be amazed that your little Leo is able to pull things off when it seemed to be something impossible. You will marvel at the ability of your child to see things to the end and finish projects once started. Encourage this and you will have a happy child!

LEO *4 a.m. to 4:45 a.m.*
First House - Cancer Rising

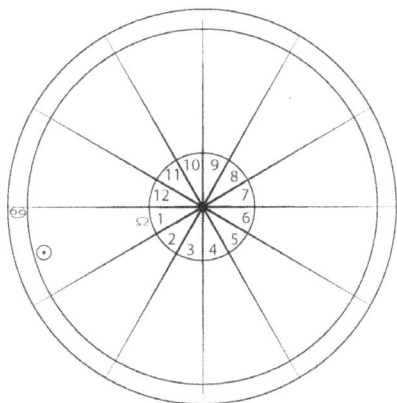

A true entrepreneur, you will be amazed by your little one's ability to get things started and make life happen early. S/He will show you that innovative streak which seems like good fortune and great intelligence at the same time. Your young Lion has the ability to be in the right place at the right time. Best of all, s/he knows why s/he is there!

It is possible that after a discussion about a certain interest, that your little one does some research and finds a book or class about the subject of interest and drag you right into the drama at hand.

Sometimes it may be difficult but for a sense of self-importance, encourage this child in those endeavors that may seem out-of-the-box for you. In the long run, you may learn something new!

LEO *4:45 a.m. to 5:45 a.m.*
First House - Leo Rising

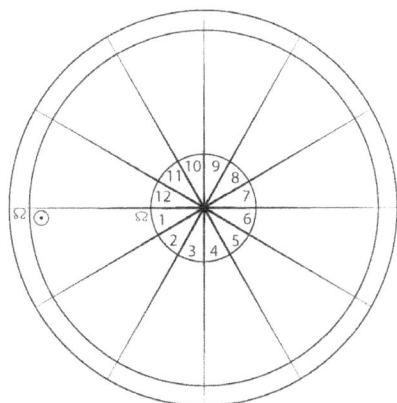

A great deal of pride follows your child. S/He should have beautiful hair and even when his/her heart is broken will still smile and make those around them happy. The ultimate entertainer and scholar, this Leo can be quite stubborn yet always savvy. Not much passes this child by so honesty is the best policy.

You will find this child is "lucky" in that things seem to always fall into place for him/her. It could be as simple as a raffle or it could be from being in the right place at the right time. In any case, things have a way of working out for this Lion!

Your child needs to feel important. Recognize and applaud accomplishments. If your Leo does something that pleases you, be sure to acknowledge it so that s/he will feel good about repeating the deed.

LEO *5:45 a.m. to 7 a.m.*
Twelfth House - Leo Rising

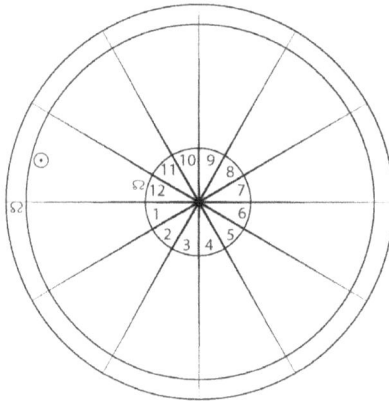

S/He isn't secretive, just knows how to keep secrets. Your Leo is introspective and imaginative. These are good traits. S/He should be encouraged to keep a journal so that s/he doesn't burst. It is good that s/he knows that there is privacy and that his/hers is kept, and that anything in the journal is sacred. This will help a great deal later in life. Trust is an important element in the raising of this child.

You may find an incredible amount of sweetness oozing from this child. Just remember that a Lion's roar can be close at hand and it is a good idea to encourage this one's lovely disposition.

Your child may be reluctant to come out in the open to stand up in front of a crowd. Don't fret. There is just a small element of shyness when s/he doesn't know if his/her audience is trustworthy. After that, you will find an eager participant in many activities.

If your child has nightmares, change up the before-bed activity and let him/her go to bed with good thoughts and peace of mind.

LEO - *7 a.m. to 8:15 a.m.*
Twelfth House - Virgo Rising

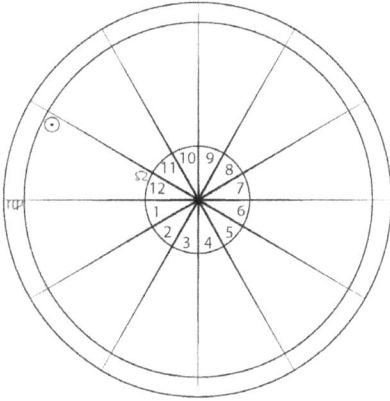

Details are important to this highly intelligent Lion. Your little Leo may ask you a lot of questions because s/he wants to know everything. But don't expect any information coming from him/her. S/He can be very secretive.

S/He can fumble when trying for perfection but that doesn't stop this child. The endeavor to do the right thing and precisely, will continue. When teaching something to this little one, don't forget to teach how and where and why (in other words, all the details).

This is one Leo who can come off as shy. Reluctant to trust is really what's going on. Once you have earned his/her confidence, you will watch your intelligent child blossom!

You have a loyal and true confidant in this child but since you still have a child on your hands, don't clog up those brain waves with too much information. S/He enjoys learning on his/her own and will amaze you with bon mots (clever remarks!).

LEO - *8:15 a.m. to 9:30 a.m.*
Eleventh House - Virgo Rising

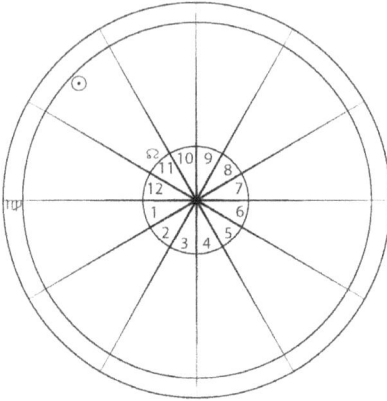

Looking for the perfect friend. Your Leo child may have a tough time finding someone who will suit his/her understanding of who is "perfect." Understanding that imperfections are a part of being "perfect" will help this child immensely.

In his/her endeavor to be "perfect" him/herself, you can teach this child that there are options and different opinions to what is perfect and what is not. It is up to the child to make these discriminating points and to choose which strengths and weakness constitute perfection.

You will hear many phrases from this child that begin with "When I grow up . . ." They have many hopes and wishes and will seek many ways to manifest them, with a wish, a prayer, meditation, etc. (whatever you teach him/her).

LEO *9:30 to 10:45 a.m.*
Eleventh House - Libra Rising

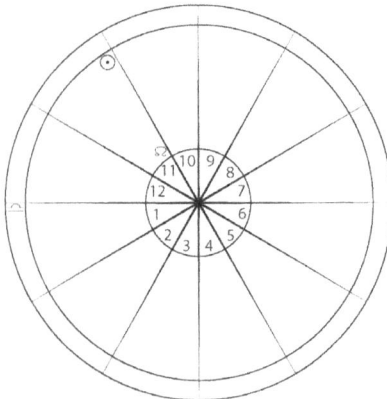

Friendly and eager to please, your beautiful Leo should have many followers. Usually, this child will bring home many others that s/he can gather. A spirit of sharing should also be apparent, and it goes both ways. Your Leo child expects others to share in his/her attitude toward dividing and participating in activities and owned items.

This is a Leo who loves to have others join in the same activities and games and who finds it easier than others to give up his/her place in line.

Your child has aspirations, but they are not yet formed. You don't need to encourage him/her to know. When the time is right, the truth will be revealed!

Expect this little one to be quite entertaining and a bit of a "ham." Let him/her enjoy it at the early stages of life because later s/he will be embarrassed by any posturing.

LEO *10:45 a.m. to 12:15 p.m.*
Tenth House - Libra Rising

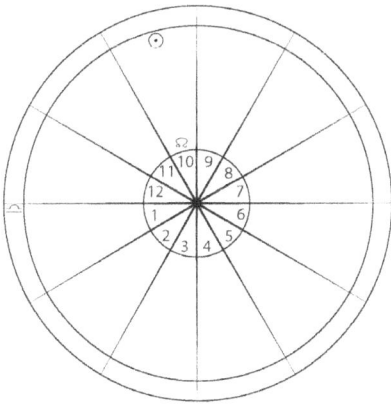

Always the entertainer, your little one needs attention and will do much to get it. If s/he cannot be the performer, s/he will be the director or producer. As long as s/he gets credit for what is being done (or performed).

This is a Leo who has a lot of pride and reputation is very important to him/her. S/He wants and deserves credit for what s/he has done but does not appreciate being publicly humiliated. If you have criticism for this proud Lion, be sure to do it in private so that his/her dignity is not lost. A good reputation is very important to your child and s/he is easily embarrassed.

You probably don't want to use any information you have as a weapon against him/her because s/he will rebel and store up information you don't want disclosed, as well.

LEO - *12:15 p.m. to 1 p.m.*
Tenth House - Scorpio Rising

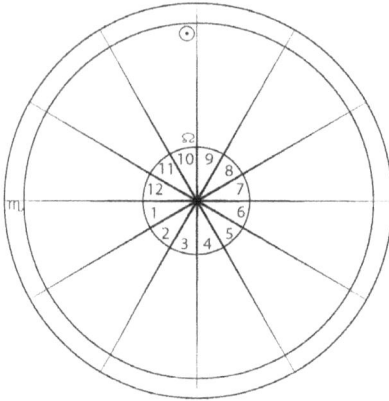

This proud and stubborn Leo may surprise you when s/he demands proof of everything. A good researcher, you will find that your child is highly intelligent and retains information. When in doubt, your Leo will look things up to prove a point and to make a point. The research and self-education will not go to waste, as you will find that s/he is able to make contributions to others with things learned.

Give this child some responsibility and watch him/her flourish. They love to be in charge and will need to know all the details of their job before taking the reins but then watch how well the job is done!

One young Leo I knew could not afford an attorney, so they went to the law books to glean the information needed to put a company together. Research and action are key words for your little one and s/he will move mountains to fulfill his/her goals.

LEO - *1 p.m. to 3 p.m.*
Ninth House - Scorpio Rising

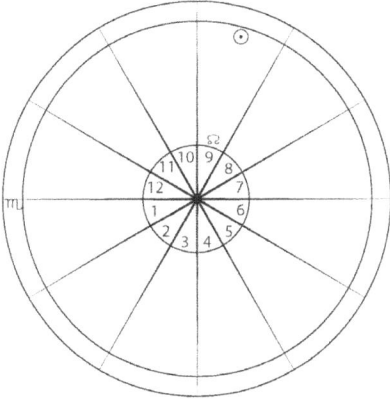

You have a scientist in your midst. Your investigative Leo wants to know "WHY" about everything. The other question is "HOW" and you may sometimes feel this child is relentless. If you go into details early on, you may find yourself repeating the same story but at least you will know it. Your child looks for answers and is a good detective. You can teach this little Lion how to do his/her own research early on. Any subject will do so don't be surprised if there is something out of left field that you never imagined.

If this little Leo is looking through your things, help. Learn what the quest is and support it. You may be thrilled at learning new things and finding answers.

Genealogy is also a good quest for your Leo, and you may want to help with the research. When you are asked, "Where did I come from?" don't jump to conclusions but go to the ancestry answer first.

LEO - *3 p.m. to 4 p.m.*
Ninth House - Sagittarius Rising

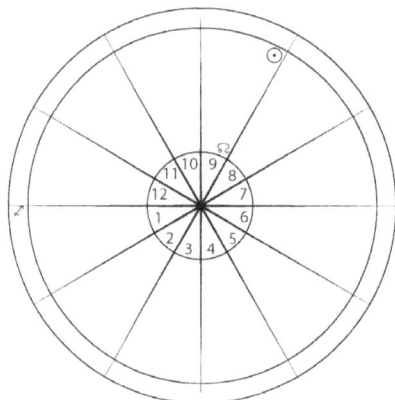

Underachieving gifted child. Your proud Leo may be easily bored and may need something to stimulate his/her interest in projects and lessons. Don't consider this child to be an underachiever because chances are there is nothing there to stimulate his/her interest.

Eddie was a straight F student. Once he went to college and was able to choose his own courses, he was a straight A student. He graduated Magna Cum Laude! It is possible that he had low self-esteem growing up.

This child needs appreciation and praise. When you see him/her doing something wonderful, acknowledge it and let your child know of your appreciation. This doesn't mean a participation trophy; it means true acknowledgment for doing something wonderful. Leo children need to know their worth and that they have value.

You can find a studious child, one who excels in an area unexpected. It is good when you are pleased with his/her accomplishments and all fields.

Chances are that you have a genius on your hands and don't even know it!

LEO - *4 p.m. to 5:15 p.m.*
Eighth House - Sagittarius Rising

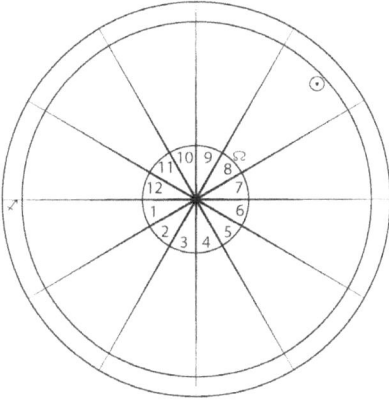

Imaginative and creative, your Leo is very good with advice. You can introduce this child to the stock market at an early age and you will find that s/he excels in such things as hedge funds.

Sometimes your child can be stuck in an idea or ideal and needs help is getting out of a particular frame of mind. With encouragement, s/he can stubbornly stick with the same dialog that makes him/her happy. That same stubbornness can continue to make this child miserable so dwelling on a subject is not a good option if the subject is one of persistent sadness.

An important part of growing up for this little one is in learning forgiveness, which may be difficult. Your kindness and love will guide him/her but understanding of other people's circumstances will help.

LEO - *5:15 p.m. to 6:15 p.m.*
Eighth House - Capricorn Rising

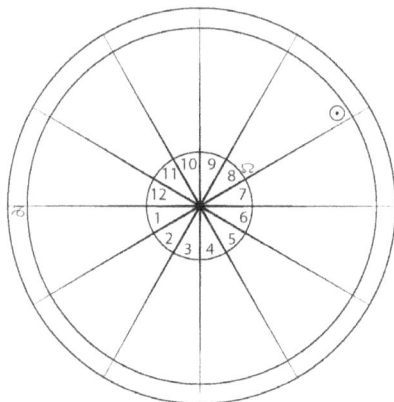

This is the child in your family who believes that s/he is the only one capable of handling all the assets.

A serious child, this Leo can assume a great deal of responsibility and wishes to have even more. A busy child, you will find your Leo caring about your needs and wants.

Your little Lion is very generous and may give away many things, but you will be happy to put him/her in charge of the valuables because these treasures will be esteemed and regarded well. If you place value on something, your Leo will do the same.

You will also be able to encourage this child to work toward goals such as scholarship and other awards and prizes. Contests are a good challenge for your little one!

LEO – *6:15 p.m. to 7:15 p.m.*
Seventh House - Capricorn Rising

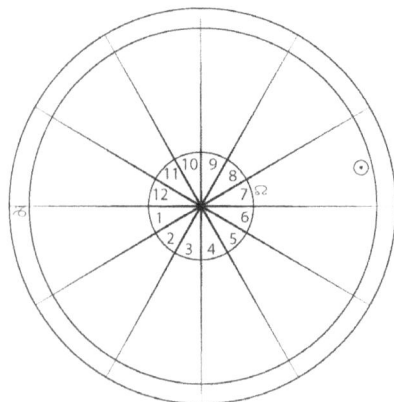

This Leo wants to be in a relationship where s/he is the boss! Should s/he want to start a business at an early age, you can encourage it, especially if a partner is involved. This is a good time to teach your Leo the importance of equality and fairness. Even you or another figure of authority can join in the partnership. You can suggest it if your little one hasn't asked you first!

Often times, your little one is drawn to those who are a generation (ten years) older or younger. Wisdom is a key lesson to this child, and s/he is drawn to those who either can teach them or whom they can teach!

A talent for mirth and laughter, your child also has a serious side. Be certain to allow the lighter side of life to enter into his/her world. There will be plenty of time for the serious stuff later.

LEO - *7:15 p.m. to 8 p.m.*
Seventh House - Aquarius Rising

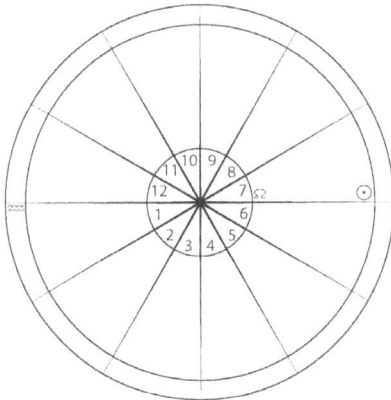

Going against the rules is easy for your Leo child. In the long run, however, it will be the rules that will be the glue holding your little one together. Don't be afraid to make rules for him/her and watch the rebellion. Eventually, these very regulations will be a cornerstone of life for your Leo child.

You can usually find your child has a good disposition, as long as s/he feels free to bounce around in the middle of his/her restrictions. Your clever child will figure out a way to make these rules and regulations his/her own.

Pay attention when you are being told something or are given an explanation. Learn to read between the lines because there could be an underlying message.

LEO – *8 p.m. to 9:15 p.m.*
Sixth House - Aquarius Rising

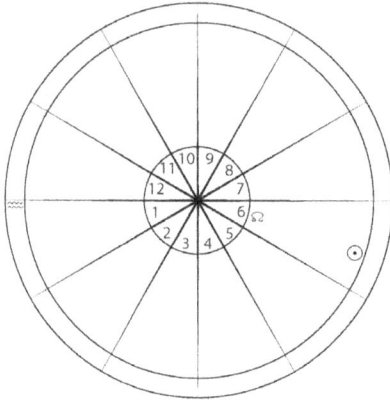

One of the most delightful humanitarians is your little Leo. Whenever and wherever s/he can, s/he will try to help and make things better for everyone else around. Be sure this child knows all the rules first so that s/he doesn't get in "trouble."

Your Lion may easily believe s/he has the talent to make things better for everyone. Watch and see that s/he does that for which s/he has been trained–this will prevent problems later. If s/he wants to learn something, by all means do your best to teach him/her or direct him/her to someone or a book so that s/he can learn.

You will find that your Leo child is a hard worker. Do not be afraid to give him/her chores to do because not only will they be done, with proper instruction, they will be done well.

LEO – *9:15 p.m. to 10:15 p.m.*
Sixth House - Pisces Rising

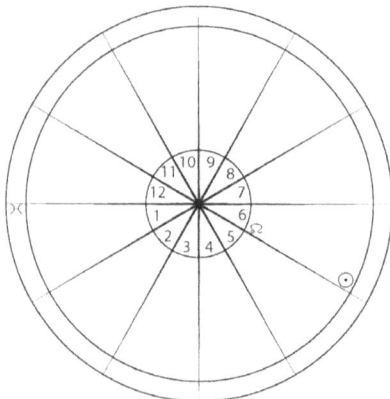

A gift for healing and great compassion leads your Leo child to be the healer in the family. Playing doctor and nurse is a sincere exploration for this little one and not one to be taken lightly. You may want to introduce your child to nutrition and other endeavors that could lead to creativity and health.

A compassionate person, your Leo may tend to want to fight for the underdog. It is good to encourage this while teaching your little one to differentiate and to be able to tell the difference between the opportunist and those who are in need.

You may also find your Pisces-rising Leo to be quite the artist and able to create new visions. Put some paper in front of him/ her early on and see what direction his/her art takes. You may find additional talent that will help your Leo be more expressive.

LEO- 10:15 p.m. *to 11 p.m.*
Fifth House - Aries Rising

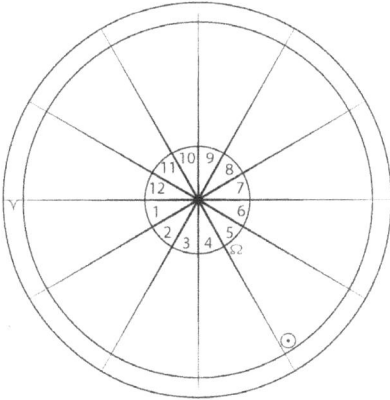

How lovely your Leo is! With an ability to be kind and also to be beautiful, life is easy, until it isn't. Your little Leo tackles problems as they come along and finds solutions right away. This child may come to you (encourage it) when something comes to him/her out of left field. If this is a problem that s/he doesn't understand, you will find a lot of questions thrown at you. Be prepared. Ask first, what the problem at hand really is and then go from there.

Innovative and creative, be sure to recognize your little Lion's talents and praise him/her for his/her efforts. A lot can be said for some of the unrecognized creations that have been made by these Leo children.

When she was five, a sweet little Linda had a hair band that was hurting her temples. Rather than make a fuss, she took some tissue out of her purse and immediately made pads for the points of the headband that were hurting her. She had the wit and ability to find a solution to a problem without bothering others with it.

Your child is creative and innovative and will make things that are "good" for others. Design of any sort is something that should be encouraged. Your Leo child is very creative. S/He can always come up with new and innovative ideas to please everyone and has a knack for finding the right thing for each person.

In spite of the fact that s/he has Aries rising, you may find that this Leo is not necessarily the solo entertainer but is great in the chorus. S/He likes to go along with everyone else but stars in his/her own circle.

Camping is a great vacation for this little one. Being a part of nature is always pleasing and adventurous.

LEO – *11 p.m. to 11:45 p.m.*
Fifth House - Taurus Rising

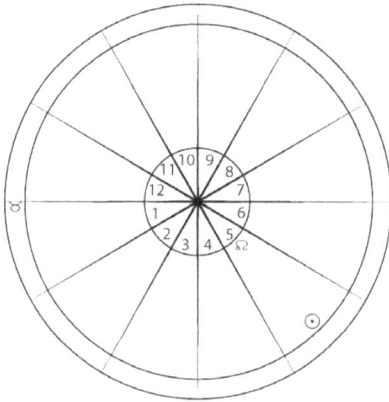

Voice lessons! A wonderful vocalist (and a large booming voice) is your child.

His/her voice can be heard everywhere, and it is a good idea to teach your little one how to modulate it. If your little one is the loudest one on the playground, you may want to teach him/her to use his/her voice carefully and prevent sore throats.

If your Leo gets sore throats often, chances are that s/he is not happy with his/her approach to life. You may want to help him/her switch directions and learn what their expectations are. You will often find that their demands are not unreasonable, and their requirements are simple. In the event they don't know, it is a good idea to give them some responsibilities that will make them feel important.

LEO – *11:45 p.m. to 1:45 a.m.*
Fourth House - Taurus Rising

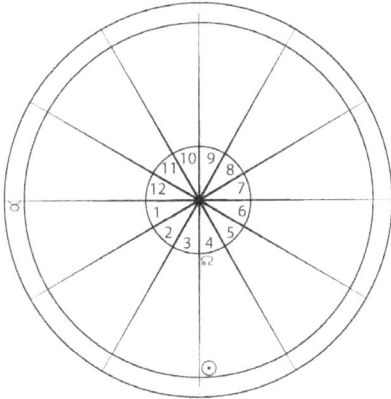

Until your child learns to be independent, nesting will be the only problem you have with him/her. The best encouragement you can give this child is through art and music. S/He may want to learn to play the drums, early on, however, you may want to steer this desire into some-thing more palatable for you that may be less noisy. The real thing here is that making more noise and being heard is what is important. Give your child an outlet where s/he can be heard, and you will have a happy child.

You may find that your little one can do anything once s/he wraps his/her head around it. S/He may be loud while attending to a challenge, but this child loves the provocation. You may have high expectations, but your Leo's expectations are even higher!

This child needs praise along the way to know that s/he is doing a job well. On the other hand, if your child is a little more mature, s/he may wait until the job is finished and then present it to you. No matter the timing, a job well-done deserves credit and praise. Your child lives for your praise!

SCORPIO

Intense. Some people say that the higher sign of the Scorpio is the Eagle. I like to think of it more as the butterfly. First, they are fuzzy caterpillars. Then they go into their cocoons and finally they emerge. Your little Scorpio asks "why?" more than any other question. There are times when you think you don't know anything for all the questions asked.

Scorpio children love to delve into anything and everything. They are not afraid to be dirty if there is an end result. They are usually quieter than most children but appear to be quite needy. The type of attention you give this child will make all the difference in his/her chances for success. If you scream "Go away", your little one will retreat and go elsewhere for the attention s/he craves.

Your Scorpio is deep and a great researcher. Introduction to the library at an early age is very beneficial. S/he may not necessarily want the story books but would rather learn about dinosaurs and outer space. They delve into the unknown.

Your little one also has a strong constitution. These children are usually quite healthy. The only physical problem they could have would be constipation. This is usually due to holding things inside and not letting go. Encourage your child to talk things out and to solve problems. Help them work out their issues and their plumbing will work. This child needs lots of grains and vegetables for a healthy constitution.

The strong-silent type is usually attributed to the Scorpio child. When they hurt, you can see it in their faces–even when they say that nothing is wrong. Encourage them to find ways to communicate. These children are good at keeping journals. Teach your little one early to write things down, be it in a letter, a diary, or the like. Do not invade his/her privacy!

The Scorpio child is usually very sensuous. S/he needs to touch and feel. Keep textures around your little one. A favorite blanket or stuffed animal may be a comfort to this child.

Scorpios enjoy collecting. You may find that they will start storing things early on. You might find crackers in a little corner of the room (in case of an emergency). If there is a favorite type of toy your child enjoys, you may find that s/he wants every type there is–this could be anything from baseball cards to dolls. Find something unusual and hard-to-get and the collection will have greater value and appreciation. Don't let anyone else mess with your Scorpio's private accumulation of prized possessions.

Anything earned or deserved is more appreciated by this little one than things simply given for no reason. Your child will value those treasures s/he has merited. If s/he made it him/herself, all the better.

Money–other people's–is always interesting to your Scorpio child. Your little one can be the banker in the family. You can teach him/her about the stock market at an early age. You can also open up a savings account for him/her and allow him/her to know what has been put in it. They will enjoy having the security of their own worth. The principle of saving for a rainy day is easily understood by this child–although, when the rainy day comes, s/he may find it hard to part with money saved. As time goes on, it gets easier, however.

When Mark was a little boy, he inherited a lot of money from a grandparent. He always felt secure that the money was there for his college education and his future. However, when he turned eighteen, he learned that his father had spent the dollars left in his care, leaving Mark with no security. Seemingly undaunted, Mark went on to earn more money and put himself through school. He forgave his father but did not forget.

Scorpios do not forget. In some cases, they hold grudges. They need to learn early to be able to let go and move on. It is with your actions, not your words, that they understand this. Forgiveness from you is the best demonstration to them. Don't constantly bring up old sins or offenses to this child. Teach him/her the importance of moving on so that s/he does not stagnate.

Affection is important to this child and at first it may feel as though your little one does not respond. Keep it up. It is paramount that your child learns early about holding and loving. It will help him/her to differentiate between sex and affection later on in life.

This child may be very clingy in the early years. When your Scorpio reaches the teens, the metamorphosis will be reflected by how they were treated earlier. As a butterfly emerges from the cocoon, it must spread its wings by itself. This is the same for your Scorpio child. If you take the wings of a butterfly and try to pull them out for it, the butterfly will not be able to fly. The same goes for your child. Let his/her wings unfold at their own pace. Do not force your child into social situations if s/he is not ready. When the time comes, s/he will emerge, with a smile and with grace.

Highs and lows are sometimes called moodiness. In fact, while solving a problem and deep in thought, your little one may appear to be anti-social. This is the time that you give them a project or a journal and leave them alone. An interesting aspect of the Scorpio is that their lows are never lower than their first. Scorpios rise to the occasion. They climb high. When they fall (and they do fall) they never go as far back as they did the last time. When they climb again, they climb higher than they did the last time.

Scorpios are uncanny in their ability to *know* what is going on about them. Don't lie to your child, s/he can read between the lines. They are like Santa Claus–they know when . . . Your Scorpio is very intuitive.

Purples, maroons, deep reds, deep blues, and mustard are colors your child will enjoy around them. Deep intense colors suit these children.

Word games and puzzles are a challenge and fun for your Scorpio. S/He should stay in his/her own age level and not be pushed into adulthood too soon. However, you can enjoy jigsaw puzzles and word games together. Growing up comes soon enough, keep the child as long as you can!

SCORPIO - *11:45 p.m. (prior day) to 12:30 a.m.* Third House - Leo Rising

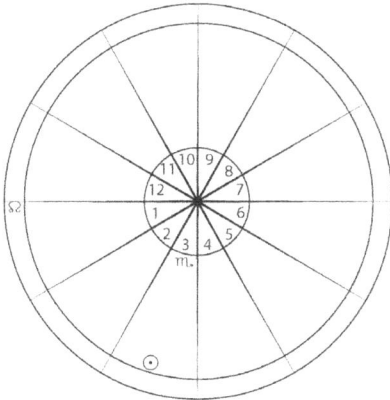

Intelligent and introspective, this child is full of questions. Good books never come too early for your little Scorpion and you will find s/he enjoys entertaining anyone who will watch him/her. An old saying, "Look, Ma, no hands," refers to riding a bike without using the handlebars. This can also be attributed to your Scorpio child. S/He needs to be noticed whenever s/he has made an accomplishment. It is your job to take notice and to acknowledge all great feats!

This child is proud and stubborn. Don't try to force him/her to do something your way once another method has been decided on. Until this little one fails at his/her way, yours will not be attempted. Afterwards, however, you can teach your little one to acknowledge and be grateful for suggestions and help doing something the "right" way!

Learning to share with siblings may be difficult. Begin with little things and then allow your child to be more generous as time progresses. Since s/he appreciates praise, it is good to heap it on in the beginning to show gratitude for his/her actions.

You probably didn't realize that children could be so smart! Your child not only has a remarkable ability to learn, but his/her retentive skills are also quite significant. If you don't see signs of a photographic memory at an early age, you will probably notice that you and others are being quoted verbatim. (My mother used to warn, "be careful what you say, the angels may be passing!") In this case, the "angels" could be your little Scorpio. There is nothing more embarrassing than to be quoted by a child when you are trying to avoid something.

Your Scorpio has a wonderful sense of humor and loves to laugh. Laugh with him/her and enjoy the mirth together. You will find you have a good deal of fun with this witty child.

SCORPIO - *12:30 a.m. to 1:45 a.m.*
Third House - Virgo Rising

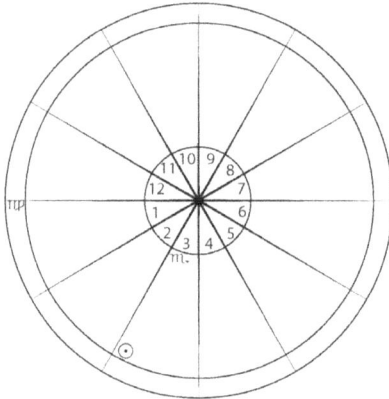

Your analytical child may question everything, but once s/he learns something, s/he retains it and does not have to be reminded. When you give a restrictive notice to this child, be sure to give an explanation as to why this applies. For example, when you tell your little one not to touch an electrical outlet, you may want to put your hand near the outlet and make a buzzing sound and pull your hand away fast, screaming "ouch." Your Scorpio child will learn the lesson quickly and will understand the lesson. The same lesson applies to the stove and other dangerous things.

Should you bleed, be sure to show your curious child so that your mistake isn't repeated by him/her. Your child is bright enough to learn by example and does not have to repeat your mistakes to get the point.

SCORPIO - *1:45 a.m. to 2:45 a.m.*
Second House - Virgo Rising

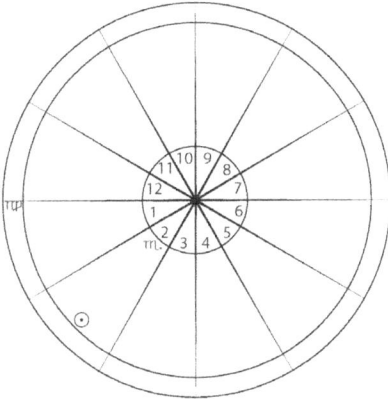

Your Scorpio child knows what is of value and what is not; you may find him/her sorting things out accordingly. It is possible the s/he makes lists or sorts things out in front of him/herself.

Your child will ask you for details. S/He is investigative and wants all the answers, weather s/he is ready to hear them or not. His/her curiosity is great and detailed answers whenever or wherever are desired. Remember, if you don't tell your little one the truth, s/he will learn it from someone else and that may not be a version of the truth that you wish to have shared. Please don't dismiss questions with "later" or "go ask someone else," unless you really don't care who answers the question.

Your Scorpio child values gifts that are given which can inspire the mind. Thoughtful gifts and those which have sentimental value will be treasured. Books are special treasures to your little one and a book that comes from the past or one about powerful and wizardly people are especially appreciated.

SCORPIO - *2:45 a.m. to 4:15 a.m.*
Second House - Libra Rising

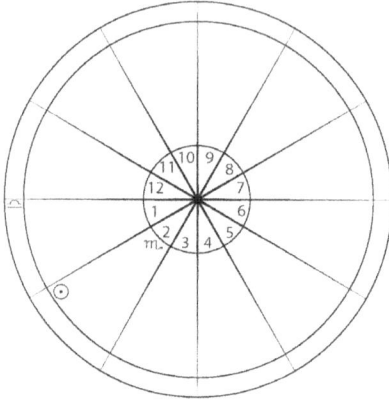

How generous your child is! Be sure s/he knows what should be kept and what can be given away because you may otherwise find yourself replacing may belongings, not only of this child's but also of your own.

Conversely, your little Scorpio, could scream, "Mine!" when someone wants something s/he believes belongs to him/her. Ownership is important and once the difference is known, the generosity begins. If something belongs to this child, it is always a good idea to let him/her know it is theirs to do whatever they choose. If, on the other hand, it is an item to be saved and one of importance, you may want to let him/her know that as well. It can also be used as a weapon of threat, should there be any anger or angst, such as destroying the "thing," or giving it away. Be sure that when you place importance on an item that the significance is to your child and not to you.

SCORPIO *4:15 a.m. to 5:30 am*
First House - Libra Rising

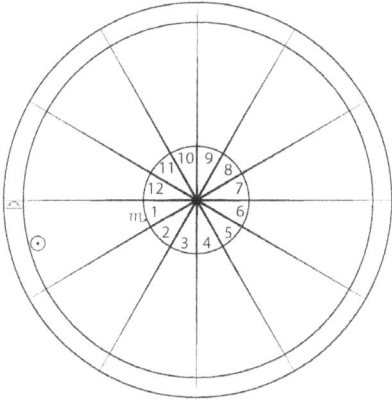

Some of the most beautiful and sensual children I have seen are Scorpio with Libra Rising. These children are very aware of their surroundings and quite instinctual. They are so lovely in the way they approach others and do their best to please. It is sometimes hard on them.

A stubborn child who wants desperately to please everyone around him/her, your Scorpio can bungle and trip through many lessons. Once a lesson is learned, however, your Scorpio child will not forget.

Your little Scorpio may want to follow his/her bliss. Whatever the path, s/he will follow. This lovely child loves both parents equally and is sad if one is away.

SCORPIO *5:30 am to 6:45 a.m.*
First House - Scorpio Rising

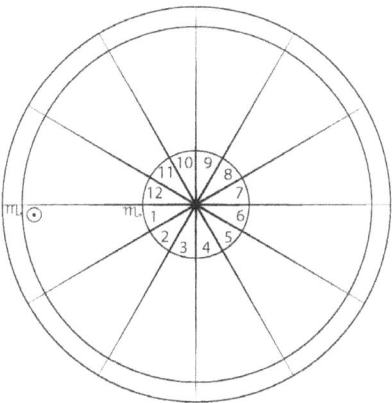

If your little one seems intense, s/he is just in the middle of a lesson.

Research is a good thing for this child. Teaching him/her how to discover new things and to then apply that knowledge to solving some great problems is a perfect exercise for your little Scorpio. Determination is a solid

73

characteristic of this child and, once challenged, s/he will move heaven and earth to get things done.

Kindness is a big thing with this Scorpio Child. S/he will respond in kind. Should someone treat this child unjustly, s/he will treat others the same way. Moreover, your Scorpio child has a long memory. Although s/he can hold a grudge, should you teach him/her early on how to let things go, it won't be as difficult for him/her. However, this child has a strong memory and will remember that adult who injured his/her pride or other throughout his/her life.

It is also good to teach this child forgiveness.

SCORPIO - *6:45 am to 8:00 am*
Twelfth House - Scorpio Rising

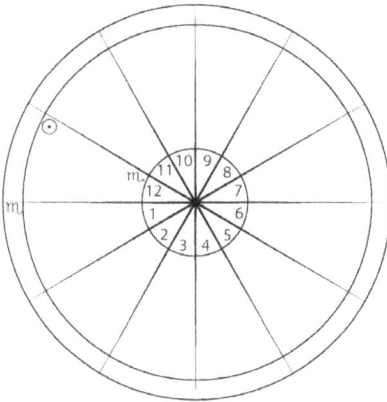

Your secrets are safe with this child. In fact, it is a good idea to teach him/her to keep a journal because keeping all that information inside could prompt your little one to burst. Holding on to too much information can be destructive. It is up to you to allow this journal to be private and for you to not "peek" into it. Trust begins at an early age and it is your responsibility to not only teach it to your child but be a trustworthy example.

If your child can learn early on in life to let go of things, such as menial problems, life will be easier. The expression, "Forget about it" applies to this child. The best thing is to teach your child how to tell the difference between what is important, what is necessary information, and what can be discarded.

Your intuitive little one has feelings about certain things. Pay attention because you may receive an important message or some great insight from this child.

SCORPIO - *8:00 am to 9:00 am*
Twelfth House - Sagittarius Rising

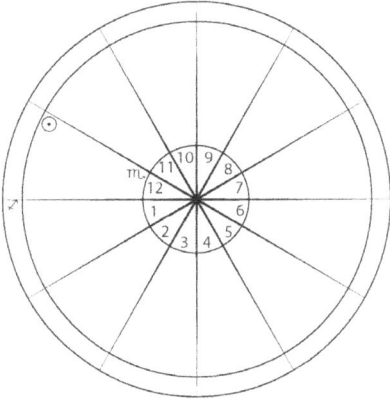

Full of insight and intuition, this child will know your moods and gauge your reactions well before you do. Your little one wants to do the right thing but can be at bay sometimes when choosing. It is up to you to guide and help mold this little one with rights and wrongs so that s/he won't be confused later in life.

S/He has a connection with his/her Higher Power and wants you to also have a belief system and understanding. If you have a belief system and practice it, you can introduce it to this child. Later on in life, s/he will find his/her own, but the practice is important in the early years, be it theist or atheist.

Your child may tend to parrot you but only because s/he wants to be like you. Teach this little one the value of having an independent thought and to have his/her own ideas rather than someone else's.

SCORPIO - *9:00 am to 10:15 am*
Eleventh House - Sagittarius Rising

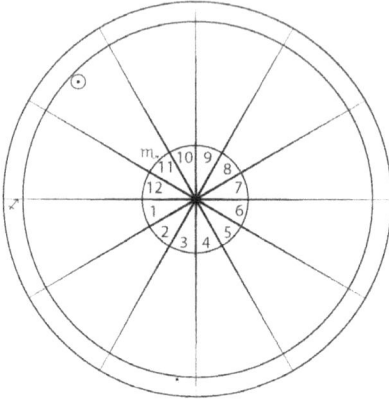

The best relationships while growing up are those learned on the playfield. If there is a sport or activity where a uniform is worn and your Scorpion can join others on the playground and be one with them, you will find a happy citizen. You will find that s/he will dive into an activity and be passionate about being a part with everyone else.

A scholar, you may find that your child enjoys scientific endeavors and research. Trips with groups to museums or other places of interest will be welcome. Even if s/he expresses disdain, you will find your little one talking about all s/he learned while attending said event.

Your child does well in groups, and you can encourage membership to him/her. Sometimes, you can make a suggestion and your little one will come to you with the right group. David wanted to be an actor. His mother told him that he would have to learn to act, sing, and dance, among other things. The next day, David brought home a brochure from an improvisational theater class. Children will step up when encouraged.

SCORPIO - *10:15 am to 11:15 am*
Eleventh House - Capricorn Rising

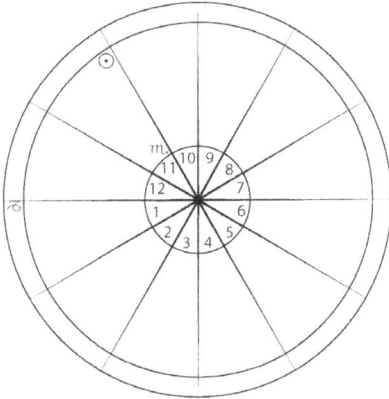

Your bold child wants to be in charge of activities with friends. This includes being the first to do things or activities. S/He wants to be the knowledgeable one and will first study that which makes him/her the lead. Don't let this be a deterrent because eventually s/he will learn how to behave with others. Discourage any form or bullying or getting even!

Becoming the Captain of any team suits your child's personality. You will find that at a very early age this little one takes the lead and is ahead of the crowd.

Friends who are a little older appeal to your Scorpio child. When older, s/he may seek out younger people to be his/her friend. This is a natural phenomenon of your child's. Don't fret, they learn . . . they teach!

SCORPIO - *11:15 am to 12:00 p.m.*
Tenth House - Capricorn Rising

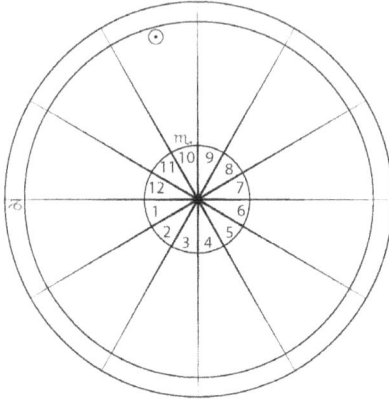

Do you think s/he is a little bossy? This child likes to be in charge and should be given roles that reflect this desire. Then the teaching begins! This is when your Scorpio child can learn that being the boss means to be fair and respectful should s/he wish to be accepted as a leader.

The best way to conquer this characteristic is to give your Scorpion a place or thing to rule or something where s/he is in charge. The key here is that you want your child to feel powerful in a good way. The best way is to give him/her responsibility and s/he will grow up generous and knowing how to make others feel good.

SCORPIO
Tenth House - Aquarius Rising

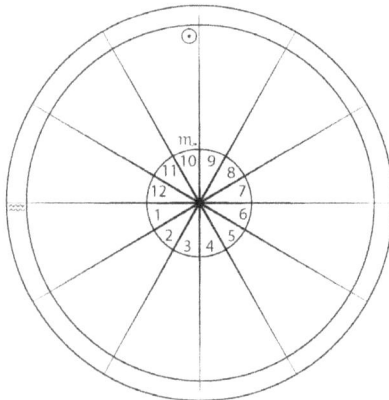

Your Scorpio child shows great leadership ability. A good reputation is important to this little one and it is good to demonstrate right from wrong to your child. Let this little one know the rules first so that the humanitarian in him/her shines. Kindness prevails with this child and you will find that s/he behaves in that manner.

There is a sense of pride that you will discover which starts in the crib. You may also find that your little one will make attention-getting sounds to see if you are paying attention. If you have been found to be ignoring this child, you will hear large wails. S/He is only saying, "pay attention!"

An internal fight exists in this child. S/He wants to be held and, at the same time, wants to be let free. Let your little one take the lead. If your child is acting out, ask if s/he would like to be held. This guileless child will answer honestly. Then you can act accordingly.

SCORPIO - *12:00 p.m. to 1:30 p.m.*
Ninth House - Aquarius Rising

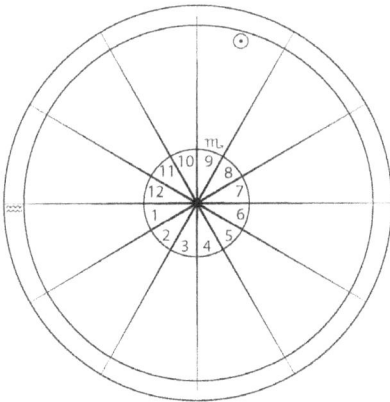

If your child learns early on how to teach others and how to learn from others, it will be to his/her benefit. Two places to take this child would be a place of worship and a foreign country. In both places, your child will learn and discard. What this little Scorpio learns will give him/her patterns throughout his/her life. That which is discarded is what your little one thinks is not necessary in his/her course of life's patterns.

If you are unable to take your child to another country or travel with him/her, introduce him/her to books and to foreign languages.

Your little one was born without prejudice. No matter to whom s/he clings, let him/her choose and you both will be happier for it.

SCORPIO
Ninth House - Pisces Rising

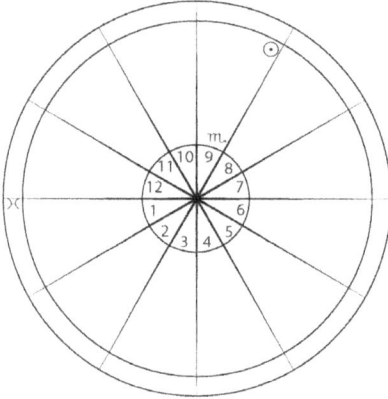

Your little one is so bright and wants to share his/her knowledge with everyone around him/her. Whatever path is chosen, it is good to encourage this child with books and journals. Keeping a journal helps your child to stay focused. Reading books about a certain passion will help your child to stay the course. If goals are set early on, your Scorpio child will find ways to further educate him/herself and feel successful at the same time.

A quest for knowledge is very great in this child and you may be asked a lot of questions about his/her passion. What you learn and impart to your child will matter later in life and help guide this child to a happy future.

Listen closely to what your little Scorpio has to say. Words of wisdom come easily for this intuitive child.

SCORPIO - *1:30 p.m. to 2:45 p.m.*
Eighth House - Pisces Rising

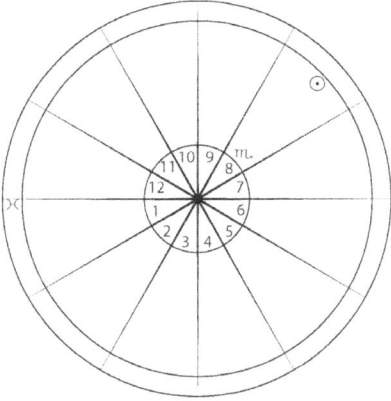

Your Scorpio child is enthusiastic about new information. S/He finds out all the information. This little one may even want to bet the horses! This child needs an allowance and needs to learn how to budget. Although s/he may show some creativity with possessions (especially someone else's), a time may come when s/he can crash and burn if not diligent. Therefore, it is important that your little one learn early that s/he can be creative but must also be practical.

You may also want to teach your child that there are consequences to every action that is undertaken. The more creative s/he is, the bigger the fall if things go wrong.

Your little one has an affinity for the bizarre. It is okay to let him/her watch a scary movie as long as your child realizes that it is fantasy and not reality. Otherwise, s/he could be the victim of nightmares. Encourage him/her to make up stories of his/her own and then you will discover what a great imagination your little one has.

SCORPIO - *2:45 p.m. to 3:30 p.m.*
Eighth House - Aries Rising

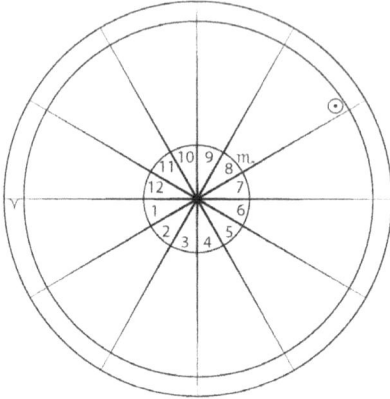

Your little one may want to trade anything at an early age. Trading up is usually a good thing, but at the same time it is just as easy to misjudge value. Be on your guard and show this child that you respect his/her choices but would like to learn about them in advance so that you can monitor his/her progress.

Since this child is curious about gambling, you can show him/her the differences in choices and how one can lose as well as win. You will be surprised when your little one begins to understand the "odds." Lessons on taking chances and the consequences are good for this innocent child so that others won't take advantage of him/her.

S/He loves to win prizes and often is the recipient of the same. This is a child who would win a scholarship or be a beneficiary of wills and prizes. Don't be surprised when s/he comes home with a certificate or other gift. These are not usually earned, as such, just won by virtue of benevolence.

SCORPIO - *3:30 p.m. to 4:30 p.m.*
Seventh House - Aries Rising

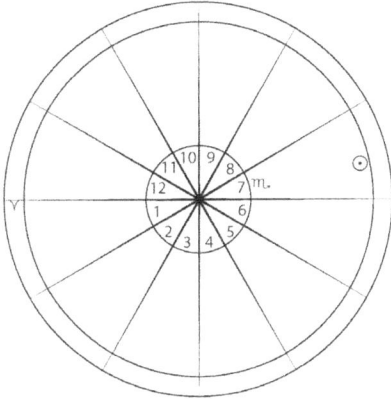

My way!!! You may find a willful child on your hands. It is good to teach compromise to your little Scorpio at an early age.

A self-starter, your Scorpio child will take the ball and run with it. Goal oriented, s/he becomes bored easily and is on the next thing, unless something is compelling to him/her. In that case, your Scorpio will see something to the end.

Although s/he can learn to stick it out no matter what, it is possible for your little one to get bored and move on to the next project. The best way to teach this little one to see things through to the end is to give small parts of a project to him/her to work out or puzzle over before going on to the next segment. After that, you will be happy to watch him/her build an entire house!

SCORPIO - *4:30 p.m. to 5:15 p.m.*
Seventh House - Taurus Rising

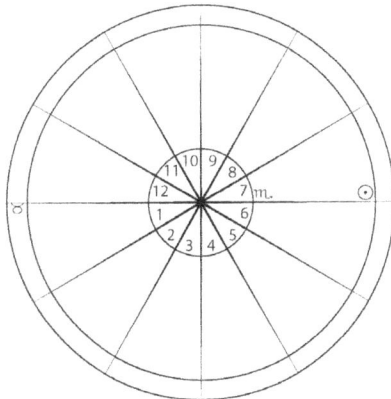

Determination!!! Your likable child can accomplish anything. If you want to see something get done, challenge him/her and see the results for yourself. Your challenge has to have good payback (not necessarily money) and the results must give satisfaction. Once that is decided, the challenge is "game on!"

Your little one may use his/her voice to convince others to do things his/her way. Sometimes it is a sultry voice and sometimes it is like a song. In either case, it will surprise you to see how very convincing this little one can be.

Should your little one have a sore throat, chances are s/he is unhappy with his/her approach to life and it is time to move on to other things!

This beautiful child loves to partner-up. It's better than doing things alone and can be more fulfilling to him/her to have some-one to share with him/her.

SCORPIO - *5:15 p.m. to 6:15 p.m.*
Sixth House - Gemini Rising

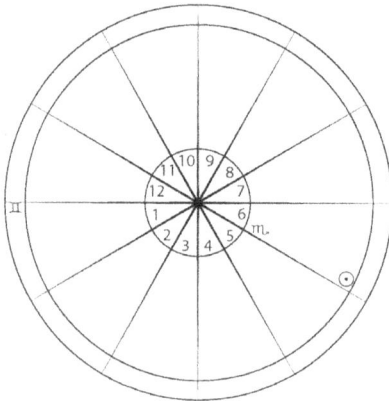

A hard worker, your little Scorpio isn't afraid of hard work. S/He may have to have a plan and scrutinize before diving into a task, but the process brings good results. There is no task too big or too small for this precious child. Be sure to assure your little one that things do not always turn out the way one expects them. There are successes and there are "so-called failures," which are more lessons than failures. It is all right to mess something up the first time, learn the lesson and continue with a different approach. Your Gemini-rising child is malleable and has the stick-to-itiveness of the Scorpio. Successes come more often than not, and this little thinker will find a way to it!

Don't give this child a task that is so great that his/her other side come out when frustrated. Be sure you start things out slowly so that s/he can feel fulfilled.

SCORPIO - *6:15 p.m. to 7:30 p.m.*
Sixth House - Cancer Rising

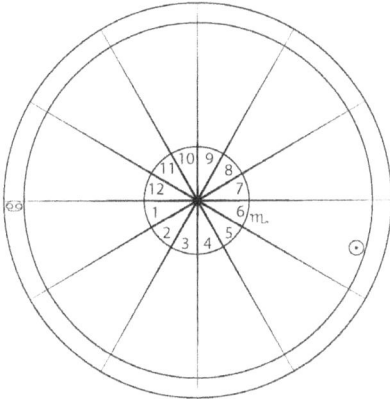

Making things work is a large goal of your little one. A true architect and builder, your Scorpio child is eager to put things together to make them work.

Another side of this child is that of the healer. Eager to make everyone better, you can be assured that nursing is in his/her genes and your little "fixer-upper" will be sure that everyone is all right and feels good!

Sometimes your affectionate child is so much of a people pleaser that it is a good idea to point out that it helps to be asked for assistance first.

Your little one may seem morose from time to time. This is only because s/he needs some affection. Just hold him/her, even rock your child. This will help soothe and calm his/her nerves. There are times when anticipation leads itself to anxiety with this child and the best way to counter this is to just hold your child. If s/he needs to cry, let him/her.

SCORPIO - *7:30 p.m. to 8:30 p.m.*
Fifth House - Cancer Rising

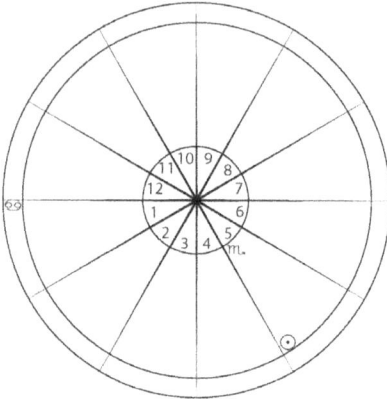

Get out the snacks, I'm bringing someone home," is a common request. With a wry sense of humor, your little Scorpio will be quite entertaining. Your little one will love to entertain and also will play with children who are brought to your home.

Teach him/her to cook early on so that when s/he brings in company, s/he can be comfortable making a spread for them. Also, you will find your youngster a whiz in the kitchen and loving the experimentation. Allow creativity and you will have a happy child. If you are told that s/he wants to be a chef when s/he grows up, encourage it. You may enjoy a meal or two out of it.

Your little one is a lover. Romantic always, don't be surprised if s/he is always kissing you and everyone else. This is normal. It isn't just the romantic aspect. You have a very affectionate creature on your hands and the best thing to do is to return the love or s/he could look elsewhere for that needed affection!

SCORPIO
Fifth House - Leo Rising

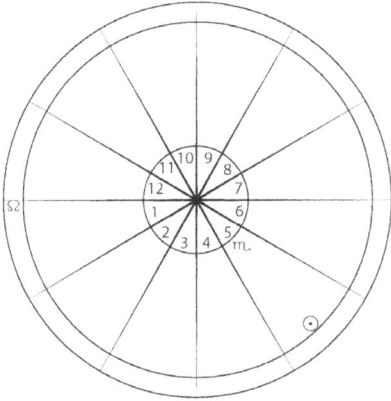

A true entertainer, your Scorpio child may originally be somewhat shy. Any kind of lessons will help to allay these insecure feelings of your proud child. Your Scorpio is a bit of a perfectionist when it comes to crowd pleasing.

Loyal to you and those s/he trusts, you will find your child quite adept at reading your underlying messages and responding accordingly. There could be a tendency to change the narrative to make you or him/herself look better and it is up to you to point out the importance of honesty. These lessons are maintained and even when they come back to bite you, you will have no problem owning it.

Be sure that you tell this stubborn child the truth because s/he has a retentive memory and anything you say today could come back to you at a much later date.

You have a proud child and it is good to show him/her how to maintain a healthy ego without injuring others. Showing this child the importance of using his/her wit to prevent bad feelings is good. You will also notice that compassion is easy to teach as it is instinctive in this child.

S/He loves to laugh so be sure there are situations to create joy. You will also find that s/he is a very good student, especially with anything that requires research.

SCORPIO - *8:30 p.m. to 9:30 p.m.*
Fourth House - Cancer Rising

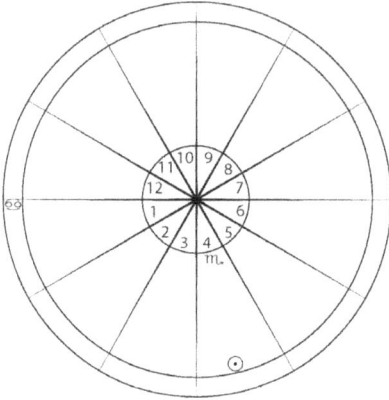

Give him/her an apron and introduce him/her to the kitchen early. Your little homebody will love to cook and prepare for everyone. Teach him/her early on to clean up as s/he goes along, or you may end up washing a lot of pots, pans, and dinnerware.

If s/he shows ability early on for entrepreneurship you can encourage it. Help bake cookies and cakes for sale so that s/he can start a business on his/her own. You will find that you can make your child quite happy if s/he is able to use skills to begin his/her own business.

Education is important to this intense child and you will find a thoughtful student. First, it will be important to you to learn what interests are his/hers. Then help him/her educate him/herself in that field.

Music will also be an important endeavor and eventual outlet for this child.

SCORPIO - *9:30 p.m. to 11:45 p.m.*
Fourth House - Leo Rising

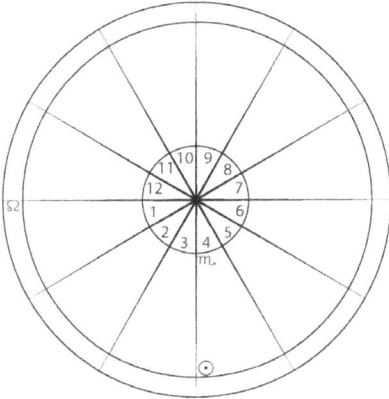

Home schooling is suitable for this child. Although, remember to give him/her a social life and allow playtime with other children. Your intelligent child will always be a good student and can even be self-taught in some subjects. Therefore, if s/he asks you a question, answer honestly. If you don't know the answer, say so. Your bright investigator will find the answer for the both of you.

There is an exhibitionist in your home, and it is this child. By this, you can be sure that s/he is quite the entertainer. Everywhere is a stage, and here is your player. If you are punked by this little one, watch as s/he grabs his/her sides and laughs him/herself silly (at your expense!).

Your Scorpio child enjoys laughing and will touch you with wonderful attempts to make you laugh with him/her. Full of mirth, you will have great pleasure if you join in with your little one rather than rebuff him/her.

AQUARIUS

Space, space, space!!! The best way to work with your Aquarian is to give boundaries and freedom within that area. In this way, there will be less rebellion on the part of this fixed child. Aquarians need to follow the rules. However, if the boundaries are too limited, your little one will push to change them until there is suitable space.

Most Aquarius children are born with symmetrical features. Your little one will always be attractive. Even should there be unusual features, there will be an enchantment about him/her.

Young David was born to very "cool" parents. They allowed him to do anything he wanted because they did not want him to feel restricted. As a result, when the family would go and visit anyone, David sat quietly in a corner and kept to himself because he didn't know what he could or could not do. At home, however, it was another story. He would stick a poker in a fire and run after his parents or any visitor with it because he was told that he could do anything he wanted. One time when the family visited me, I told David that we had rules. He could do this and that and had to show respect and kindness to the other children. He played happily with the other children and had a wonderful time. The moral: Give your Aquarius his/her dos and don'ts and allow him/her freedom within those guidelines. You will have a happy child who grows with good self-esteem.

What this Aquarius child retains will not be forgotten. Sometimes, you can become frustrated hearing about something you said or did a long time ago. You should use care in what you say around your Aquarian because it can come back (in some cases) to haunt you! Your Aquarius child will challenge you and what you say so be aware of what is said around him/her. If you say something like, "I really don't usually like . . ., but this time, I found it quite enjoyable." Your Aquarius child may retort with, "then that means you like it." You can be frustrated by this and try to argue back, but you will be badgered until you agree just to stop the conversation. Teach your little one to be kinder to people who have made changes in their minds.

Aquarian children are usually obedient. Once they are seven, however, they begin to create their own parameters and will fight tooth and nail for the right to something they believe in. "My way," is a common phrase heard from your Aquarius child. Once that little mind gets a fixed notion, there is no sway. They know! And that's all right. Rather than question what your little one is doing, ask why. It allows your child to think it through and in some cases decide on a different course of action.

You will find your little Aquarius seeking friends. A social creature, and often an old soul, your Aquarius needs companionship of his/her own choosing and liking. You can set up a play date with your best friend's little one, but there are no guarantees that they will be bosom buddies. Your Aquarius is very selective.

You will also learn that your Aquarius stays within his/her generation. That is to say, that if your child is born during the 20's s/he will stay in social pace with others of his/her generation. Because your Aquarius is social, s/he will conform to the norm.

Aquarius rules the ankles. Should your child have a few ego problems or feeling sorry for oneself, s/he may have sore ankles or heels. They may complain about their shoes or socks not fitting well or being uncomfortable.

Honesty is a characteristic of your Aquarian child. Sometimes, almost too much honesty. It is your job to teach your little one to temper honesty with kindness.

Blues, lavenders, and aqua are good colors for your Aquarius child.

AQUARIUS *12:30 am to 2 a.m.*
Third House - Scorpio Rising

A great need to communicate and an ability to retain. What you say to your little one will be remembered so be certain to speak carefully and kindly. Your words could come back to haunt you at a later time. Your Water Carrier will be a better adult if taught early on to be considerate of others' feelings. S/He can start by learning to be on time and consider how others may feel if left to wait and feel abandoned.

This is a child who enjoys siblings and does not do well as an only child. If your Aquarius child doesn't have any brothers or sisters, don't be surprised if s/he brings one home (in the form of a "close friend.") Pets are also a good addition to his/her family.

Your little one enjoys going places. There are times, though, when s/he may lose him/herself in something else and lose perspective and time. In that case, you can teach this Aquarius child that it is good to consider the other person's feelings if s/he keeps others waiting; otherwise, s/he will be thought of as selfish.

AQUARIUS *2:00 a.m. to 3:00 a.m.*
Third House - Sagittarius Rising

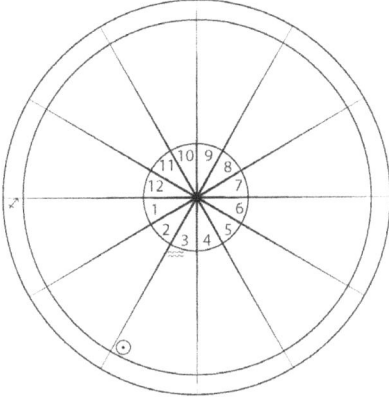

You have an adventurer on your hands. No need to leave this child home alone because s/he is ready to go with you anywhere you go. Very philosophical, you will find your little one loves to learn new things and finds spirituality in many things in his/her surroundings. A lot of wisdom will come from the mouth of this babe. Read nighttime stories to this child. A love of reading will develop, and you will have a good student, as well.

If you don't wish to introduce religion to your child, s/he will find it later in life. Don't be surprised if you find a very spiritual child underneath wolf's clothing.

Your child's retention may not be so great in the earlier years, however, by the time s/he gets to school, you will have a good student. Try, try again is a good thing to teach this child who has great determination and yet so many interests.

A little chatterbox, you may want to encourage conversation and teach listening. You may find that if your child doesn't learn early on to also give others a chance to speak, that s/he could become lonely.

Short trips (like camping) and hikes are great for this nature-lover. Take him/her with you whenever you are able!

AQUARIUS *3 a.m. to 4:30 a.m.*
Second House - Sagittarius Rising

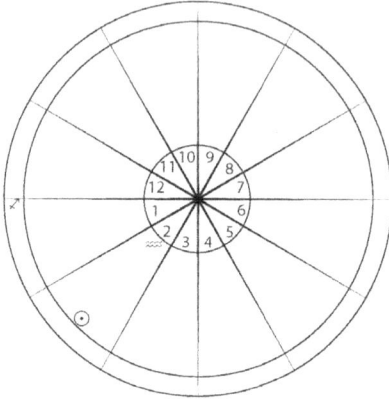

Your child could be in rags and still look classy. This Aquarian will never want for much, will always appear to have plenty, and believe in abundance. Once something is given to your little one, it will be treasured.

Give lasting gifts that will have meaning. Your little one may give a toy a name or an identity. An airplane or a map will eventually be meaningful but at an early age, something unusual and colorful will have more impact. If you want to make an impression, help him/her make something special such as an ornament or picture frame. This is a treasure that will last a lifetime.

Make lasting memories with your Aquarius child. S/He will savor those times and revisit them throughout his/her lifetime. Take lots of pictures and encourage adventure.

AQUARIUS *4:30 a.m. to 5:30 a.m.*
Second House - Capricorn Rising

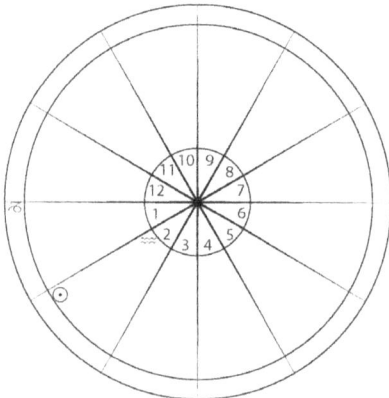

You can entrust your checkbook to your responsible child. If your little one is over-indulgent (say with candy), teach him/her the benefits of less sugar and a healthy diet. The earlier your adorable and very serious child learns the benefits of good health, the better later in life.

94

Your serious child will question everything, ad nauseum. You are not being judged; you are simply the teacher. S/He feels very responsible, and it is up to you to help him/her to differentiate between his/her responsibilities and yours.

You can give gifts of value to this child and know that they will be kept forever. Should you have a piece of jewelry you wish to gift to your Aquarius, know that it will be valued and prized as a wonderful possession.

Your child wants to be heard and in control. Set the rules and guidelines early!

AQUARIUS *5:30 a.m. to 6:30 a.m.*
First House - Capricorn Rising

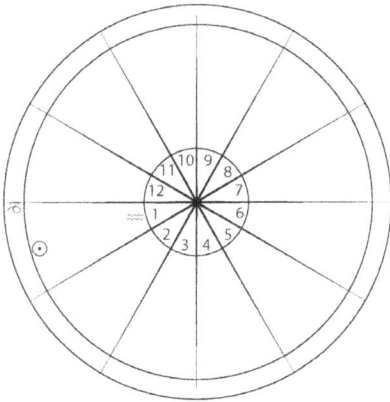

If you want to be called out, this is the child to do it. Once you tell him/her the rules, you can be expected to follow them as well. This means that if you "break" any of these rules, you can be called to the carpet! Don't tell this little one to not do something that you wouldn't do. In other words, follow any directives you give and don't bother to waver because you will be in trouble.

Your child may seem to be quite serious but only while contemplating a problem or new puzzle. The rest of the time you may hear a lot of laughter because s/he has a good sense of humor.

Your child may want to be in charge and be the responsible adult. Let him/her have a childhood first!

You will find that this little child wants to be in charge. If s/he was not born with a silver spoon in his/her mouth, s/he will question why. Keeping up with the upper crust is his/her goal and you will find that s/he has a lot of pride. Once s/he feels that s/he is "there," you will find a child who is generous in all ways. S/He just likes to be on top.

AQUARIUS *6:30 a.m. to 7:45 a.m.*
First House - Aquarius Rising

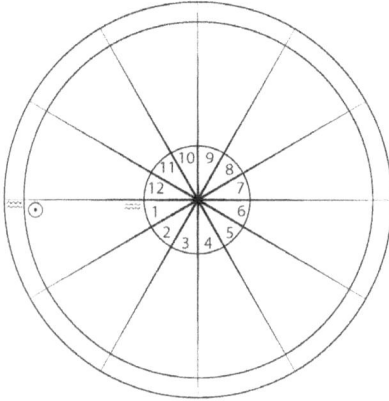

If you keep saying, "We don't do this," the response eventually will be, "Well, I do!"

Don't fence me in would be a popular theme for your young one. Unless there is a lot of freedom within those rules, your little one can feel trapped. Be sure to make reasonable requests and house rules and stick to them, then let her/him run free inside the walls you create. Space, space, space! It is necessary that there is freedom and your barriers will then be respected.

Consistency on your part is important in this child's rearing. You have a beautiful child who will do anything to make you happy. Be certain to maintain levity in the things you do together.

Your Aquarian takes things to heart and therefore honesty and integrity are important to him/her. Little white lies don't fly with your honest little water-carrier. Whatever you tell this child will be implanted in his/her psyche so be honest and save yourself and your child from future grief.

AQUARIUS *7:45 a.m. to 8:15 a.m.*
Twelfth House - Aquarius Rising

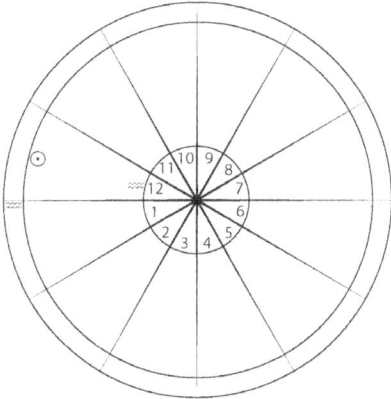

Want to keep a secret? Tell him/her that it is a secret and it will go nowhere. Many will come to him/her for advice. In most cases, the "psychiatrist" with keen senses will be helpful to those who come for advice.

Almost shy about being in the public eye, you will be surprised at how your child performs as taught. This little Aquarius is able to mimic quite well and has a strong understanding of other people's actions.

S/He is spiritual but doesn't necessarily need a formal religion to teach him/her a moral code. You may discover that good morals are built in and come for a deep resource.

You may find that your child has a "secret" code for things. Don't search for it, let it flow to you from your lovely child.

AQUARIUS *8:15 a.m. to 9:00 a.m.*
Twelfth House - Pisces Rising

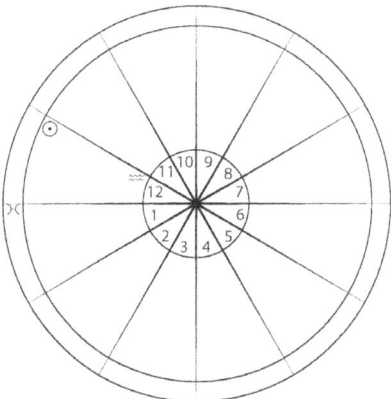

Listen closely to what your child tells you. Some things may be secrets, and some may be psychic emanations.

Your little one is very sensitive and may not do well with scary movies as they could cause nightmares. On the other hand, you will find there is a fascination with the bizarre and/or unusual. Although it is not easy to balance the two, find a way to interest your little one in storytelling so that his/her imagination can run away. Visual nightmares (such as movies) can cause real nightmares. Whereas a story can trigger the imagination and lead to a new or imagined interpretation.

This child will tell you in the morning about a dream s/he had the night before and the story can go on and on. Before you hush your little one up, ask what the lesson of the dream or the message of the dream was. In other words, "where are you going with this?"

AQUARIUS *9:00 a.m. to 10:00 a.m.*
Eleventh House - Pisces Rising

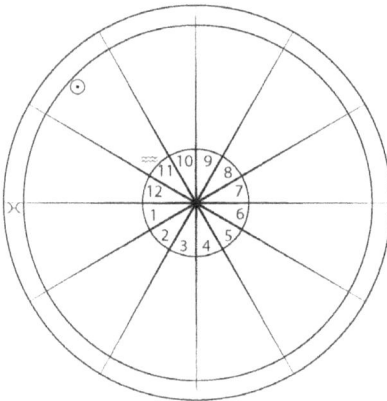

A friend to all, chances are that a pet will be very welcome in your home with this little one. Don't be surprised to find strangers in your home as your generous child will welcome any and all. If your little one wishes to join a group or club, encourage it, as it will open more doors.

It is possible that this child has a "secret" friend or an "invisible" friend. Just because you cannot see this other friend does not mean that s/he doesn't exist. It is fine to ask questions about this companion and to ask your little one to ask questions of his/her friend so that you may learn more about the nature of their relationship. You could learn a lot about your child this way.

Should your child have feet problems, it is possible that s/he is lonely and feels friendless. Your little one could also have a feeling of hopelessness.

AQUARIUS - *10:00 a.m. to 10:30 a.m.*
Eleventh House - Taurus Rising

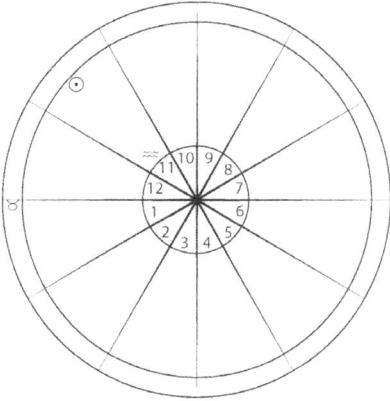

Singing lessons will go well and you may find your little one has good pitch. If s/he gets a sore throat, s/he is not happy with the way things are going.

You may find your Aquarius to be strong-willed and rather stubborn. This is natural and you can teach him/her how to be tenacious, rather than stubborn. The best way is to give a project that has an ending. Should your child complete the first project, s/he will welcome the next task.

The same goes with friendships. A pet, and the responsibilities associated with having one, can be very beneficial to this child. When given certain responsibilities, this little Aquarian will respond favorably. If you cannot have a pet, a plant or other responsibility will be favorable.

AQUARIUS - *10:30 a.m. to 11:30 a.m.*
Tenth House - Taurus Rising

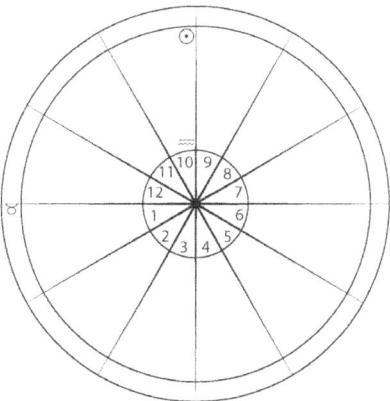

Don't be surprised if s/he wants to go into some form of public speaking or the entertainment business. People will recognize him/her by his/her voice. At one point or another, your little one could be in line for fame. Prepare him/her for this so that s/he doesn't shrink from others, especially strangers. Explain that they do not have to be a movie star to become famous, but that they will likely excel in whatever field is chosen, and others will seek out their advice or direction.

Once your child has determined a career choice, chances are s/he will stay the course and not be swayed. This child has grit and determination and is able to do anything s/he puts his/her mind to doing. The term "follow your heart" may have been written for your little one!

Your child is certain that s/he already "knows" all things. S/He may be a bit stubborn and a bit bossy. That is because s/he is louder than the rest and uses his/her voice for power. Teach him/her to sing and you will have a happy child who can put his voice to good advantage.

AQUARIUS *11:30 a.m. to 12:15 p.m.*
Tenth House - Gemini Rising

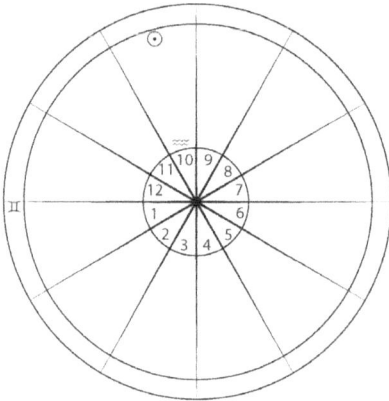

A good teacher and communicator. You may want to allow your little one to use his/her imagination as much as possible. Encourage him/her to write!

Remember that whatever this child is taught, s/he will take to heart. Be sure that you are there to guide and monitor the curriculum being presented to this sponge. Your little Aquarius may trust you enough to allow you to conduct the course of his/her studies, however, once a flaw is found, or you disagree with something learned, you may find that you will not be doing the choosing in the future.

You will discover that your child is quite popular and memorable. A great communicator and quite flexible, your little one will fit in where s/he goes.

AQUARIUS *12:15 p.m. to 1:00 p.m.*
Ninth House - Gemini Rising

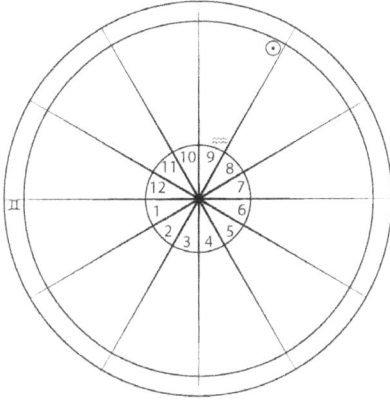

If s/he wants to be an astronaut, encourage it. Bring him/her to a space museum if possible. Whatever your Aquarius' dream may be, encourage it and you will be glad.

Your little one is quite philosophical and would one day make a good professor or teacher. A good student him/herself, you will find your Aquarius child wanting to learn more and more and eventually educating you and all around him/her.

Encourage travel to foreign lands so that your child is able to discover how others live. Languages should come easily to this little one and it is always a good idea to have a second language spoken around him/her.

A journal is always a good tool and your child can learn a great deal about communication this way. Should you encourage your Aquarius child to keep a journal, s/he will have more insight into him/herself. It will be very useful.

AQUARIUS - *1:00 p.m. to 2:00 p.m.*
Ninth House - Cancer Rising

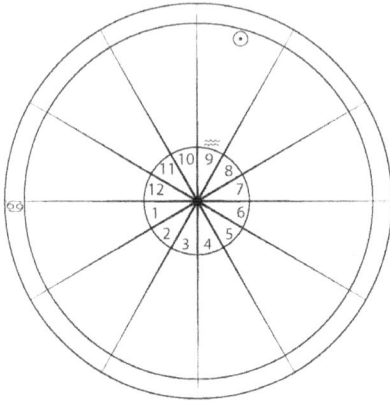

"*I don't want to go home. I just want to know it's there*" is the cry of your Aquarian. Your little one will make a home no matter where s/he goes. Travel is a joyful perk.

Maps are good for your warm and fuzzy Aquarian. You will also find an entrepreneur lurking inside the head of this child. Encourage open-mindedness. You may feel that s/he is wishy-washy and unable to make a decision; however, your little one is simply weighing all the options!

You may find that your child has a unique idea on how to present him/herself. Either by dress or other forms of attention-getting techniques, your little one wants to be different from the others and will show you and everyone else just how special s/he is!

AQUARIUS - *2:00 p.m. to 3:30 p.m.*
Eighth House - Cancer Rising

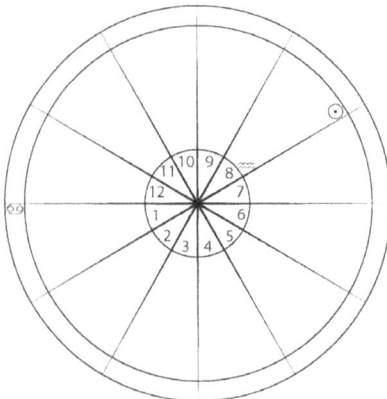

Your Aquarius child would be a good visiting nurse, always ready to help other people. S/he needs to be rewarded for these services but is worthy of the reward.

Chances are that your child will make friends with another child who would be a "business" partner and that they together will be able to work well. This will prepare him/her for the future. Working as a broker or with other people's money or property is excellent. Some entrepreneurial efforts on ways to earn money begin at an early age.

You will find an entrepreneurial spirit in this child and should not be surprised at any new ideas presented to you. It is your job to encourage. You can guide but you may also learn a few things along the way.

AQUARIUS - *3:30 p.m. to 4:30 p.m.*
Seventh House - Cancer Rising

Partnership is important to this child, who will usually choose someone who is more of a homebody. If your child is absent from home, seek him/her out at the home of a good friend (even an elderly neighbor) who makes him/her feel special. You can show your little one all the love and affection you have and then be surprised to see that love is sought elsewhere. Don't be hurt, embrace the individuality of your Aquarius child and be grateful that someone else is also taking an interest in your lovely child.

Business partnerships will begin at an early age. Your little one will love to have a partner in crime, as long as s/he is the boss!

Easily bored, your Aquarius can march to his/her own drummer. Don't expect him/her to be on time because that doesn't always happen. However, s/he won't be late for dinner! Just know what to schedule (likes not dislikes) and see how responsive this child can be.

AQUARIUS *4:30 p.m. to 5:30 p.m.*
Seventh House - Leo Rising

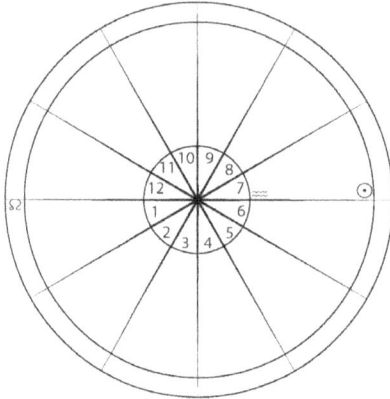

Entertaining with a partner will be utmost. "*Let's do . . .*" will be a common sound. Your Aquarian child does not prefer to do things without a partner to share the joy!

Don't be surprised to learn that after starting school your little one comes home and announces that s/he is the class clown. "What does that mean?" s/he may ask.

Many times, the seventh house describes your partner. In this case, you would not be thinking of your child as having a business or marital partner. However, you can observe (and take many pictures) whom your child chooses to be a partner-in-crime as s/he is involved in one escapade or another. In this case, your little one should find partners who are vivacious and energetic. In some cases, even a clown. Your little one may be a bit of a show-off him/herself and will look for someone who is willing to aid and abet without being the star attraction. Kind of like the person in the box being sawed in half in a magic show.

AQUARIUS - *5:30 p.m. to 7:00 p.m.*
Sixth House - Leo Rising

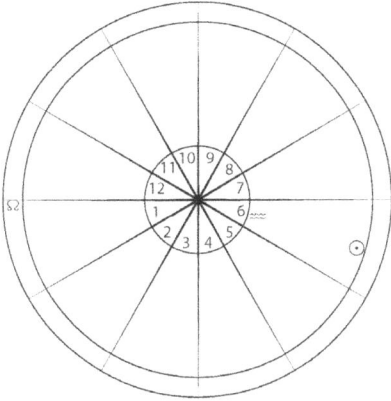

A real helper, and eventual healer, your wonderful child will grow into a caring person if shown how to care for others and to work hard. An approach to care will be with humor. Your little one could become an evangelist!

You may notice that your little one has a great mane of hair and maybe even a "widow's peak" on his/her forehead. This is a definite sign of Leo Rising. Something satisfying for this child will be to visit and entertain at places where people are less fortunate than s/he.

Some type of lessons are in order for this little one and you will find hidden talents that emerge from something simple. You may also find an athlete in this child and it is good for him/her to learn team spirit and how to play well with others.

AQUARIUS - *7:00 p.m. to 8:00 p.m.*
Sixth House - Virgo Rising

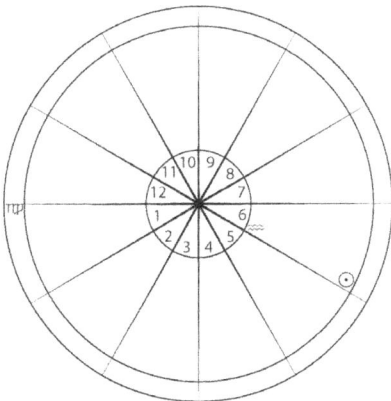

Details are important, even though your Aquarius child seems to ignore them.

A natural healer, you need to stock up on bandages and other fix-it items because your little one will be bandaging up the pet cat and siblings or friends when any suffering is witnessed. A perfectionist who follows the rules, you will have a workaholic on your hands! This child is a true humanitarian!

Sheri was sure she broke her finger. Her friend put an ice-cream stick on it to set the bone and told her it must stay on for a month. There were times when the ice cream stick could be seen on the other finger, but she waited an entire month before removing the bandage.

AQUARIUS - 8:00 p.m. to 9:30 p.m.
Fifth House - Virgo Rising

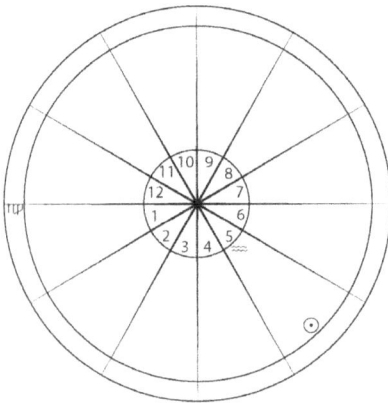

Many times, this child will have natural talent and beauty but might be reluctant to entertain anyone for fear of not being perfect. It is good to show your child that s/he doesn't have to be totally perfect. Also, encourage practice for performance and it will come easier to him/her.

Taking care of other children will be an important responsibility for this Aquarian child. If you watch how s/he responds to other children, you may see either how s/he has been treated in the past or you may see how s/he wishes others to treat him/her.

Your child may feel alone or lonely, no matter how many people call him/her "friend." With a devil-may-care attitude, s/he is actually shy. S/He wants to perform and show him/herself worthy of your praise; however, she is too reticent to do so for fear of criticism or not being good enough. Confidence may not come until adulthood.

AQUARIUS - *9:30 p.m. to 10:30 p.m.*
Fifth House - Libra Rising

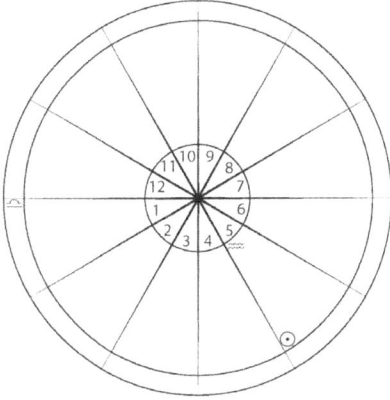

This is the child who gives the parties and/or soirees. S/He is adept at keeping harmony around all the activities. A gracious host, your little one will make everyone comfortable.

On a visit to Japan, I was one of several guests at a traditional dinner party. The little three-year-old, Chuichi, graciously led us to our seats, humming, "Dozo (Please)" as he showed each guest to a seat at the table. This is the graciousness of your Aquarius child!

You will find that your child loves to please and will go to lengths to be sure that everyone is happy and comfortable.

Your Aquarius also enjoys the spotlight and will usually fare well in a situation where s/he is the star of an occasion or event. It is good to highlight accomplishments of your child's life (to date) by pointing out his/her qualities.

AQUARIUS *10:30 p.m. to 11:30 p.m.*
Fourth House - Libra Rising

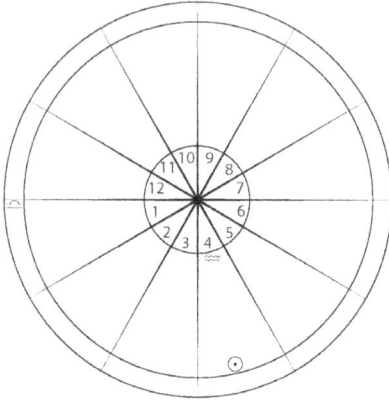

My home must be lovely, and I need to have my alone time there. Keep this in mind when you ask your little one what s/he is doing, and the answer is: *Nothing.* This Aquarian can be quite contemplative. Usually, your child will have a great deal of beauty, both inside and out. Remember that everything needs to be "fair" in his/her eyes. A place for everything and everything in its place is a mantra you will feel from this Aquarius child.

S/He loves sweets and can learn early to curb these cravings. Be gentle and supportive. Alternatives, such as fruit, can help curb the desire for sugar. As your child grows, understanding the rules of good nutrition will make a difference in his/her life. You can teach this little one to cook at an early age.

AQUARIUS *11:30 p.m. to 12:30 a.m. (next day)*
Fourth House - Scorpio Rising

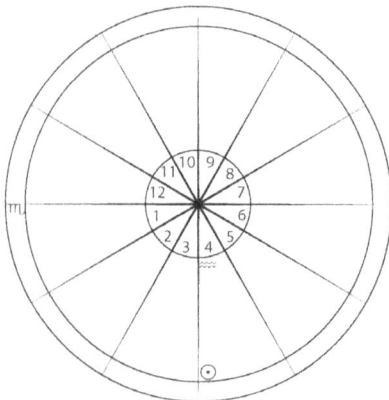

However you decorate this child's room, do it carefully because your little one may wish to keep it that way forever. Change is difficult for this child and once rooted in a home, your little boy/girl will not want to move or change his/her environment in any way.

Your child may tell you early on that s/he wants to be a scientist. Your Aquarian child enjoys delving into things and studying something to the end. This child will be a good astronomer or scientist. Whatever project strikes his/her fancy early on will continue as time goes on.

Your Aquarius child is the ultimate humanitarian and wants to welcome everyone into your home! It is good for him/her to learn discrimination early in life.

PART THREE

MUTABLE SIGNS

Your Mutable Sign child is the child who will go along to get along. These children are usually the most flexible. Their need to please is important, but mostly, your child will enjoy being part of the "crowd." Mutable Sign children are usually sensitive and do not necessarily like to stick out in situations.

These children have a way of fitting in anywhere they are. You will hear the comment, "S/He is so easy to be with," often. It is true. Your Mutable Sign child becomes one with his/her environment.

The time of your child's birth gives additional understanding into his/her needs and what area of your child's life is important to him/her.

It is a good idea to remember to deduct one hour for daylight-savings-time (i.e. if your child was born at 8:41 PDT, subtract one hour and use 7:41).

If the time is close to the hour, it is possible that the definition prior to or following the one given will apply. Also, if your child is born in a very northerly area or in a very southern hemisphere, the same may apply.

GEMINI

Duality is usually associated with this sign. On one day s/he's this way and the next day it's that way. How frustrating to you the parent. "I never know who he's going to be tomorrow," a frustrated parent related to me about her Gemini son. Does this mean that your child will go through life without a defined personality? No.

To start, it is important to teach organization to your little Gemini. They need to know where everything is located. They need to have order around them. This helps them to organize their thoughts and actions. Early on, they should be taught–this goes here and that goes there. It is a simple thing but important to how their lives are ordered as they grow.

A Gemini child who has disorder around him/her walks in confusion. Their minds wander and they are easily confused about the smallest details. Their teachers in school will complain that they do not concentrate on one subject at a time and usually are miles away from the subject matter.

If your child lives in a mess and cannot find things, his/her mind follows with confusion. The lack of concentration forces your child to move on to other things that are easier to comprehend. That is why it is important to start your little one at an early age with a sense of where and what everything is.

Under-achieving gifted children can fall into this category if they are not taught early on how to tackle one project at a time. In the beginning, long-term projects should be avoided, as it is too much for your little one's mind. Accomplishment in short-term projects help them establish self-esteem and eventually become good scholars.

This Mercury-ruled child is usually quick-witted and can amaze you with the potpourri of knowledge s/he possesses. Their minds run rampant when given a mental challenge. They enjoy puzzles and board games. You can teach your Gemini chess at a very early age.

Initially, your Gemini will not want to know all the details–just the end result. Once reasoning begins to develop, s/he will amaze you with clear understanding of problems.

Your Gemini child wants to talk, talk, talk. You can also encourage him/her to keep a journal to put down his/her thoughts. This again helps with the orderliness.

The duality of this sign also shows itself in social situations. Each group associated with your child will see him/her in a different light. To one group, s/he will be one person and to another group completely different.

These children are very versatile and will amaze you with their ability to adjust to situations. They will often go with the flow if it seems "right" to them.

Your Gemini has high morals but can also be very weak when pressured in social situations that do not conform to their teaching. It is up to you to instill the ideals which will place him/her above his/her current confrontation. This will help him/her at a later time in life as well.

Computers are easy to understand for your Gemini child. S/He can even fix it. All form of communication will be a thrill. S/he can always enjoy social media, which will be a source of pleasure.

Your Gemini child does not like to sit still. Short trips are always enjoyable and your little one will always be ready for that trip to the beach or to the mountains. Wherever you take your Gemini, be sure s/he has his/her own pack for the trip with his/her belongings to take along. This gives your child a sense of identity, individuality, and belonging.

Mental puzzles are especially enjoyable to your Gemini child. A good start is a jigsaw puzzle. Word games and crossword puzzles will eventually present a challenge as will Sudoko, etc. There are many puzzle games available that are challenging and fun for your child. S/He can spend hours working on just one item.

Yellow is a good color for your Gemini child. They also like colors that oppose one another, such as Green and Red.

GEMINI - *4:00 a.m. to 4:30 a.m.*
First House, Taurus Rising

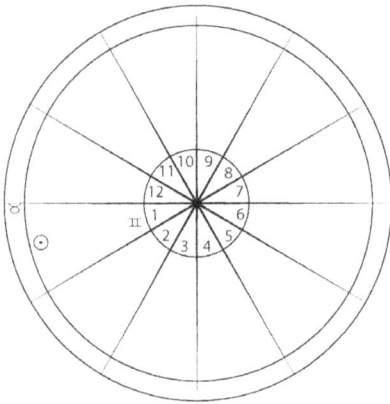

You may be surprised at how firm this versatile child can be about certain subjects. S/he will also display a firmness and stubbornness about certain matters, surprising you that this usually easy-going child could be so determined. The good thing about this is that this very determination will give your child focus to do anything.

You are able to give a task to this sweet little one and know that it will be done before s/he emerges again for the next project.

S/He likes keepsakes and especially enjoys heirlooms. If something is an important family relic, you can entrust it to this child who will cherish it and put it in safety. You may also find that your little one needs to feel cherished as well and appreciated for his/her differences and versatility.

GEMINI - *4:30 a.m. to 5:30 a.m.*
First House - Gemini Rising

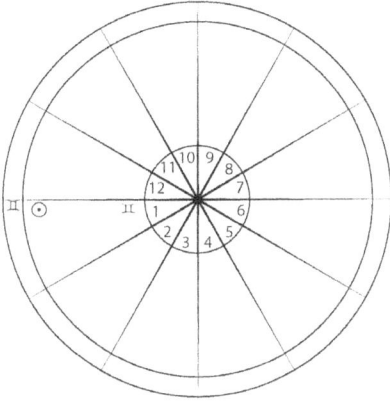

Once this child finds his/her voice, you will find that s/he is a quick learner. Your Gemini child is a quick learner and an able student.

If you find your little one is slow to grasp something, find the emotional side of your child's psyche and you will be able to help reduce the mental block.

Help your child to avoid confusion by being direct with him/her. If you are asked a question, answer it to the best of your ability. You can also teach this little one how to look things up. They love knowledge and the more s/he knows, the happier s/he is. You may have to be on your toes during these times of discovery, but eventually, you should be able to say, "I don't know, look it up," to your bright child.

Remember this little one needs a lot of affection, so don't be afraid to share it with him/her.

GEMINI - *5:30 a.m. to 6:15 a.m.*
Twelfth House - Gemini Rising

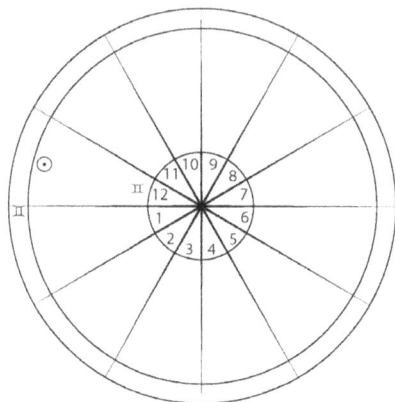

It is hard to keep a secret for this talkative Gemini. You may find that "I've got a secret" and "Guess what?" are common remarks from this child. In spite of the desire to hold in information, your talkative Gemini child may be inclined to confide in you. Once it is established that s/he has your confidence, the secrets will come your way.

You may be able to teach this child the importance of keeping a confidence but because s/he likes to talk so much, it may be hard.

On the other hand, if your little one feels strongly (or has a strong bond with the person who owns the secret) and cares about the information being held, you may have an advocate for your own causes. Then, you won't worry about your privacy.

Discretion is the rule to teach your child and then you will feel best about what is held in confidence.

GEMINI - *6:15 a.m. to 7:30 a.m.*
Twelfth House - Cancer Rising

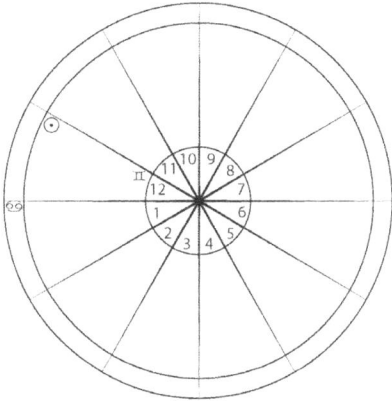

This child is a great self-starter and is able to pull rabbits out of a hat. With the quickness of his/her Gemini mind and the ingenuity of Cancer Rising, you will be amazed and how easily your child is able to solve problems and how glib s/he is about them.

Your child is very much the entrepreneur and can easily begin new projects. Being able to stick to it will be on you and your training. Starting at page one is easy but proceeding to the end is the challenge. Show your child the benefits of a finished project

A good outlet for your Gemini is in the kitchen. Teach him/her to cook and the value of knowing what nourishes and what satisfies. Then, let him/her loose. You will enjoy some tasty dishes from your creative child.

GEMINI - *7:30 a.m. to 8:45 a.m.*
Eleventh House - Cancer Rising

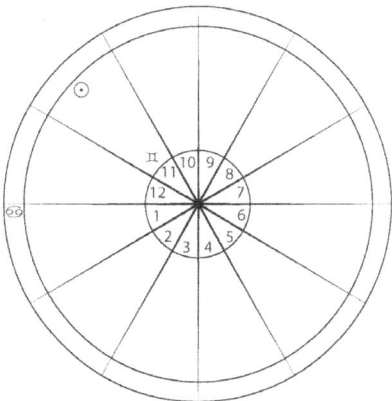

At an early age, your Gemini child will very likely tell you his/her plans for the future. Usually, this is something creative and innovative. It is a good idea to guide your child to expand his/her horizons by demonstrating how an idea can be turned into a reality.

S/He may want to include friends in his/her plan, and you should welcome this type of interaction. However, it is a good idea to teach discrimination at an early age.

A home where friends can converge is important to this child and is good to make everyone feel welcome.

Keep the pantry and refrigerator full so that your Gemini feels comfortable entertaining friends (with food).

GEMINI - *8:45 a.m. to 9:45 a.m.*
Eleventh House - Leo Rising

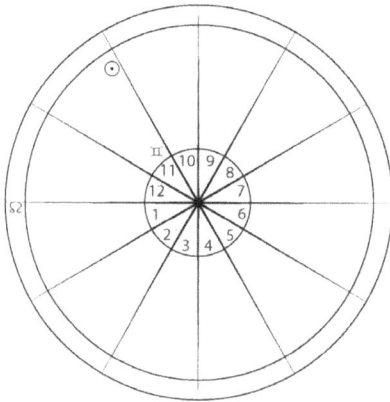

You have such a friendly child and it is to be encouraged. You will find that your Gemini child enjoys entertaining friends and is always quick-witted. Chances are you will hear a lot of laughter around your little one. This is due to a fine sense of humor and a desire to entertain others.

Your Gemini child is quite intelligent, and often excels at school. Don't be surprised if there are times when this little "Twin" begins to tutor others. You may find that once you have taught your child something, s/he may repeat your lessons to others, especially should your little one find the information interesting!

These children enjoy playing outside with friends, and it is a good idea to teach your little one outdoor activities that you once enjoyed (or would have liked to enjoy). Running and playing with others are good physical and social activities for this little Twin!

GEMINI - *9:45 a.m. to 11:15 a.m.*
Tenth House - Leo Rising

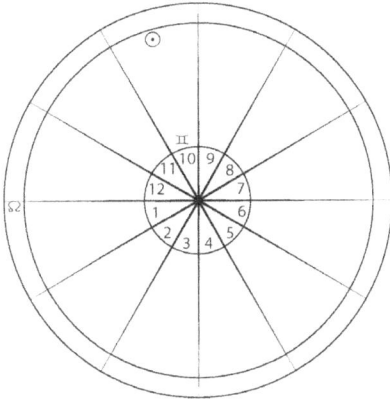

Being noticed is very important to this versatile child. Often glib, s/he will in some way, manage to entertain others. If s/he doesn't get enough attention, s/he could bully others to pay attention. The best way to ward this behavior off is to teach your child early on that as a leader of others s/he has a responsibility to protect others and not to push them or punish them to do his/her bidding. Setting a reasonable example will make a big difference.

There are times when you will see single-minded determination. S/He is not stubborn but is proud. As long as reputation and your pride in him/her is evident, your child will not act out. However, s/he needs attention and will get it in one way or another. Usually, the attention is garnered by showing how smart s/he is!

Your little one needs recognition and appreciation for his/her accomplishments and abilities. If not received by you (the most important person in his/her life) then s/he will blow his/her own horn and be sure to get recognition from those around him/her. In some cases, bribery may be involved.

This versatile child loves to laugh. Teach him/her to laugh at him/herself first before attempting to laugh at others. It is a good idea to teach your little one some compassion for the feelings of others as well so that later in life s/he won't be judged.

GEMINI - *11:15 a.m. to 1:00 p.m.*
Tenth House - Virgo Rising

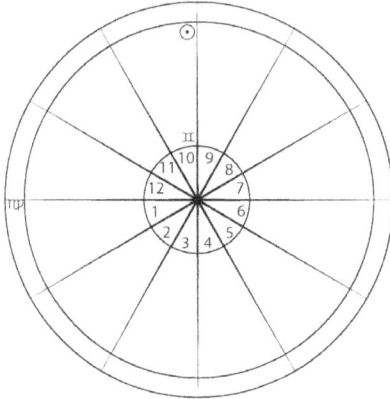

With a desire to be a leader because of his/her great mental capacity, it may be difficult for anyone to take this Gemini child seriously enough to follow him/her. It is a good idea to show your Mercury-ruled child how to use his/her intellect by being a good example.

Encourage him/her to write and to find means of communication at an early age. This will help more with a feeling of self-worth and identity than if s/he should try to be followed by others. Your Virgo-rising child will be a shining example and may be somewhat shy and reticent to display any forms of grandeur. Let him/her take his/her own lead.

Your child is convinced of his/her intelligence and it is up to you to show him/her the difference between book smarts and street smarts. As bright as this child is, s/he may have to be outsmarted from time to time so that s/he can find his/her place in the world.

It is a good thing to give praise to your child for his/her accomplishments because self-worth is valuable and important to him/her. In spite of the fact that s/he may be put in the limelight, there is a shyness to your child that also has to be appreciated. Therefore, when put on stage, applaud his/her brilliance and don't speak of the audience.

GEMINI - *1:00 p.m. to 1:45 p.m.*
Ninth House - Virgo Rising

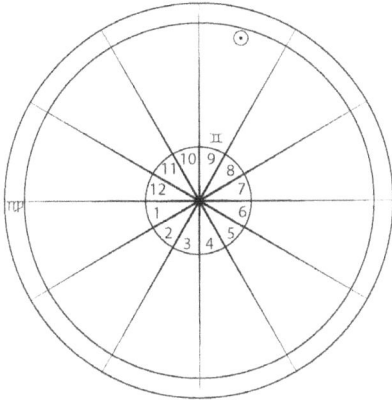

You can encourage this intelligent child to learn languages. You will find great mental acumen and a wise amount of understanding of what is going on around him/her.

This analytical child will surprise you with solutions to problems that confuse many people. S/He will enjoy puzzles, both mental and jigsaw (physical). At an early age, your Gemini may want to solve crossword puzzles. Games are especially enjoyable to this child, especially chess and backgammon. Board games that require thinking and schematics are especially enjoyable.

Higher education will be important to your child but don't be surprised if s/he bores easily. It is good to keep informative books around for his/her further education and enjoyment.

You can encourage your youngster to keep a journal with thoughts that are private. Since s/he is always thinking, this will not be difficult.

Your youngster may also feel a strong desire to travel to other countries. You could begin this type of education keeping your child active in his/her own country and learning more about it before going about to other places. Ask him/her which language is most appealing and encourage him/her to learn that language. It will be good for this child to be able to speak more than one language.

GEMINI - *1:45 p.m. to 3:30 p.m.*
Ninth House - Libra Rising

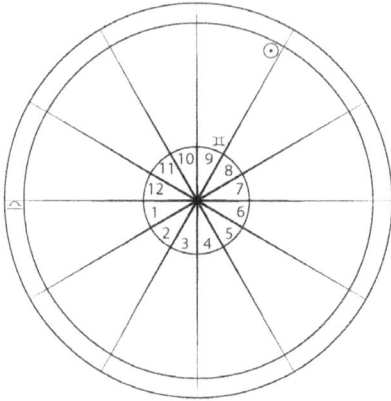

Playful and filled with mirth, your lovely child should bring joy to your life. S/He is interested in learning and in all things that are fair. Your little one will fight for peace and believes and equality at any price. S/He will fight for the underdog! S/He also believes that you should treat him/her fairly and should s/he feel something isn't right, s/he will voice it with, "that's not fair!!"

Your little twin may at times mimic you. Remember to keep order in his/her life!

Prepare him/her for a college education early on in life. Explain and show why more education will be necessary for life's endeavors.

GEMINI - *3:30 p.m. to 4:30 p.m.*
Eighth House - Libra Rising

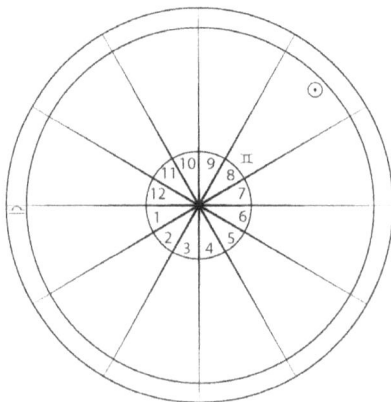

S/He knows what s/he wants and who s/he wants in his/her life. Let him/her figure it out.

Your Gemini child looks for fairness and wants order and peace. If you want someone who is not greedy but who divides things fairly, this is your child.

If your little one comes home with a gift and says,

"Look what I got from . . ." don't be surprised. This is a child to whom people wish to give presents. People know and understand when certain others will treasure and care for precious items and, when ready to part with it, will give these things to someone else who will treasure it.

Your child is often the recipient of gifts, scholarships, and other benefits. This is natural for him/her and you will find that s/he is also quite generous. Teach your child to keep what is treasured before distributing to others.

GEMINI - *4:30 p.m. to 5:45 p.m.*
Eighth House - Scorpio Rising

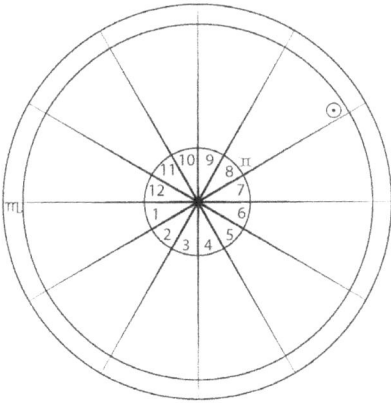

A taste for the bizarre keeps your little one on edge and enjoying the ride. Introduction to a scary movie and the knowledge that it is just a movie, will keep your little twin on the edge of his/her seat. It is a good idea to teach that not everyone has the fortitude to withstand these features.

Put a pen or paintbrush in his/her hand and see what unusual images come up on paper.

You may see that your little one wants to talk a blue streak explaining a thought or an idea. In this event, if it is overkill, refer to your own knowledge of the subject and show your child how to have an intelligent conversation about the subject. This will teach him/her how not to bore others with certain knowledge.

It is normal for your child to appear sensual. S/He is completely in touch with his/her senses and will respond in kind.

GEMINI - *4:45 p.m. to 7:00 p.m.*
Seventh House - Scorpio Rising

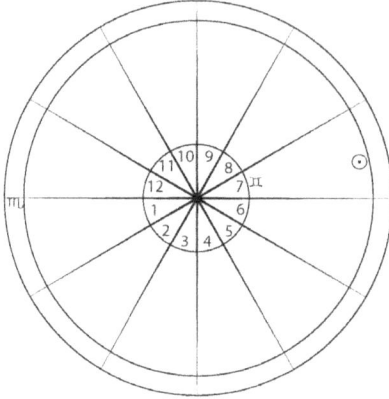

Your intelligent and diverse child with show you just how strong s/he is by overcoming many obstacles. You will revel at how well s/he retains information and how quickly s/he learns new things.

Your little "twin" is affectionate and enjoys physical contact. Don't be afraid to show love to this child, as it will frame life later.

Your little Gemini has an uncanny ability to understand other people and their strengths and weaknesses. Compassion comes naturally and disdain is learned. Allow your child the right to make his/her own judgments. You can teach differentiation and how not to be led down the wrong path to this child, but first find out from him/her what his/her instincts are. You will receive a good education from your little one.

GEMINI- *7:00 p.m. to 8:15 p.m.*
Seventh House - Sagittarius Rising

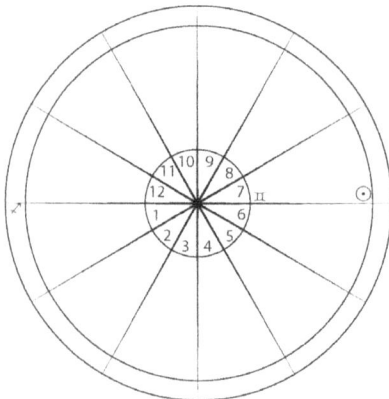

Quite the scholar, you have a child who needs constant stimulation as his/her little mind keeps ruminating the world's solutions. Your child will look for balance and equality to maintain his/her identity.

If your little one tends to exaggerate, don't worry. It's natural. Early on you can teach the difference between an exaggeration and a lie. "It was a big big tree," vs. "It was the biggest tree ever." "A big big tree" which could describe a sapling is still not the "biggest" tree. By learning these differences early, your little "twin" will be able to differentiate, and life will be easier later on.

You may not want to put this child in a uniform at an early age. Somehow or another, s/he may change it up and make it unique to him/her. Yellows are great colors for this child, and it is possible that you will be initially taken aback by his/her choice in wardrobe.

A lover of design and color, you can teach your receptive child early on how to put things together or at least get some books on the subject for him/her. They may love to construct things while they are young and Legos or (an old one) Tinker Toys are good for them as outlets for their architectural abilities.

Drawing is also good for this child.

GEMINI - *8:15 p.m. to 9:15 p.m.*
Sixth House - Sagittarius Rising

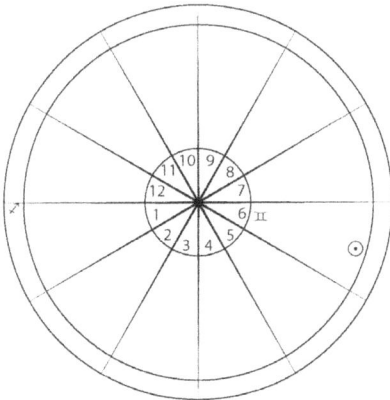

Compassion is his/her middle name. You will find that this child is kind and caring and willing to care for others.

Should s/he have a hip or thigh pain, you will know that your child is not happy with his/her approach to life. This can be conquered by putting a map on the wall and having your child stick pins of one color on the places s/he wants to visit and replacement pins on the places that have been visited.

This Gemini is a good worker and looks forward completing a task. It is a good idea to check the work and make certain that things are done well the first time so that there isn't the necessity of a do-over!

Reconstruction projects are good for your child and don't be surprised to see him/her take something apart to see how it works, only to put it back together again.

GEMINI - *9:15 p.m. to 10:15 p.m.*
Sixth House - Capricorn Rising

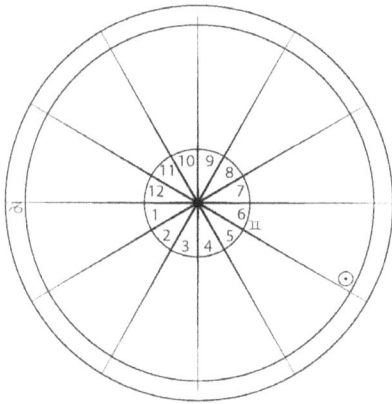

Your Gemini child is interested in health and fascinated by it. You may find a healer in your midst. It is a good idea to show him/her charts, from food charts (pyramids) to acupuncture charts. A strong interest in health and the body is evident in this child. S/He always wants everyone to feel good!

S/He should have a strong jawline and could have a jutting chin. A trip to the orthodontist early on could be helpful if his/her teeth are not lined up into a good occlusion. If you take care of this problem in early childhood years, you can prevent years of adult pain.

If s/he was on a construction site, s/he would be the boss, telling everyone what to do and how to do it. S/He needs to learn all the jobs before doing any of them so that s/he can tell everyone else what to do and how to do it!

GEMINI - *10:15 p.m. to 11:15 p.m.*
Fifth House - Capricorn Rising

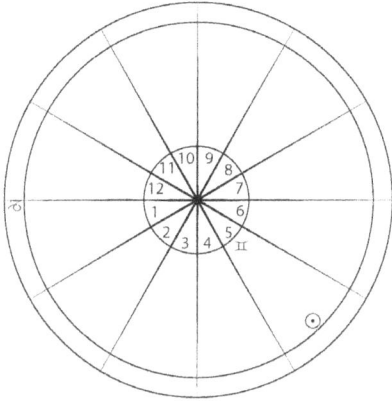

If you wish to be entertained by this sprite, you need a plan. Your child needs to learn a routine. Off the cuff isn't always easy to perform for this little one and rehearsed and planned routines are easier and more suitable.

With a strong, determined jaw, you may find your child likes to take the lead and be in charge of events, rather than actually entertaining others.

When playing house, your little one may take on the role of "Mommy" or "Daddy" and then you can see how YOU behave in his/her eyes. You may find your child a little "bossy!"

Your child is the "producer" or "master of ceremonies" in many performances or "shows" s/he wishes to put on for you and/or your friends. Don't worry, it is usually well-thought out and your child has a plan in mind. You will applaud your little one's ingenuity and talent for finding good entertainment. S/He is a good entrepreneur and will show many talents while growing up.

GEMINI - *11:15 p.m. to 12:15 a.m.*
Fifth House - Aquarius Rising

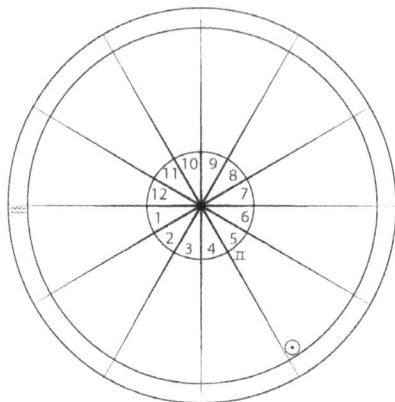

There was a song once that described your Gemini with Aquarius Rising. It was called "Charlie Brown," and one line in it described him with, "He's a clown, that Charlie Brown." Filled with mirth, your Gemini child can possess some of these characteristics and you will find much pleasure if you laugh along with him/her and not AT him/her. Your beautiful smiling child is quick to entertain you and only wants to see you smile as well.

This is definitely a child who loves and enjoys all forms of entertainment. In some cases, s/he is the entertainer and, in other cases, the one who attends all the concerts. In either case, it will never be too early to introduce him/her to any form of entertainment or fun!

You will also find that games are a good diversion for this child so keep plenty on hand! Games, such as charades, allow your child to express him/herself freely and with abandon. You will find a great entertainer in him/her.

GEMINI - *12:15 a.m. to 12:45 a.m.*
Fourth House - Aquarius Rising

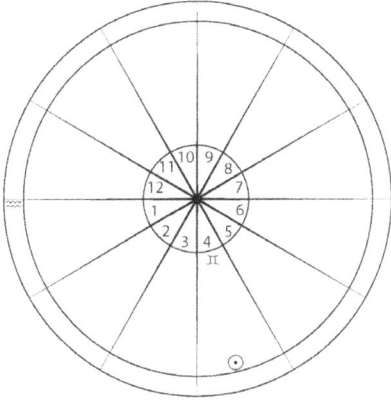

Your little Gemini likes order around him/her. If there is chaos, his/her mind will also have chaos. That is why it is a good idea to educate your child early on about what goes here and what goes there.

You may find your little twin enjoying the kitchen and feeling inclined to cook, especially if the dishes are unusual or uncommon. Don't be afraid to introduce new and unusual tastes to this Gemini and then have a need to find the recipe for him/her.

Sometimes moody, your Gemini will keep a smile on to make you happy. If you notice that s/he is busy contemplating, ask if you can help. They may need some answers to questions that may have haunted them in the past. It is also possible that they are questioning their own futures and "what will I be when I grow up?" These are normal questions and it is hard for you to really answer, except to offer encouragement and love.

GEMINI - *12:45 a.m. - 1:15 a.m.*
Fourth House - Pisces Rising

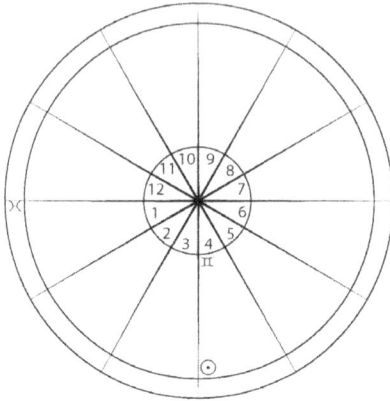

You may find your child dreamier and less organized than other Gemini children. A cheerful child, you may find that s/he has his/her head in the clouds more than other children. But do be happy at how happy your child is as s/he goes blithely through the day.

In spite of the fact that you have such a dreamy and lovable child, know too that you have a good student and brilliant mind on your hands. Some things that pop out of his/her mouth are profound and mind-boggling. You will enjoy learning new things from your wise and amazing child. Don't discount insights that you may have missed. These are gifts that are brought to you from your amazing child.

GEMINI - *1:15 a.m. - 2:00 a.m.*
Third House - Pisces Rising

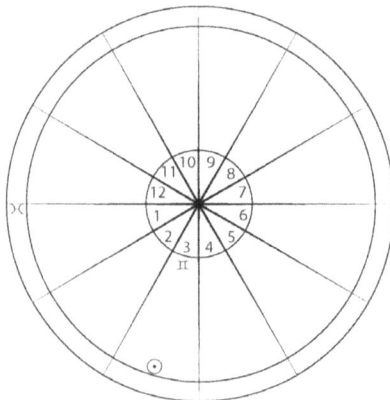

An amazing student, you will find that your little one is very ethereal in thought. S/He works at intellectualizing but begins to go off on a tangent. Your problem is whether or not you bring this little one back to reality. In fact, you do, but gently. Don't tell him/her that s/he is dreaming. In fact, it may seem that way with

130

those puppy-dog eyes looking at you. If you teach too much reality to your child, you may find s/he has lost some creativity. Instead, give him/her a piece of paper and something with which to write and you will get most of your answers.

Your child loves siblings and can be very loving and caring. However, this is not the child you would want to make responsible for other children while still a child him/herself. It is best to wait. In the meantime, your little one is a great playmate and enjoys a sister or brother. If this isn't possible, a pet is not the same, but a definite alternative. Someone to share is important to this lovable child. Cousins and other relatives are always welcome in your little one's circle.

GEMINI - *2:00 a.m. - 2:30 a.m.*
Third House - Aries Rising

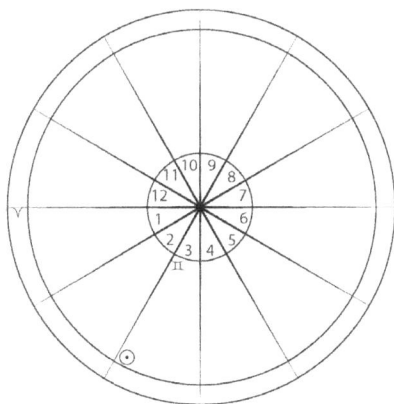

"Let's go out and play!" will be often heard from this child. Running and playing are lots of fun for your versatile child. At the same time, you have an unassuming student who is ready to learn anything you wish to teach him/her.

A very good sibling, your child will love his/her brothers and sisters and any pets that come into your home. S/He has a special affinity for small pets and will be a good provider for them. You will see a lot of love poured into other children and pets.

Everything is of wonder to this child and you will find discovery with him/her. Don't be afraid to try new places and new activities because they will be welcome. This child is an innocent and has fresh eyes for discovery. Go along and you can learn together!

GEMINI - *2:30 a.m. - 3:00 a.m.*
Second House - Aries Rising

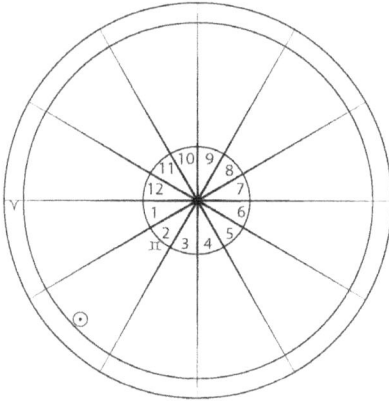

You will be responsible for teaching your child when to be generous and when to protect his/her belongings. It is possible that every gift or prize is given away, and it is up to you to teach your little one when to give and when to share!

Your child values everyone and everything. It is good for you to help him/her to learn to differentiate and to know how to place value on an item. Most value for this child comes from sentiment more than monetary value. If s/he can learn the difference from you, it will make life easier for both of you.

There are times when your very bright child will enjoy playing more than anything else. Puzzles are so appealing, so if you must keep your child inside for any reason, find some puzzles that can be solved. Remember that your little one does not have a long attention span and prefers those things that are accomplished quickly.

Books can be valuable treasures for your lovely and intelligent child. In the beginning, you can encourage a new appreciation for books by reading to him/her. Eventually, as your child begins to learn to read, s/he will enjoy reading on his/her own. Audio books will be of great comfort to him/her so that s/he can multi-task.

GEMINI - *3:00 a.m. - 4:00 a.m.*
Second House - Taurus Rising

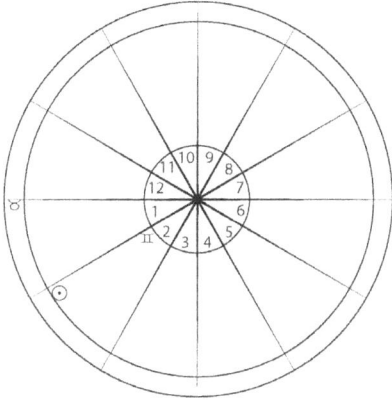

What is of value to you may not be the same for your Gemini child. A library can be important as your child enjoys stories. However, a library does not necessarily have to consist of simply books. A music library is also as valuable, as your little one can enjoy singing along with the music s/he hears.

You may find that your lovely, smiling child has a wonderful voice that is distinctive. No one else sounds like him/her and you can pick him/her out in a crowd just by the sound of his/her voice.

Singing lessons are of value to this child of wonder and you will hear lovely sounds emanate from him/her. You can also give this child music lessons.

VIRGO

This child is very self-reliant. Although s/he is on a quest to find the perfect partner because of his/her independence, s/he may wait before making any commitments to anyone else. This includes working together on a project or trusting anyone into his/her circle. You will also find your Virgo to be shy in the face of strangers.

This little Virgo will become impatient and want to get things done immediately and alone. So, if s/he recruits someone to help him/her fulfill a project, don't be surprised if s/he becomes impatient and leaves the partner in the dust. Your Virgo child may tend to put things off until the very last minute. But, s/he is sure to finish those things that were started.

The nitpicker of the zodiac, every little detail is important to your little one. If there is a thread loose, teach her/him to tie a knot, rather than pull out the seams. The same is true in life situations. Your Virgo child can pick a thing to death while it completely unravels. This comes from worrying too much. No matter your course of action, your little one can worry it to death. Assurances are not always enough, unless there is great trust. Prove you are right and soon the worrying can stop.

If you make a promise, keep it. Even if you make a threat, (like taking away a treasure) keep the threat. You will have more mutual respect. Your Virgo child trusts you (and sometimes you alone) and will believe everything you say to him/her. Be honest, be firm!

Your lovely child will remember every detail of every occasion. This can either vex you or thrill you. If you tell a fib or embellish a story, your little Virgo will correct you with the facts. If is in your best interest to remember the details so that your child won't feel compelled to correct your narrative.

Your Virgo child will seem shy until s/he feel comfortable with the people in his/her environment. So, if you introduce him/her to someone new, don't feel surprised if s/he falls back completely shy and quiet. Once s/he warms up to someone, the opposite is true. Your little Virgo will love to see the new person all the time. It just takes time with these children.

Your Virgo child likes irony. Mysteries that make sense are also appealing. Things that puzzle are appealing and when a solution is not obvious, your child is delighted because s/he enjoys the challenge.

Do your best to teach your Virgo to finish a project before starting a new one. Since s/he bores easily, it may be difficult, but in the long run you will both be happy – your child with a sense of accomplishment and you with seeing something through to the end.

It is said that Virgo has a lot of knowledge of many things but has not mastered anything. If you teach your child early on to finish projects, you will find a happy and accomplished child. "Jack of all trades, Master of none" only applies when you don't teach your child to finish what s/he started. A great sense of accomplishment comes when you honor your child with the opportunity to complete a project.

Should your Virgo child seem impatient, it is only because s/he is a perfectionist and tries hard to correct things to make them better. Find out what is so frustrating and perhaps you can help!

As soon as your Virgo child begins to socialize, you will find there could be a self-deprecating nature about him/her. Your little one may feel unworthy of any attention heaped upon him/her. This is a case more of wanting approval. Although too much praise is not necessary, it is always good to take notice of even small accomplishments. You don't necessarily have to heap praise, but it is a good idea to notice when an accomplishment is presented to you.

Navy blue is a good color for Virgo, as is brown.

VIRGO - *9:00 a.m. to 10:15 a.m.*
Eleventh House - Libra Rising

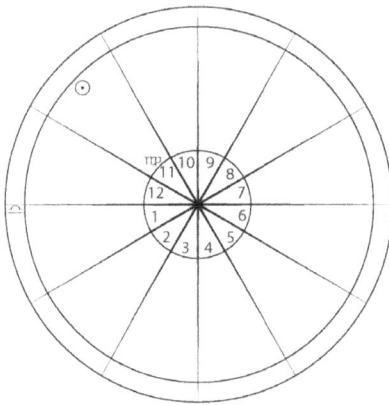

A scholar and leader, your little one will want to share everything s/he has learned with others who do not have the same advantages. Your bright child will begin teaching others at an early age and will share ideas and ideals. Usually a good orator, your little one will get on a pulpit to any and all who will listen. Encourage education and learning, and don't hesitate to introduce your child to good books at an early age.

Conversely, this child could easily take the easy way and take advantage of any situation that will benefit him/her. It is important to teach this child to differentiate and to learn the difference between doing good or not.

Encourage mirth in this child so that s/he doesn't grow up to be too serious. Your child has a natural sense of humor, and it is up to you to point it out to him/her.

VIRGO - *10:15 a.m. to 11:15 a.m.*
Eleventh House - Scorpio Rising

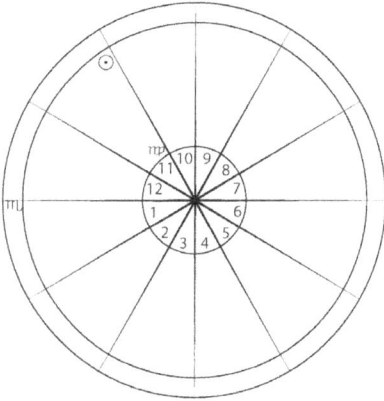

The story will never change. This child will fight for everyone's rights and for the good and well-being of all around him/her. The Virgo in your little one will show itself with his/her concerns for the health and welfare of all around him/her.

The Scorpio rising will assure that this child will not be wishy-washy or change his/her mind. Once on an idea or ideal, there will be no sway! Pay attention to what your child has to say because you will hear the same thing over and over until changes are made but not to his/her mind. If your child decides to lead others in a cause, s/he will have many who follow him/her.

VIRGO - *11:15 a.m. to 1:00 p.m.*
Tenth House - Scorpio Rising

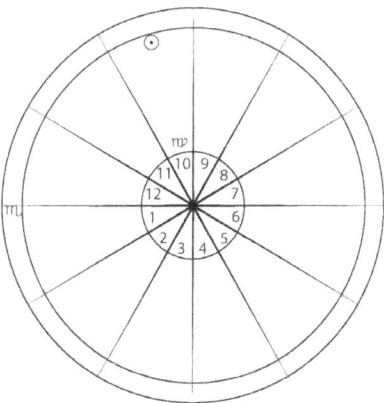

Happy and willing to learn new things, your Virgo is a good student. His/her desire to be the boss can sometimes be frustrating. This child will retain everything! Whatever is taught or witnessed will be remembered so it is a good idea to set good examples in front of your little one.

137

In spite of the fact that your Virgo wishes to be the boss, it is difficult for him/her to lead with too much authority. As a boss or leader, s/he will get down in the trenches with everyone. Your Virgo is not afraid to work and still doesn't want to hurt feelings. Instead of correcting someone, s/he will do it him/herself. Since leadership is important to him/her, it is a good idea to demonstrate how a leader does not have to be a despot!

VIRGO
Tenth House - Sagittarius Rising

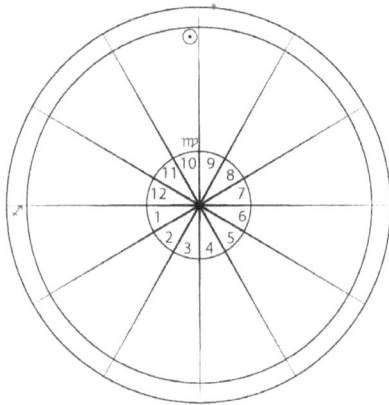

Wise and a good leader, you will find your young child gathering followers. With good instincts, s/he will be an inspiration to others. Although quiet and seemingly modest, your little one has good instincts and is able to inspire and help others in a very positive way.

Your young Virgo is quite spiritual and is an inspirational to many. A desire to be a spiritual leader may come while your child is quite young. In spite of the fact that s/he may outgrow this, you will find that your little one is an inspiration to all around.

The world will see him/her as a wise and talented child. Easy to take center stage, your little one is still shy but willing to entertain and/or lead others. S/He will bring great joy to those around him/her and will always do his/her best to please.

VIRGO - *1:00 p.m. to 3:15 p.m.*
Ninth House - Sagittarius Rising

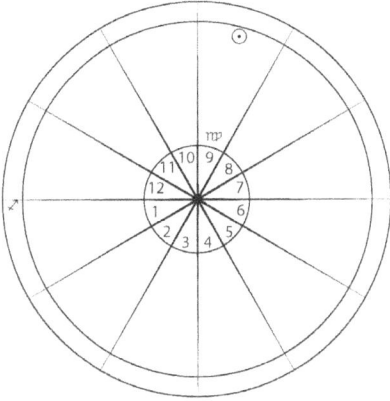

Your Virgo is a good teacher and an excellent judge. Often lovely with long and beautiful legs, travel is a plus, and your intelligent child will usually attract peoples from foreign countries.

It is important to this child to be able to finish what s/he started. If you give him/her swimming lessons, let your little Virgo complete the course. A job half done will be frustrating. Certificates of completion are very fulfilling for this child and are signs of acknowledgement to them. So, don't be afraid to allow your child to finish what was started and enjoy the satisfaction.

Don't be surprised if this child is fascinated by foreigners and foreign countries. Encourage him/her to learn to eat other dishes from what is common. Experimentation goes a long way with him/her, and you can enjoy some of the adventure as well.

No matter what, your Virgo child will figure things out. If it is important to this fair child, s/he will find a way to make things work. Sometimes it takes trial and error, but once something is perfected, you will find a sense of satisfaction present.

VIRGO - *3:15 p.m. to 3:45 p.m.*
Ninth House - Capricorn Rising

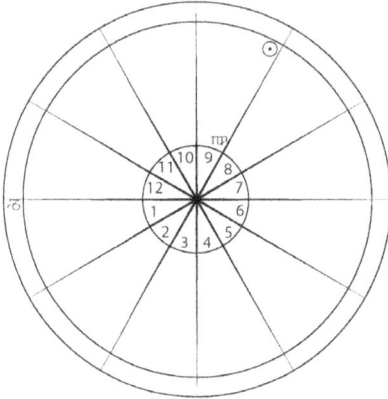

Bold and proud, your Virgo is the ruler of all s/he surveys. Eventually a good lawyer and judge, s/he may try early on to exercise these "characteristics." In another country, your child would be known as royalty. In fact, your young one carries an air of superiority, especially when traveling.

A classroom where s/he is in charge is a good fantasy game for him/her. Also, role playing a judge will be a hobby or pastime enjoyed.

The desire to be in charge is very great, and it is a good idea to teach this child early on the difference between taking responsibility and pushing others around.

Sometimes, your little one may take on some of your responsibilities, whether prepared for the tasks or not.

VIRGO - *3:45 p.m. to 5:15 p.m.*
Eighth House - Capricorn Rising

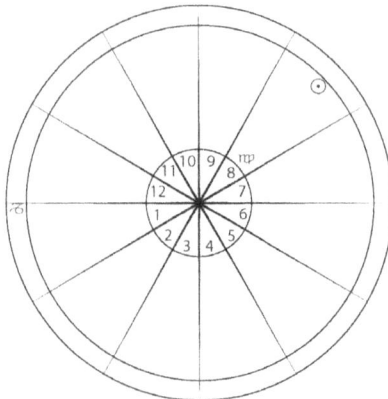

This Virgo is usually a good banker and you can teach him/her value. S/He needs to learn to discriminate and how to save without being selfish.

Although inclined to earn, you may find your child enjoys winning and receiving some things for free. S/He loves a good bet, and a good win, and could easily become a gambler. You will see this characteristic early on and can teach the value of earning.

Even when your little one is the recipient of gifts and prizes, you may want to show him/her that nothing is free, and that s/he will need to earn in one way or another the gifts. A good example is a scholarship. It is earned with good grades or exceptional work and/or talent in a particular field.

VIRGO - *5:15 p.m. to 5:45 p.m.*
Eighth House - Aquarius Rising

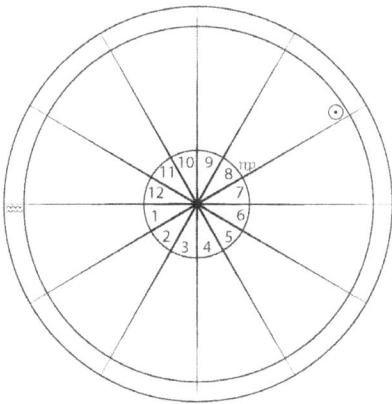

There are times when you can expect the unexpected from your child. S/He stands out from the crowd, either with his/her unusual looks or a special talent. In any case, you will find that your child is pointed out and noticed by many. Your Virgo needs rules and regulations to follow and walls to climb. Goals are especially important to this child and success is rewarding on a personal level. Personal best is always a good goal!

Generosity can be a characteristic of this little one. If s/he knows what to save, and what to give early on, life will be easier for him/her.

Expect everything to be done with great precision.

If your little one is late all the time, you may want to teach him/her consideration for others. Rather than blame your child for not being on time, ask your child to consider the feelings of the person kept waiting so that s/he can understand why you want him/her to learn to respect other people and their time.

VIRGO - *5:45 p.m. to 6:30 p.m.*
Seventh House - Aquarius Rising

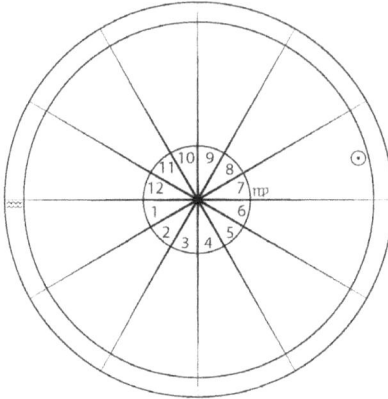

Your child is very observant and will follow the examples of those s/he respects. Your Virgo enjoys being in the presence of structure. Once s/he grasps the reason for a rule or regulation, s/he will follow it to the "T."

Virgo by nature is very neat. However, you may find piles of things or papers and not understand why this child doesn't seem orderly. However, you may also be surprised to learn that your little one knows what is in each pile and where everything is situated. Ask for a certain item and it will be the "third one down in the blue pile." Don't underestimate this child and his/her form of filing. If you wish, you can give him/her places to put those important items.

There are times when your little one will want to clean things out. At this juncture, you can be on hand to help sort the "keep it" from the "toss it" piles. Once they let go of an item, Virgos will seldom regret the disposal. Once it's over, it's over!

VIRGO - *6:30 p.m. to 7:15 p.m.*
Seventh House - Pisces Rising

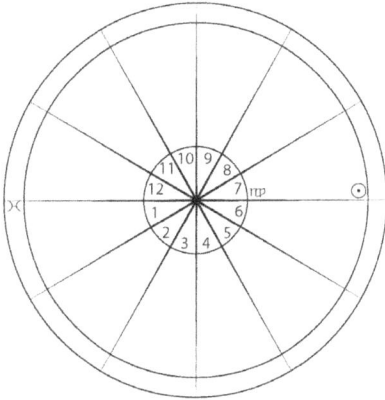

A partner is what your Virgo wants. That partner may be a dreamer or your little one may be the one who looks for a perfect mate. Don't be surprised if mock weddings are staged or eventual contracts are made with another "perfect" person. Until such time as your child grows up, s/he will idealize the perfect person to go through life with him/her as a partner in life or a partner in crime!

In the meantime, don't be surprised if this person comes to your little one in a dream or is an "imaginary" friend. You may learn some interesting things and it is always a good idea to ask questions. Be interested and you will find your child respects you more and confides more in you. You will also learn about another life of another soul, be it from your child's imagination or from what is perceived to be real. You will learn more about your child when you ask questions, such as: "Then what did you do?" or "What did you think about that?"

VIRGO - *7:15 p.m. to 7:45 p.m.*
Sixth House - Pisces Rising

You have a natural healer in your home with this little Virgo. S/He will work hard at any job because no job is too menial. This child should be appreciated for a job well done, more than the type of job s/he does or is doing.

Sensitive and intuitive, you will be amazed at how tuned in this child can be. You can enjoy his/her opinions when presented with a problem. Your little one seems to know a lot at a very young age. If you watch closely, you will see that s/he is also very observant and paying attention.

There seems to be no problem too big for your little one to tackle. However, it is more informative when you can promote small tasks and allow them to be completed before tackling the larger scale assignment. When someone says it can't be done, know that this child can do it!!

VIRGO - *7:45 p.m. to 8:45 p.m.*
Sixth House - Aries Rising

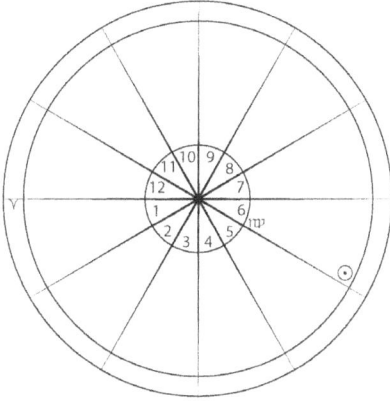

An eager helper, your Virgo is prepared and at the ready. Very handy and able to do all things, you will find more and more people relying on your child. Your little Virgo is the perfect engineer and/or handyman and can do many things. S/He will strive for perfection and amaze you with his/her many talents. This child enjoys how-to manuals and enjoys working.

Your self-starter will do unexpected things for you. You may find him/her cleaning out a closet or organizing the pantry. Whatever s/he see that "needs" to be done, s/he is on the spot, doing it.

Approval and appreciation are your role. If you wish to teach this little fix-it child, it is best done in a positive manner. Suppose you wanted the junk drawer to stay a junk drawer, show by example that things you don't know where to put go there. That way there will be no confusion on either side, and you won't have a need to reprimand this helpful child.

VIRGO - *8:45 p.m. to 9:00 p.m.*
Fifth House - Aries Rising

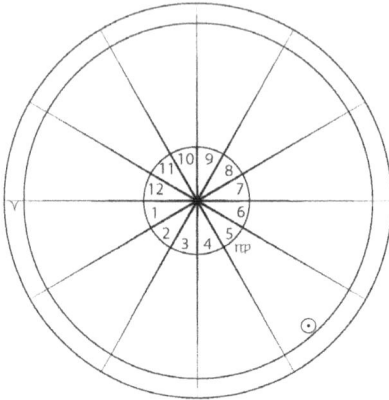

You have a true romantic in your home and your Virgo child will usually find the good in his/her surroundings. This child loves to laugh, and your humor will be a blessing in situations that seem helpless.

You will enjoy giving some sort of music or other lessons to your entertaining child. You will find that s/he delights anyone who walks in with a recital of some kind.

Also athletic and a bit competitive, you may also see a child who is willing to challenge others (even you) to something of mutual interest. Don't be afraid to let him/her lose. It is a good lesson to see that s/he is not always the one on top.

VIRGO - *9:00 p.m. to 10:30 p.m.*
Fifth House - Taurus Rising

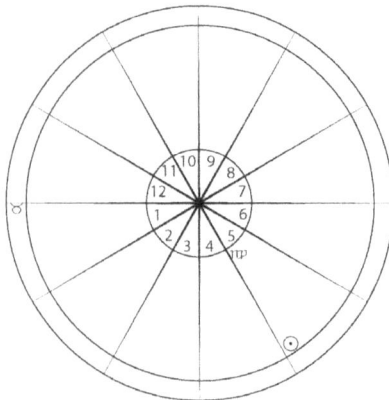

This Virgo needs to find his/her voice. S/He may be reluctant to sing in the choir because being a perfectionist s/he is unwilling to take the chance at being criticized. However, should you take the time to show this child that s/he is no different from any of the others, then you will find an excellent vocalist.

Your little Virgo enjoys performing and/or entertaining. You will know when s/he is ready because you will be told. You do not need to force your little one to entertain guests and friends. When s/he is ready, it will happen!

You may be surprised to see such determination come from a usually flexible child. However, once something is in his/her head, s/he will pursue the idea or subject to the end, and s/he has a finished project.

VIRGO - *10:30 p.m. to Midnight*
Fourth House - Gemini Rising

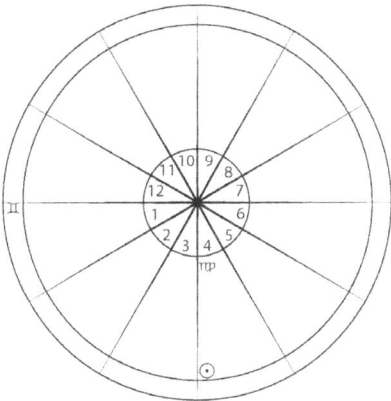

It will be entertaining for you once you keep the door open and allow your child's acquaintances in the house. You will usually find interesting conversation and great mental rapport among the visitors, who may be all ages and come from all walks of life

Your Virgo child is a people-gatherer and will find peoples of all walks of life and of all ages coming to your door. The depth of this child attracts many and you will find a variety of eager participants in conversation with your bright child.

Chess and Backgammon are challenging games for this child and many other intellectual games that require thinking are enjoyable. S/He loves puzzles. Pull one out!

VIRGO - *Midnight to 2:00 a.m.*
Fourth House - Cancer Rising

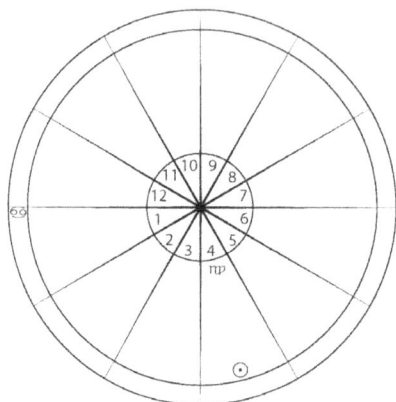

Have you taught his/her favorite dishes to him/her yet? You can start off in the kitchen early.

When only four, Em saw that her siblings were hungry. Her mother was in the other room and on the phone. She didn't know where her mother was, so she decided to cook lunch for herself and the others. She dutifully put a stool to the stove and began with everything from the refrigerator. When her mother finally came into the kitchen, exclaiming, "why is everything so quiet in here?" she saw the young Em feeding her younger siblings cooked eggnog. She had some of the ingredients right but what a mess!

Somewhat of a nester, it takes a good adventure to get your child out the door. Once on the road, however, it is hard to get him/her to go home. These children enjoy having a home and like to know it is there; however, taking a trip to someplace different is good too, as long as s/he can go home.

VIRGO - *2:00 a.m. to 2:30 a.m.*
Third House - Cancer Rising

S/He may be moody, but you'll find that your Virgo child often wants to be on the go. If you announce a "road trip," s/he is usually the first one packed and ready to take off.

Your intelligent child is also clever and able to make something out of nothing. Creative and detailed, s/he will make your time enjoyable.

S/He also enjoys books and it is a good idea to read to this child while s/he is young so that once s/he learns to read. You will find yourself being the recipient of stories that have been told or read.

Shy, but not retiring, your little one may not warm up to everyone until s/he trusts. Then you will find affection is a part of his/her pattern. Although this child's trust must be earned, once it is, your little one will always be there.

VIRGO
Third House - Leo Rising

"Let's have a party!" you may hear. It is okay to have that party in the park or in the woods or at someone else's home. Going out and doing something is the most fun for your Virgo.

You will find an intelligent student who excels in anything taught to him/her.

Great determination will keep him/her at "it" until the lesson is learned. You may also find that once a lesson is learned, s/he will do his/her best to pass on the information.

Lisa was taking a cookie from the cookie jar (really!). When Gary walked in, he began praying immediately "And lead us not into temptation . . ." to guilt her. But she was already determined to eat that cookie and faced him as she began munching away. They are (respectively) Virgo and Leo.

VIRGO - *2:30 a.m. to 4:15 a.m.*
Second House - Leo Rising

Frugal and careful, your little one could have a death grip on the money in his/her pocket. It is good to teach him/her to circulate the money so that more will come; however, it is also good to teach him/her how to save.

There is an extravagant side to this child, like an old song says, "The drinks and the laughs are on me . . ." After you start with a piggy bank, you may want to introduce your little one with a savings account so that s/he can learn values.

You will find this child needs to know his/her parameters so that s/he can feel free to express him/herself. Otherwise, s/he may sit in a corner unable to come out of his/her shell.

VIRGO
Second House - Virgo Rising

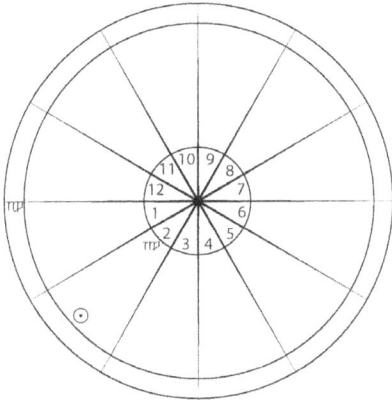

If you have lost something, don't fret. Just tell your Virgo Child what you have lost, and s/he will find it for you. S/He has an uncanny sense (or nose) for detection and is able to readily find missing objects.

If you assure your child that something is of value, s/he will learn the value and treat the object accordingly. Your Virgo child enjoys placing value on things and following through with research on the item.

If s/he could, you would find your little one inspecting an Egyptian tomb. S/He enjoys antiquity and the stories that accompany. Accordingly, you will find that s/he has an interest in history and the value of historic items and placements.

An opportunity to visit museums and historical points of interest will always keep your child's curiosity in check and you will have a willing party to investigation.

VIRGO - *4:15 a.m. to 5:15 a.m.*
First House - Leo Rising

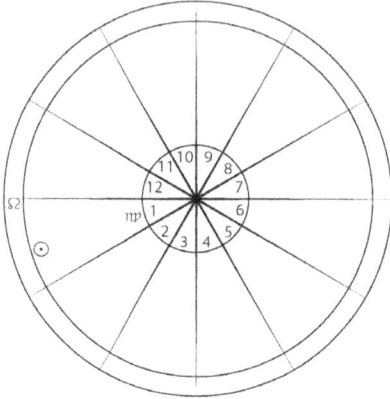

Your little Virgo feels responsible for everyone's happiness and needs to learn to allow others to create their own joy.

An effervescent child and so entertaining, s/he may seem a bit shy. Once the door to entertaining is open, watch a new child emerge.

Your child wants very much to please you and is already self-deprecating. Rather than criticize, it is good to praise first and then discuss later any changes that could be made.

VIRGO - *5:15 a.m. to 6:30 a.m.*
First House - Virgo Rising

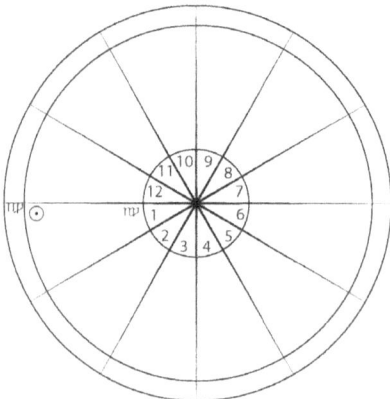

Picky, picky, picky. You may find your child can be somewhat of a germaphobe at an early age. S/He may want to wear the same outfit day in and day out—usually in brown or navy blue. It is normal. Once they find something that works, Virgo children like to go with it.

You may also find that your little one doesn't like to mix his/her food and that separating the peas from the carrots is normal for him/her. The reason for this is that this child likes order and likes to know what is what and where it is.

When a toy is given to your little one, it may be pulled apart and put back together again before it is ever played with. This is normal. S/He just wants to see what makes it work. Don't be alarmed.

VIRGO - *6:30 a.m. to 7:45 a.m.*
Twelfth House - Virgo Rising

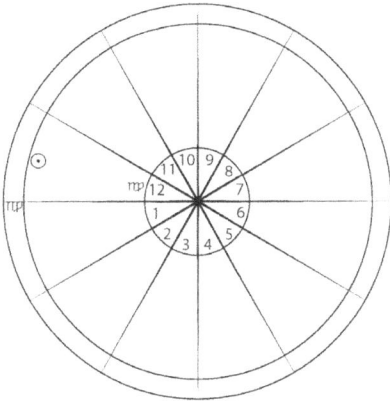

If you have ever heard the term, "a memory like an elephant" you will find it in this child. You may say something, without thinking about it, then find it repeated back to you much later. Although it doesn't seem fair that you must watch what you say around this child, know that you are important to him/her and what you say is golden. Therefore, your words and actions are very important to this child.

You will also find comic relief when your child mimics other people. Just remember that you are also being impersonated, and it may not be as funny.

A good keeper of secrets, this child will not betray you. Return the compliment and let him/her know the importance of being trustworthy. Don't fill him/her up with too many secrets, s/he could burst. Let your mutual confidences be held to a minimum so that his/her little head doesn't explode.

VIRGO - *7:45 a.m. to 9:00 a.m.*
Twelfth House - Libra Rising

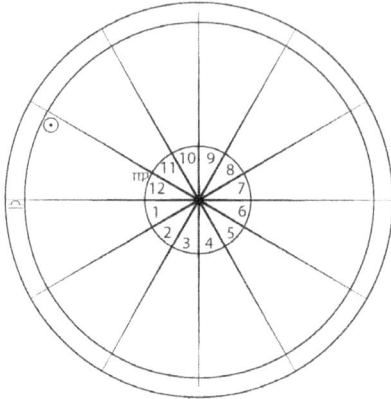

Hide and Seek is a favorite game of this little one. One minute s/he's there, the next minute, you cannot find him/her. Although s/he enjoys "entertaining," s/he is also shy about it and can pull back when it is time to perform. Applause and praise are important at this juncture.

Your child loves a mystery; keep puzzles around. If you enjoy puzzles, your bright Virgo will enjoy them with you. Introducing your Virgo to all sorts of puzzles will not only stimulate his/her mind but will keep him/her interesting and interested in new things.

This child will not betray you and expects the same in return. If something is a secret, keep it!

Dixie used to walk as if on a cloud, heel to toe on each step. She managed to delight everyone in her presence at all times. An introspective child, she paid close attention to what everyone around her had to say or do and would approach that side of the person.

SAGITTARIUS

World traveler, philosopher, teacher, judge. Your child has wisdom beyond his/her years.

Larry was nine when his parents divorced. He took it in stride and went on with his life. An excellent scholar in school, he appeared to not have parents. He related to his friends of like kind. Other students who were serious about studies were his companions. When he was twelve, he spent a lot of time home alone. This did not upset him, he just went home, studied, and then played intellectual games with his "elite" band of friends. Wise beyond his years, his friends brought all their problems to him. He went on to become a lawyer and a judge.

Gentle in their approach, many Sagittarius children have a quiet demeanor. Conversely, if their lives are out of order, they are seemingly loud. They speak out, at times, embarrassingly so. Whatever pops into his/her mind at the moment flows right out of his/her mouth.

Your Sagittarius child needs the truth only. If a lie is detected, rebellion is great. But trust is lost with this child.

If there is someone in your home or who visits regularly, and that person speaks a foreign language, encourage your little one to learn it because languages come easily to this Sagittarius child, as s/he is a good mimic.

Your little one is fascinated by things and peoples foreign. Long trips are not a bother to him/her. You will find that s/he adjusts to new environments and circumstances quite well.

This child has a thirst for knowledge. At an early age, s/he can learn languages, and can easily adjust to different accents and sounds.

Religion is also important to this child. A belief system with structure gives security and purposefulness to your little one's life.

To your Jupiter-ruled child, things are larger than they seem. They are awed by nature and history. They are fascinated by elephants, whales, and other large animals. A large dog is a good pet for this child.

These children love the outdoors. Nature is an important element. Hiking and camping are good outlets for them. Be certain to put a book in the backpack.

You can read to your Sagittarius child early on. They love stories and will enjoy reading as they grow. Books are great gifts for your child.

Purples and lavenders are colors you can find on a Sagittarius. However, any combination of clothes that stand out, such as a hat, that can make them unique is preferable.

SAGITTARIUS - *3:15 to 5:00 a.m.*
Second House - Scorpio Rising

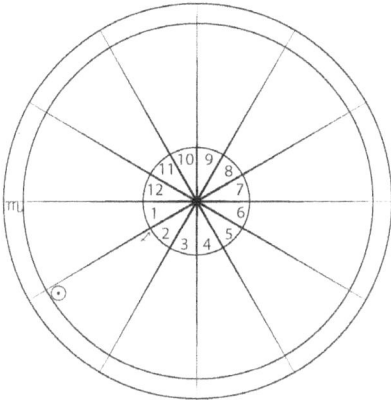

A gatherer of knowledge, you will have the constant question, "why?" asked by this curious little one. Books are really good gifts for this child. You will find a desire for "things" that pertain to a special interest and anything you can give to extend that knowledge to him/her is greatly appreciated.

(A young lawyer once had a case where the opposition was an astrologer. He researched the subject so well that he later became an astrologer himself. He quit his law practice and moved to another state and began to take astrology clients.)

Anytime you can teach this little one how to research is a good time! Many questions do not necessarily have to be answered by you but can be answered by other experts. Your child will appreciate you and respect this method of learning very much.

SAGITTARIUS - *5:00 a.m. to 6:00 a.m.*
First House - Scorpio Rising

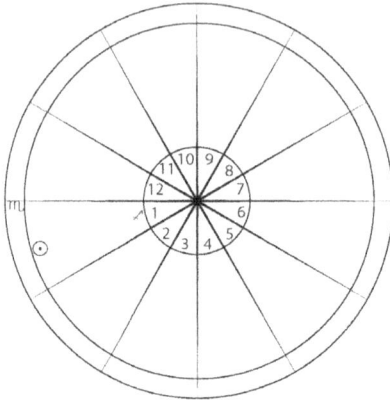

You do not want to be judged by this child, and yet, you may feel that the eyes of your Sagittarius are always upon you. This is simply curiosity at work, and your child wants all the answers now. There are times when you will have to go into detail in order to explain. Once satisfied with an answer, your questioning Archer will let you off the hook. If you teach this child at an early age how to look up things, you will not feel the prying eyes upon you!

Scrutiny may be uncomfortable; however, if you should invite him/her to learn something you can do, you will have a happy companion/co-worker. Your child enjoys being your mirror and being just like you! Take time to learn more about this curious and wonderful child. You will find a wise old soul in your midst. Nurture and enjoy this gifted angel.

SAGITTARIUS - *6:00 a.m. to 7:00 a.m.*
First House - Sagittarius Rising

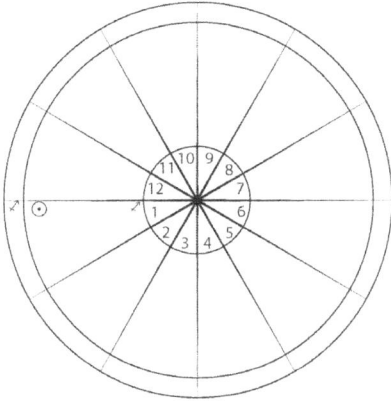

Your most creative and imaginative child will make you ask yourself how you managed to have such a gifted child! Your little one can wax philosophically and astound you with his/her insights. You can bring your little one, at an early age, to international events and s/he will fit right in. No one is a stranger to this child, and s/he will adapt to his/her environment wherever you take him/her.

A paintbrush early on will be a lifeline to this child. Creative and visionary, your child has a keen eye and is able to create visions that others may be surprised to see. You will also see a good deal of maturity in your child's creations. You will also be able to determine your little one's mood and what is going on in his/her life through the eyes of the pictures depicted.

Later on, as your little one matures, you may find that his/her interest goes in another direction, such as statuary. Eventual work with larger items may come to play with maturity and as your child continues to move on.

SAGITTARIUS - *7:00 a.m. to 8:15 a.m.*
Twelfth House - Sagittarius Rising

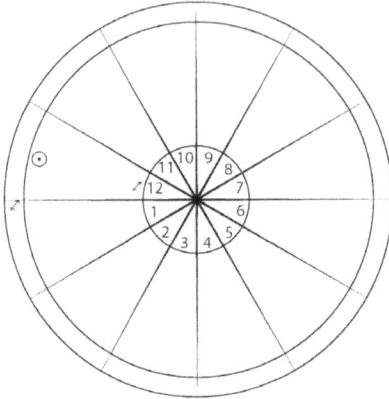

Introspective and/or contemplative, your child's curiosity will be vast. Try to keep him/her from holding things in for too long so that s/he doesn't burst!

Journaling is a good thing for this Sagittarius. Expression can be taught and then, at some point, let go. Give your child the opportunity to feel safe in his/her own mind and with his/her thoughts.

Your little one needs to be encouraged to join in activities that are physical. S/He could keep him/herself in his/her own head for hours and needs to be in touch with nature. At every opportunity, let him/her enjoy nature, the benefits of the outdoors, and physical activity. It will be very beneficial later in life!

SAGITTARIUS - *8:15 a.m. to 9:00 a.m.*
Twelfth House - Capricorn Rising

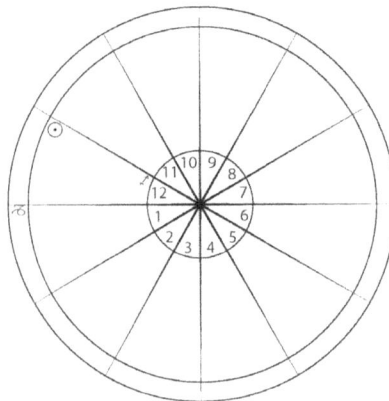

Frustrated that s/he is not always in control, you may find that Journaling is a good thing for this Sagittarius. Expression can be taught and then, at some point, let go. Give your child the opportunity to feel safe in his/her own mind and with his/her thoughts.

Your little one needs to be encouraged to join in activities that are physical. S/He could keep him/herself in his/her own head for hours and needs to be in touch with nature. At every opportunity, let him/her enjoy nature and the benefits of the outdoors, and physical activity. It will be very beneficial later in life!

Determined, your little boy or girl will live up to your expectations. If you teach him/her something that is important to you, it will become important to him/her. Michela was a vegan from birth. Her daddy taught her not to eat anything from an animal. One day, in the grocery store with her daddy, she pointed to some cheese crackers and told her father that they tasted good. He told her that the cheese came from a cow. When they went home, she ran to her grandmother and yelled out that her grandmother should not have given her anything from a cow. This learned behavior is what you can expect from your child in the early years, until his/her mind forms its own ideas. The more rigid you are, the less flexibility you can expect from your child.

SAGITTARIUS - *9:00 a.m. to 10:15 a.m.*
Eleventh House - Capricorn Rising

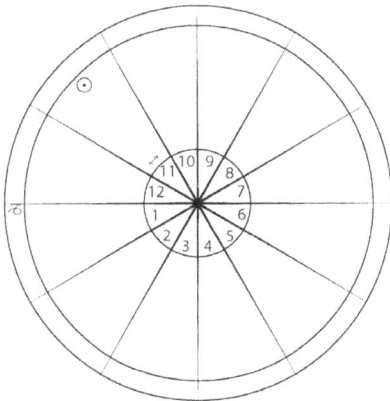

Don't be surprised when your little one brings home an "army" that will follow him/her as their leader and/or "general." Being in charge is important but it is mostly important among peers.

With a strong jaw, your youngster will forge ahead, mastering any task. S/He has many plans for when s/he "grows up" and you can learn and perhaps help to set the stage for future endeavors.

Your Sagittarius child is a delight to be around. People like his/her company and enjoy looking up to and admiring your

161

Archer. Having a childhood is imperative to this little one, even though s/he acts as if s/he wants to be just like you. Don't forget to remind him/her that once they are grown up, they can be whoever and whatever they choose. In the meantime, it is okay to be a child.

SAGITTARIUS - *10:15 a.m. to 10:45 a.m.*
Eleventh House - Aquarius Rising

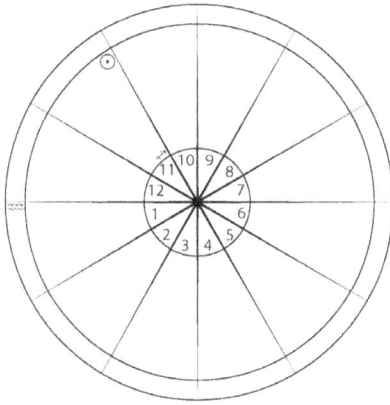

A friend to the end, your Sagittarius child will want to be social and always play according to the rules. It is best if this child is taught games and/or activities that have rules and regulations because that is where s/he is most comfortable.

There are times when s/he seems to behave a little "off the wall" or not like everyone else. It is perfectly alright, as s/he is expressing his/her individuality. Some of his/her friends may also seem a little different to you. Your child enjoys the diversity and can find it in his/her friends. There is a part of your child that wants to stay within the mold s/he thinks has been created for him/her, however, s/he will find it in his/her friends and will bring those friends around for your approval.

Give him/her the rules early so that there are no mistakes when s/he passes them on to others.

SAGITTARIUS - *10:45 a.m. to 11:45 a.m.*
Tenth House - Aquarius Rising

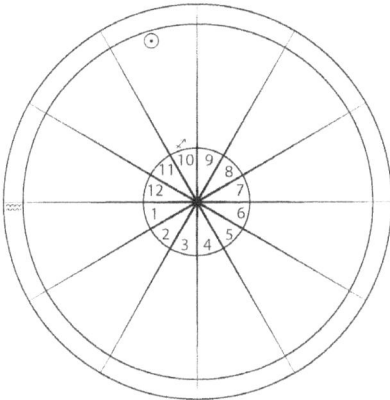

This child may perform remarkable feats. Don't allow too much praise to go to his/her head so that they don't believe in their vulnerability. Once shown the right way to do something, you can watch your little one shine in the glory of accomplishment.

Lessons are good for this curious child. When there are subjects where you cannot teach, it is fine to get a tutor. Your imaginative little one should be quite good in the arts, such as music or drawing. Current events are always of interest to your child and s/he can be exposed to the news early on.

If something isn't right, your little one will be the first to cry, "that's not fair!" Pay attention to what you are hearing because you'll learn quickly how your child thinks. A very moral and strong advocate, your child will be there for the underdog.

There is a daring part of your child's psyche. You will find that s/he does his/her best to make changes in the atmosphere. Should there be household rules, you will find that s/he does not necessarily want to follow them but rather would want to make his/her own set of guidelines that make more sense to him/her. Teach your child diplomacy and how to institute new laws that make sense.

SAGITTARIUS
Tenth House - Pisces Rising

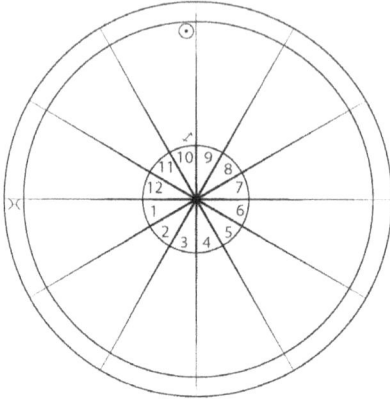

Your little Sagittarius was born to preach. Ideals are important to this child and any platform is acceptable.

Teach your child to stand up for him/herself. S/He can be easily discouraged. It is not a good idea to allow him/her to feel sorry for him/herself. Instead, it is good for this child to learn empathy.

S/He should learn how to laugh at him/herself. Little Denny was three when he went to the airport with his Mom to see his uncle off. For a moment, she lost sight of him. Suddenly, she heard, "Mom!" She turned and saw him throw out his arms and run to her. She dropped down and threw out her arms. He ran right past her and skidded on the floor, laughing as hard as he could. He then ran into her arms and started laughing with great joy. He grows up with a great sense of humor.

A spiritual outlet is important to your child. Whatever your belief system is can be passed on to your impressionable child. If your little one begins to ask questions (usually at the age of seven), be prepared to have answers. It is possible that s/he begins to develop his/her own belief system. Don't fret, it isn't anything you said, it is simply your child growing up and finding his/her own way!

SAGITTARIUS - *11:45 a.m. to 12:45 p.m.*
Ninth House - Pisces Rising

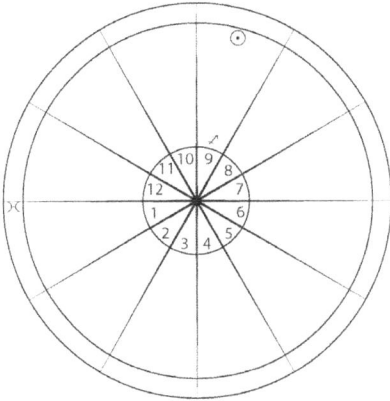

A true philosopher, your little one will be able to conceptualize at an early age. It is always good to introduce this child to a belief system, as you will find that s/he wants some higher power in his/her life.

You may find your little one is a good psychologist and is quite understanding of the human condition even at a very early age. S/He has a good deal of empathy and is able to understand the human condition. You may find your child doing deeds for others with no expectation of a reward. You can encourage this type of behavior and let your little one know how much you appreciate his kind and empathetic soul.

You may learn that your child's generosity extends very far. S/He may want to take care of everyone, and you can encourage kindness and emphasize the good things that s/he may be doing.

You have a real child of delight!

SAGITTARIUS
Ninth House - Aries Rising

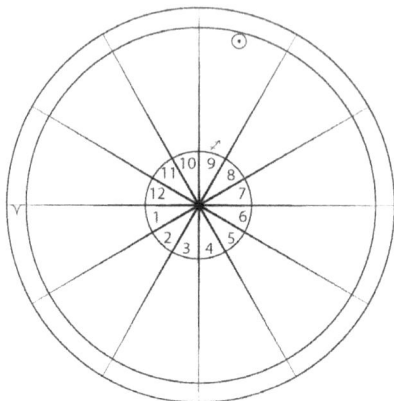

Eager to travel, this is not a child you leave at home while you go away somewhere. Your child is a delight to all who meet him/her and therefore will fit in anywhere. If you have taught him/her to do some research, you may be delighted to learn about a new place that you are visiting.

Your Sagittarius child should have a talent with languages, and you may be thrilled to learn that if you visit a foreign country that you have an interpreter!

No matter where your child is, you will find him/her to be comfortable in his/her surroundings and others will be comfortable around him/her.

On the go and quite athletic, your young archer will show a good deal of energy. There is also a serious side to him/her and usually it is found in learning.

You will also be pleased to see a talent in artistic endeavors. This is a true child of wonder!

SAGITTARIUS - *12:45 p.m. to 1:15 p.m.*
Eighth House - Aries Rising

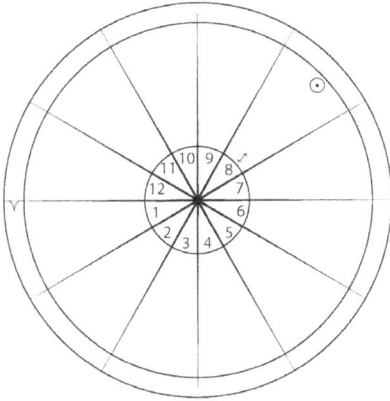

Psychic and intuitive, your Sagittarius child has a gift for understanding the psyche of others and having a close association with the dead. A lover of history, your child can surprise you with insights into the past that are significant in day to day activities.

Your child is a self-starter and is able to get things off the ground, once s/he has made a determination.

Teach your child that aggression is not always the answer to his/her problems. Help him/her to show patience and to allow others a chance. Once this lesson is learned, s/he will find his/her own leadership ability and happiness among his/her peers.

It is fine to bring your little one to funerals and also to let him/her watch scary movies because it is a genre that s/he is most curious about.

SAGITTARIUS - *1:15 p.m. to 2:45 p.m.*
Eighth House - Taurus Rising

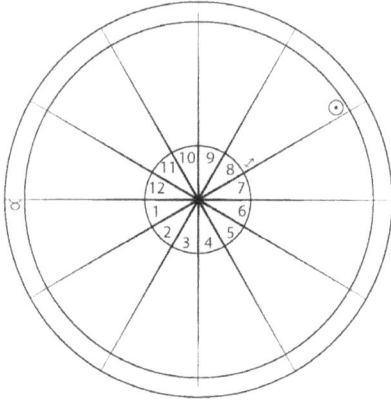

Money from others - gift receiver. There will always be enough and "more from where that came from . . ." Your little one has an uncanny ability to receive whatever s/he believes is needed. You may from time to time hear him/her say, "I knew I would get that!" It is because invariably s/he will want something badly enough that it will come to him/her.

Your child has an uncanny ability to understand value, especially the value to and of other people. S/He will appreciate what others can do and will not be afraid to ask for favors or gifts when asked what s/he would like to have.

If there is a certain school s/he wishes to attend, it is good to apply because chances are there will be a way for him/her to go there. Don't be afraid to ask for something for your child. You may be happy with the answer!

SAGITTARIUS - *2:45 p.m. to 3:45 p.m.*
Seventh House - Taurus Rising

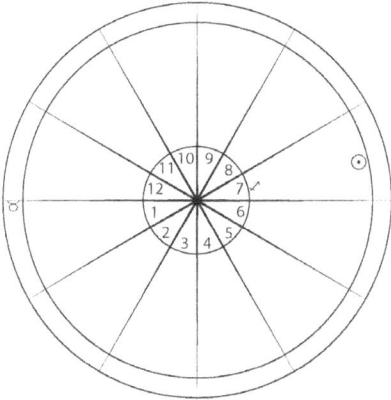

Lasting partnerships are always there and available for your Sagittarius child. S/he will want to learn about legalities at an early age.

Legal matters are always of interest to this inquisitive child and s/he does not lack tenacity. What this means to you is that once you tell him/her something and you have convinced the child of your truth, s/he will absolutely believe and follow your directive. If it is something that can be proved, s/he will check it out first and then be comfortable in your opinions. Don't be surprised if everything you say is initially scrutinized until your child is comfortable with your thoughts or opinions.

Stubbornness can be turned into determination. The best way to encourage your little one to find his/her hidden talent is to give him/her a project that will take time and patience. You will see your little one shine once a project is accomplished.

SAGITTARIUS - *3:45 p.m. to 4:15 p.m.*
Seventh House - Gemini Rising

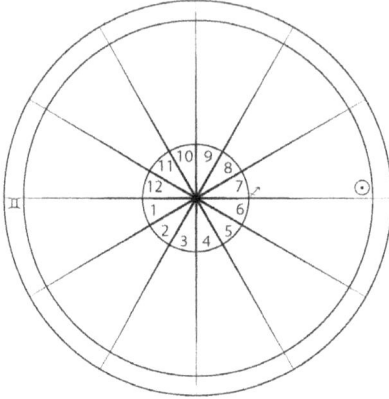

Your child could bore easily and will always seek out the most interesting people to be in his/her environment. S/he will make pacts and have terms with these individuals and call on them for advice and amusement. This child will allow someone else to do the speaking for him/her and enjoys being amused by such another person.

With Virgo, Sagittarius is the bachelor of the zodiac. However, you will see that other children will seek out this intelligent child to be his/her partner in many endeavors. Your child is more sensitive than s/he seems. S/He will plow through things with much bravado, however, that is just a show. Watch those feelings!

A good scholar, this Sagittarius child could easily want to emulate someone who is already a scholar or businessman. S/He will want agreements and even contracts to make everything proper and right. The partnership will last as long as the "project" lasts. After that, it will be on to the next.

Your Sagittarius child will not forget his/her first love and could carry the torch well past puberty. This is not unusual and should a shrine be set by your child to this "love" allow it. Discovery will be a painful but beautiful part of his/her life.

SAGITTARIUS - 4:15 p.m. to 5:30 p.m.
Sixth House - Gemini Rising

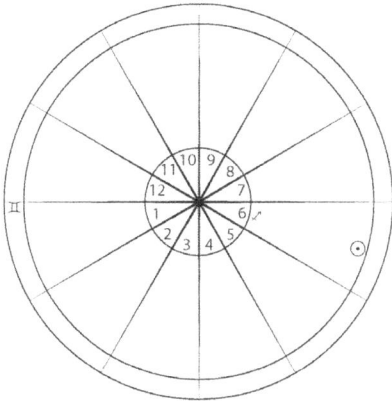

An interest in healthy habits and how to serve his/her fellow citizen, your child will show altruistic grace. S/he will read everything possible about health and what is best for one's well-being.

An instinct for those who hurt, your little one's empathy will be great. Keep the bandages ready because your child will always want to fix up anyone who is hurt.

With a lovely smile s/he will plow through whatever needs to be done to fulfill a goal. You will be gratified to see this child has a good deal of success completing projects. This is one thing (completing) that must be taught because initially, your little one could lose interest part way through. Your encouragement will teach your lovely child how to complete something s/he has started.

Your Sagittarius child is very versatile and can do many things. Be sure to pay him/her for any "work" that is required of him/her. You will have a grateful and hard-working individual.

SAGITTARIUS - *5:15 p.m. to 6:00 p.m.*
Sixth House - Cancer Rising

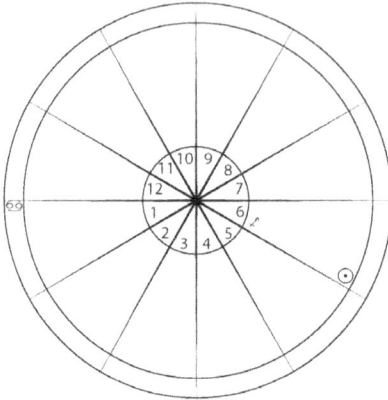

A true healer, your Sagittarius child may want to be a doctor of sorts at an early age. You can encourage this behavior by directing him/her to learn about not only healthy habits but also about the care of others. A pet is usually good for this child.

You will find this child tending to anyone who needs his/her attention. With an intuition for healing, your Cancer-rising Sagittarius will be able to pinpoint the problem in someone else. It will not always be the same for him/her. This child will sometimes be sad and not know what is really wrong with him/her. The best way to work with this type of problem is to ask how s/he feels. Many times, it is simply a mood thing (check and see if there is a full moon) and not a physical ailment.

SAGITTARIUS - *6:00 p.m. to 7:30 p.m.*
Fifth House - Cancer Rising

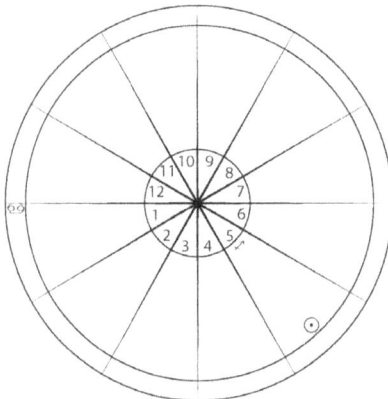

If your little one arranges the entertainment, you will find an entertainment industry leader in the making. An entrepreneur at heart, your Sagittarius child can be an arranger of ceremony. If you are having a get-together of any kind, you can ask your intuitive child to help and make the plans.

"I'll be back soon," is a common sentence coming from your child while rushing out to the next adventure. As long as you make him/her feel secure that home will always be there, your little one will feel free and adventurous.

Should you have any kind of financial problems, it is a good idea to keep it from him/her. Little children don't need to know everything! There'll be time enough to tell them when they are older. In the meantime, you can just keep a "home" for him/her.

If you home school your child, you may find a desire for a social outlet. So, it is a good idea to encourage playdates and other social activities for your little one.

SAGITTARIUS - *7:30 p.m. to 8:45 p.m.*
Fifth House - Leo Rising

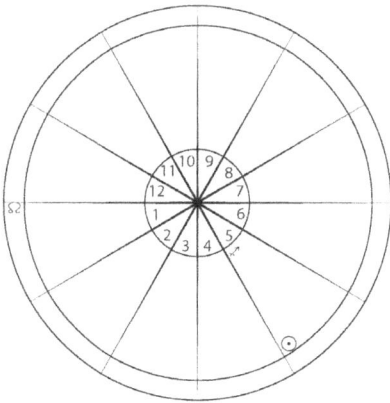

The entertainer in the family with a great mane of hair is this little Sagittarius. A magic kit is a good gift for this little one, who will do his/her best to create illusions for you.

You may find that even as a toddler, your Sagittarius is doing his/her best to entertain your guests with his/her special "talents" and that s/he needs positive feedback. Let him/her know that s/he is appreciated. Applaud the show that s/he has put on for you!

A good student, it won't be difficult for your studious child to learn new things. You can introduce new subjects and points of interest to him/her.

With strong legs and athletic ability, your little one will advance quickly in dance and athletics. It is possible that once older, that s/he will entertain others with his/her stardom in his/her chosen field!

S/He may have a very dry sense of humor. One thing for sure, you have a good student and wonderfully entertaining child on your hands. Pay attention so that your little one doesn't become a hermit!

SAGITTARIUS - *8:45 p.m. to 10:00 p.m.*
Fourth House - Leo Rising

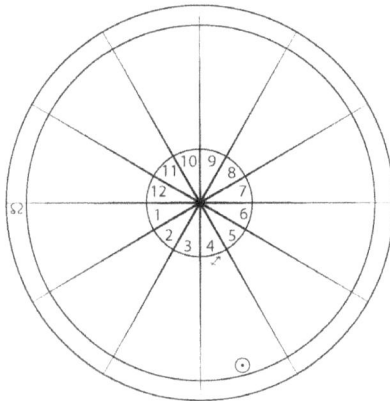

Parties at home are a favorite of this Sagittarius child. The entertaining that s/he prefer comes in the preparation. Then you will see the "host" or "hostess" who has grace and charm. Your guests will be entertained, as will your child be entertaining. Loves home, loves family, loves to be somewhere else.

Once you venture away from home and teach your child that anywhere s/he hangs his/her hat is home, you will have a true adventurer on your hands. You may find that wherever s/he goes, there will be a few items that s/he takes along to make the new (or temporary) residence his/her own.

SAGITTARIUS - *10:00 p.m. to 11:45 p.m.*
Fourth House - Virgo Rising

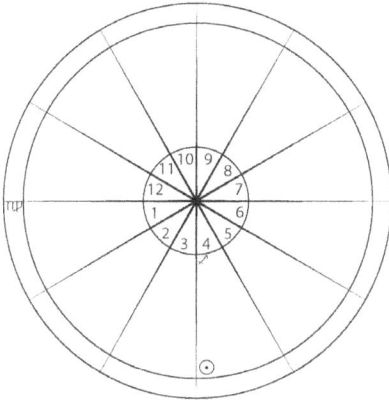

Mirth is important and your Sagittarius child may be too serious. Puzzles are a great challenge to this child. Although it may be difficult, it is a good idea to introduce your little one to the outdoors early on in life. Fresh air and sunshine are his/her friend and the sooner s/he knows this, the healthier s/he will be.

Your little one is not only interested in good health but can be taught at an early age the benefits of a healthy lifestyle. Activities that encourage this will be of great benefit to you and your child later on in life. You may want to encourage good eating and other healthy habits.

Take your Little Sagittarius with you when you go shopping. His/her discerning eye will be very helpful as time goes on and you will be pleased that your little one is able to differentiate one item from another or even one color from another.

Puzzles are a great challenge to this child.

SAGITTARIUS - *Midnight to 1:15 a.m.*
Third House Sun - Virgo Rising

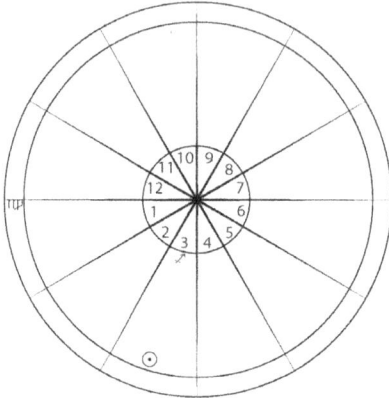

A good scholar, your Sagittarius child will be a good sibling and a good student. Particular about his/her appearance, your little one may tend to be fussy. Even if a little messy, your little one knows where everything is.

You may find this bright child teaching others what s/he has already learned. Therefore, books will be an important asset to him/her.

Eager to go out and play, although shy, your youngster wants to have friends and is amiable. Your Sagittarius child enjoys games and is a good participant in certain intellectual games.

SAGITTARIUS - *1:15 a.m. to 2:15 a.m.*
Third House - Libra Rising

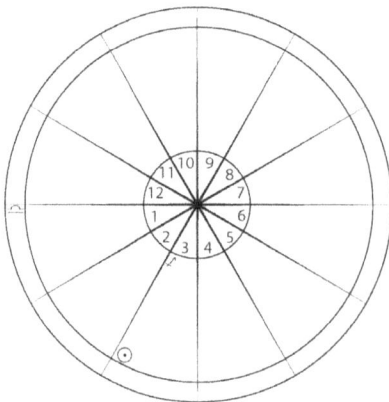

Procrastination is easy for this impatient, quick-minded child. So busy to be "on with the next" thing, s/he doesn't have time to wait around for life to happen.

Appearances matter to this lovely child. Although s/he may not conform to your sense of style, you will find that your Sagittarius will quickly develop a style completely suited to his/her personality.

You will find your child outspoken and an advocate for the underdog. S/He will fight tooth and nail for what is fair and if s/he doesn't think something is right, you will find that s/he is quite vocal about it. Play attention to what is said, it may be important or at least give you a clue as to the character of your lovely child!

SAGITTARIUS - *2:15 a.m. to 3:15 a.m.*
Second House - Libra Rising

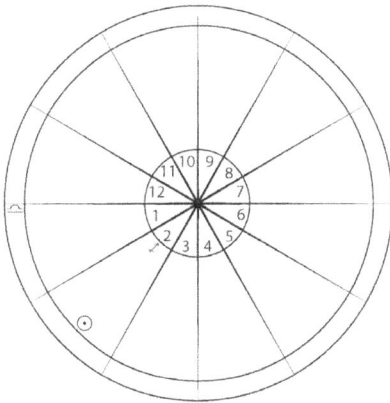

Pretty little things that will enhance the looks of this child's environment is how money will be spent. Possessions will be harmonious and lovely. They should also be colorful.

Your little Sagittarius loves to study new things and enjoys learning with friends. S/he enjoys the company of others with a like mind.

All things should be equal around this child. You will find that fairness is very important to him/her. If you give a gift to another child (say for a sibling's birthday), include another, perhaps smaller, gift for your Sagittarius child. S/He enjoys receiving presents and always feels deserving of all rewards and gifts.

PISCES

Your child of wonder will amaze you with his/her insight into everything in his/her surroundings. Should you voice a problem out loud, your wise child will tempt you with solutions. I say "tempt" because the solutions are not always the best answers.

Many times, this child will have an imaginary friend. They will tell you about this friend as though it was someone you have known and have had a relationship with. The friend will fade when new friends come into your child's life and there is no need to worry. One niece of mine used to play under the table with her friend. Eventually, she stopped playing with "her" when she attended school and made newer companions.

Nothing is strange to this child and you don't have to hide anything from him/her. With vivid imaginations, these children are able to conceive anything. They are great storytellers and can fascinate you with details that you once forgot.

Your Pisces child loves history, especially his/her own story. You can tell them about their genealogy to pique their interest. They enjoy learning about their own ancestry and can also share it verbatim. Be sure you have your facts right before imparting information to this sensitive child.

Your little one must be told the truth and needs to learn to differentiate what is true and what is almost true. This may be a problem if s/he considers a lie to be a truth. Once reality is learned, you could be blamed for misconceptions. Further, if your little one is taught that it is alright to color reality, you will never know if you are being told facts or embellishments.

Little white lies don't work, either. If s/he asks a question, s/he is ready for the honest answer! But don't be fooled by the "where did I come from?" question. Usually, the answer is the name of the city where s/he was born!

If you find your child being dreamy and slightly unattached from reality, a good idea is to give him/her something creative to do or a problem to solve. Then ask your little one to get back to reality or prompt him/her in that direction. There are times when rewards and/or goals are warranted.

Most Pisces children have long eyelashes and dreamy eyes. You will find that people comment on their beautiful or mysterious eyes. You, too, will see this. There are times when you can feel your Pisces child looking right through you! Don't be alarmed. As long as your relationship with him/her is an honest one, you have no worries.

Pale pastels (especially lavenders) are especially good on your Pisces child. Should your child have problems with his/her feet, there is an ego problem.

PISCES - *5:00 a.m. to 6:00 a.m.*
First House - Aquarius Rising

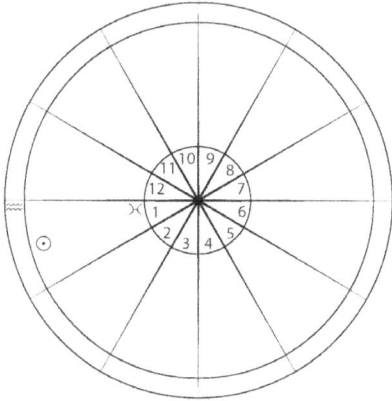

Sometimes you may wonder if this child came from the future. Interested in so many different things, s/he has a great deal of insight and enjoys the bizarre and the unusual.

It is always a good idea to know what your child has learned and who is his/her primary influence. His/her rules may be different from yours, as are ideals and philosophies. Listen to this child and you may learn a lot.

You will also find determination in your little one's makeup. There are times when you may want to sway your little one's attention, but once his/her focus is determined, it will be hard to change it.

PISCES - *6:00 a.m. to 6:30 a.m.*
First House - Pisces Rising

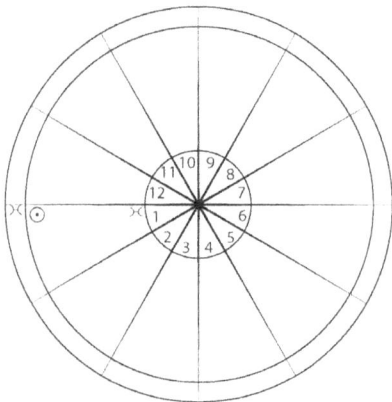

The dreamiest of children, your double Pisces will amaze you with information that seems other-worldly. Your creative Pisces is very insightful and understanding.

This child usually goes along with whatever is put before him/her. Therefore, it is good to teach your sensitive little one to be able to differentiate between that which is good for him/her and that which is not, as s/he is easily influenced.

Encourage your child to use backbone and stand up for him/herself. In spite of the fact that s/he is eager to please everyone and to go along with everything, teach this wonderful sprite that it is all right to stand up for him/herself and to think for him/herself. It is a good idea for your child to have an opinion!

PISCES
Twelfth House - Pisces Rising

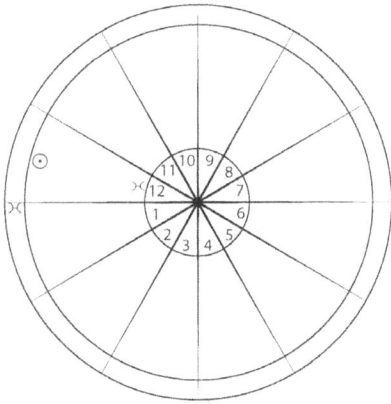

Introspective and intuitive, you may be surprised to learn just how knowledgeable your youngster is. If you said something even before s/he could talk, it may be remembered and quoted back to you later.

This is the child who is psychic or intuitive. You will find that s/he has the ability to finish your sentences and thought processes before you do.

Besides this great attribute, your Pisces child will be like a little elf. Dreamy and wise at the same time, you can enjoy the ethereal atmosphere that is ever present around your little one.

Creativity and artistic ability come quite naturally with your lovely child and you can give him/her art supplies and allow them hours of pleasure.

Just remember that your secrets are safe with him/her! If s/he complains that his/her feet hurt, you can be certain that your child is not happy with the way things are going or with his/her approach to life.

PISCES
Twelfth House - Aries Rising

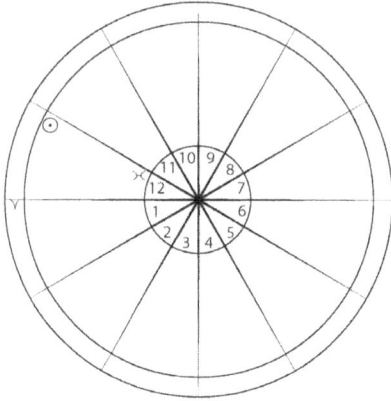

Your little child has more energy than you could ever imagine. And yet, with all of this, once s/he looks at you with those puppy-dog eyes, you melt. It is easy to let him/her be free. There is so very much innocence and yet an unmistakable naivete about your child, that you may feel s/he is clueless. It is not that. Your child is curious and needs to know and to learn and looks to you for the answers.

With all of this, your little one has a sixth sense about things and is uncanny in his/her understanding of mysteries and secrets around your home. An old saying, "Pull the wool over one's eyes," doesn't work on your child. You can try to fool him/her all day long, but surprisingly s/he is aware of what is going on. S/He seems to have an inner detection when you are trying to keep something from him/her so you may as well spill the beans.

Remember that if s/he is old enough to ask the question, s/he is old enough for the answer. Be gentle and understanding that your child is innocent and fewer details are necessary.

PISCES - *8:00 a.m. to 8:15 a.m.*
Eleventh House - Aries Rising

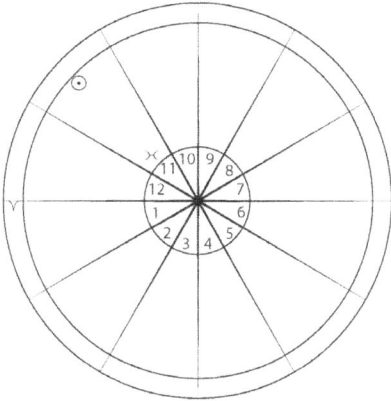

A born "hero," your little one is fearless and brave. You will find your child championing the underdog and very much in favor or the causes of those who are less fortunate and/or not as strong as s/he. Coming to the rescue is his/her forte and you can learn a lot from this child. A believer in "truth and justice for all," your Pisces child will always be there to protect.

This child is usually a good swimmer and athletic. Swimming and track are good pursuits for this child.

If you find that this sensitive child is acting out and looking for a form of discipline, ask if s/he needs to be held. You may be surprised that s/he needs to cry. Just hold him/her and let him/her cry. It is a cleansing and a form of rebirth.

PISCES - *8:15 a.m. to 8:30 a.m.*
Eleventh House - Taurus Rising

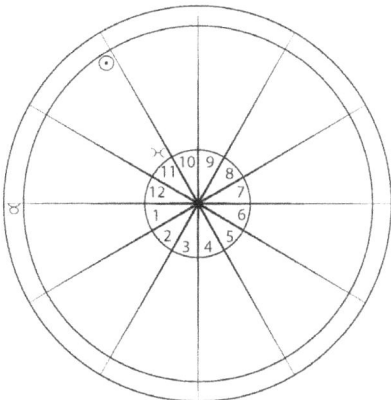

BFF (Best Friends Forever) are usually established at an early age. This child will stick like glue to all aspects of a relationship. Your little one's hope and wishes are quite tangible, and s/he wants material, rather than esoteric, things.

Betrayal is a bitter pill to swallow for your sensitive

child. At the same time, your little one is a loyal supporter of anyone s/he deems a friend (and in some cases, acquaintance). Should your child learn that this person is not who s/he thought, there will be disappointment and then total cut-off. However, remember that your Pisces is loyal to the end and it will take a good deal to convince him/her of anything that could hurt. The biggest part of the hurt comes from self-ridicule. Let your little one know that finding things out early is better than a later disappointment.

Your child may have some lofty expectations. It is your job to teach realism to your guileless child. Reality can sometimes be tough, but the earlier it is learned, the easier it will be to understand!

PISCES - *8:30 a.m. to 9:45 a.m.*
Tenth House - Gemini Rising

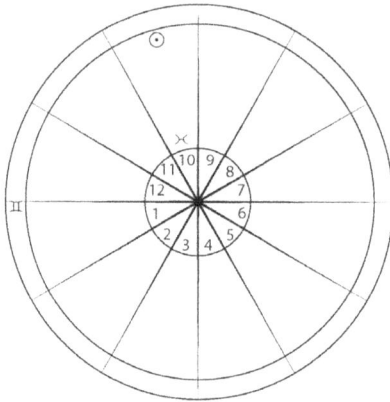

Wise beyond his/her years, your intelligent child will reluctantly take the helm and do his/her duty. Responsibility can sometimes be difficult and yet your child needs to be taught that a job or title of importance does not necessarily mean that s/he can abuse his/her powers. It is nice to be the boss, but caution calls and fairness is important.

Being in charge is something that comes naturally to your child and it is your duty to teach him/her kindness and respect so that when the time comes to rule the roost, s/he will be considerate to others around.

Your child is very glib and enjoys verbalizing everything. Part of this is so that s/he can understand it, the other part is for confirmation. Your Pisces knows things beyond his/her realm and needs confirmation.

PISCES - *9:45 a.m. to 11:30 a.m.*
Tenth House - Cancer Rising

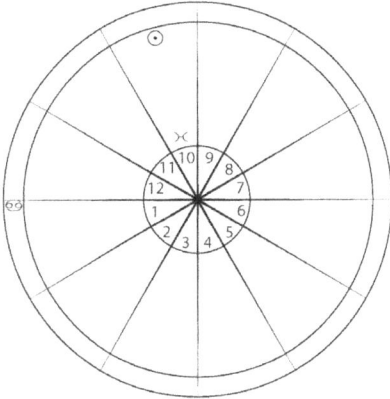

True leadership ability and sensitive to the needs of all. Your child will amaze you with his/her entrepreneurial skills and ability to get others to do his/her bidding. Let him/her learn some of the tenets of business and leadership and s/he will be a great leader in the future.

Be careful, however, to not allow yourself or others in the household to be pushed around by this dreamy child. It is important for him/her to know the difference between right and wrong and also to learn to listen.

How others think of him/her is somewhat important, but what is most important is how you think of your child. Reputation be damned, acceptance is most important.

PISCES - *11:30 a.m. to 12:15 p.m.*
Ninth House - Cancer Rising

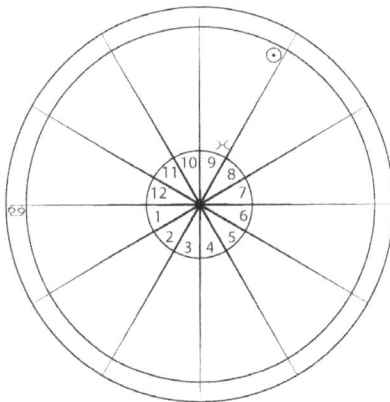

Your child connects with those who are alone or downtrodden. Your little Pisces is very compassionate, and you can't be surprised if s/he brings home a stray (person, pet, etc.).

Anywhere s/he hangs his/her hat is home. Your child loves to know that there is a home where s/he belongs but is happy to call anywhere home.

If you find him/her staying at a friend's house more than your home, learn what the features and benefits are there that are not in your home. Then decide if it is worth changing the environment for that purpose!

PISCES - *12:15 p.m. to 2:00 p.m.*
Ninth House - Leo Rising

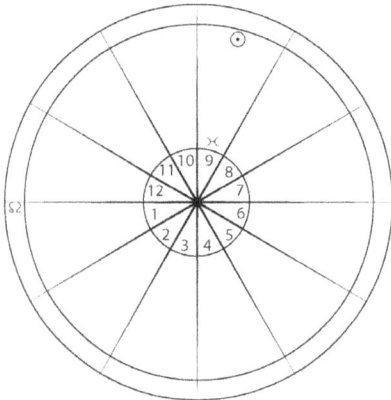

There is never enough to learn. A need to know more is apparent in this child. Books and education are the things that will occupy the mind of your little one. The quest for knowledge is very great.

A true scholar, your Pisces child has great retentive powers as well as powers of observation.

S/He may be a little bit stubborn but that is something that will eventually even itself out and with some prompting and laughter, s/he can learn to have an open mind!

PISCES - *2:00 p.m. to 3:30 p.m.*
Eighth House - Leo Rising

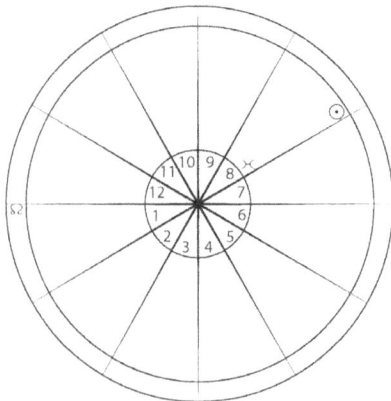

It is important that your child is praised for his/her outstanding behavior. S/He has a great deal of talent and showmanship and needs to be noticed and appreciated for it.

A taste for the bizarre can even scare you. Your little one should enjoy a good practical joke and creepy crawly animals (or insects). The rubber ones will do well in the beginning; however, as s/he matures, so will the nature of the beast(s).

Scary movies won't really scare your child into not wanting to see more. S/He loves mystery and suspense and anything that may seem "strange." You will discover your little one's mirth coming out on the occasions where "odd" things are introduced!

PISCES
Eighth House - Virgo Rising

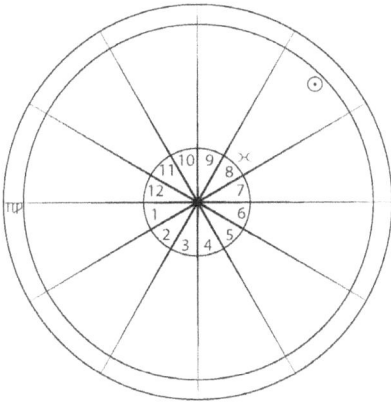

Your child is very generous. His/her need to bring good things to others is embedded into his/her DNA.

When your child is not satisfied with his/her work (s/he is a perfectionist), s/he breaks out in the strangest diseases. As soon as your child can forgive him/herself, s/he is suddenly well! It is very important for your child (who can be prone to OCD behavior) to learn to forgive him/herself. It is the key to his/her existence.

Your little one is a healer and his/her giving nature won't allow him/her to give bad vibes. Therefore, it is necessary for him/her to be in a state of grace (as you will) and display kindness and generosity. This state of mind is what keeps him/her healthy. It is up to you to teach this to your lovely child.

You can introduce your little one to books early on and marvel at his/her pleasure in the bizarre.

PISCES - *3:30 p.m. to 4:30 p.m.*
Seventh House - Leo Rising

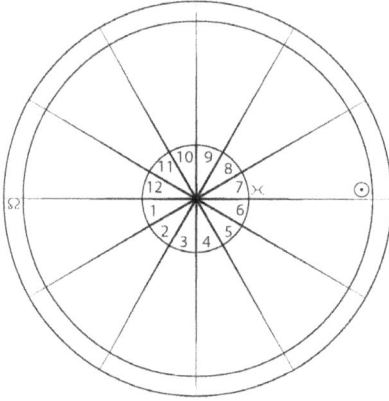

Your sensitive Pisces loves humor. With a great imagination, s/he will surprise you at how funny s/he can be. You may find that s/he is firm (some call it stubborn). However, when going after a goal, the single-minded determination of this child will always win out and you will see that s/he gets results almost all of the time.

It is good to teach this lovely child (does s/he have a widow's peak on his/her forehead?) how to live and let live or better yet, how to be less judgmental. You may find that your sensitive child might jump to conclusions because of a pre-determined idea, usually learned from a respected source, which may color his/her opinions. Try to be neutral around your intelligent and insightful child and let him/her come to his/her own conclusions.

PISCES - *4:30 p.m. to 5:30 p.m.*
Seventh House - Virgo Rising

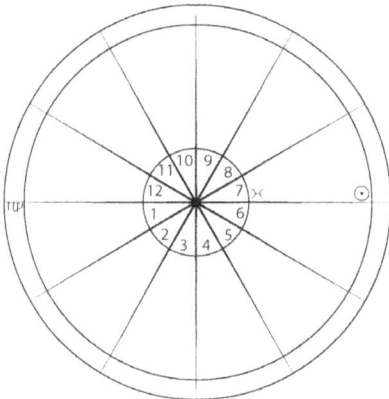

Sometimes, your little Pisces sprite is very serious. More organized than most Pisces children, your little one may display a need for charts and diagrams. The more organized s/he is, the happier. Even when things seem messy, your

Pisces knows precisely where everything is situated, and don't you change a thing.

In the event that you deem his/her belongings messy and you decide to straighten things out or (heaven forbid) toss out things, you may experience a rant for this sensitive child. It is only because s/he has wrapped his head around his/her own organization and therefore does not like to make the changes. If instead, you organize with him/her and s/he can re-organize in his/her head, you will enjoy a happy child.

Teach your Pisces early to fit other people into his/her equation and to not change anyone!

PISCES - *5:30 p.m. to 7:15 p.m.*
Sixth House - Virgo Rising

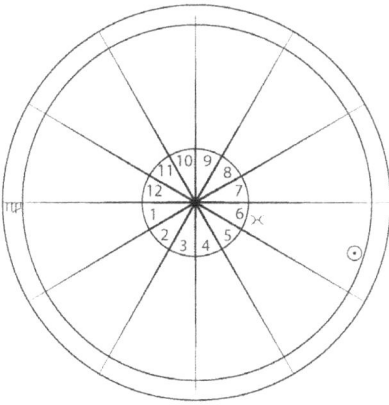

You will find a very compassionate child who wants to fix everyone and everything. Discrimination is a good lesson for your sweet child. A first aid kit and how to use it will be a good and valuable tool for this gentle soul. Don't be surprised if little birds with broken wings or squirrels, etc. find their way into his/her "laboratory."

Mostly, you have a healer on your hands, and you will find your gentle child wants to repair all things that are broken. With detailed precision, you may find that s/he pulls things apart to learn how to put them back together. The same applies to people who may seem broken to your sensitive child.

Patience is a virtue and it's important that your little one learns this attribute. When you first tell your sensitive child that "patience is a virtue," you will get defiance and may even have a standoff. However, once patience is learned, your child will be happier with the way things are happening. Otherwise, your child could grow up pushing others around and making people feel uncomfortable.

PISCES - *7:15 p.m. to 8:15 p.m.*
Sixth House - Libra Rising

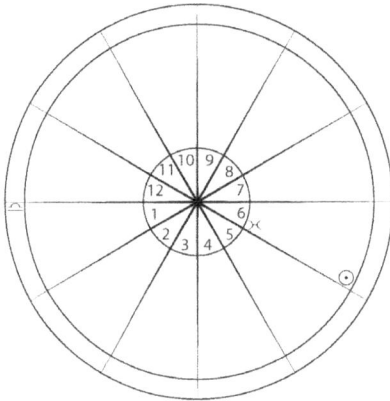

S/He may have a good sense of humor which you notice after the age of three. There is merriment in your child, as well as loveliness and beauty. Eager to work and help with chores, you may also find that there are times when your child is lazy. S/He simply needs prompting to know that his/her help is necessary.

It is important that your Pisces child feels worth for a job well done. If there is recognition for what has been done well, then you will see it happen again and again. However, if your child does not feel that what s/he has done is up to par, then attempts will be slow repeating themselves.

You do not need to "praise" you child as much as you need to show appreciation. A simple "thank you for a job well-done" does the trick and is enough to satisfy your little Pisces. On the other hand, should you heap praise on him/her, s/he may either not believe you or s/he may think you are being phony and that you are not really satisfied with a job well done.

PISCES - *8:15 p.m. to 9:45 p.m.*
Fifth House - Libra Rising

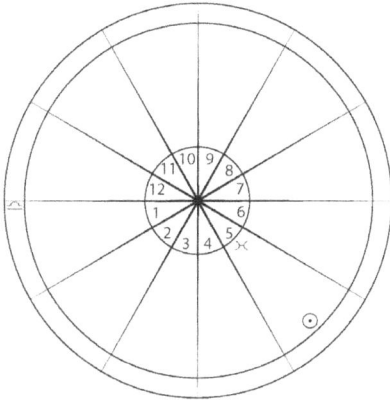

It is good to let your lovely child take dancing lessons. Music lessons are also good. The music in his/her soul will soar out as your child feels a purpose as well as talent in his/her life.

You will also find that your lovely child is quite patient with little children. It is a natural instinct that your child has as a patient and loving nurturer.

This child loves to play and being with children gives him/her the opportunity to return to a seemingly happier time as a baby. You may find that s/he enjoys being a baby again, looking for the attention that is perceived as given only to younger children. You can demonstrate to him/her what life would be like by showing him/her the advantages s/he has as an "older" and more-knowledgeable child. Once s/he discovers his/her powers from being older, s/he will no longer wish to be treated like a baby.

Affection is important to this little one and it is good to pour as much on him/her as you can. You will be informed by your child when it is time to stop. You don't need to determine this for yourself. Just keep loving him/her and let him/her grow into him/herself!

PISCES - *9:45 p.m. to 10:30 p.m.*
Fifth House - Scorpio Rising

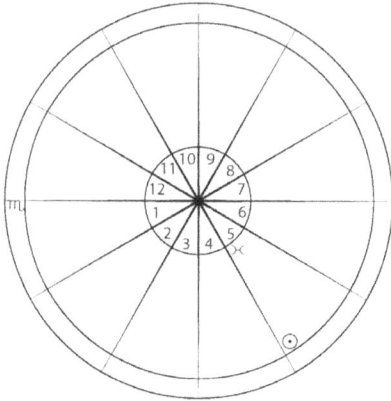

"Why?" You hear this question so many times, that you can find your own patience waning. The best thing is to not make an unfounded statement. If you are going to say something, let there be something substantial to back it up. "Because, I said so!" is not always the best answer!

In an argument, your child is very challenging. For example, you say "we have to do this, even though I don't like it." The retort is: "Then you must like it, since you are willing to do it!" You get frustrated. Your child feels powerful for being right. You are powerless because you don't want to explain. It is a round circle! I don't know the solution. Simply that there are times when you can say, "I still don't like it. Period!" Not that it will quiet him/her, but it may help him to drop the subject and try to understand. You could later explain that there are things that we must do, whether or not we enjoy those things, but that doesn't fully explain to a stubborn mind.

PISCES - *10:30 p.m. to 12:15 a.m.*
Fourth House - Scorpio Rising

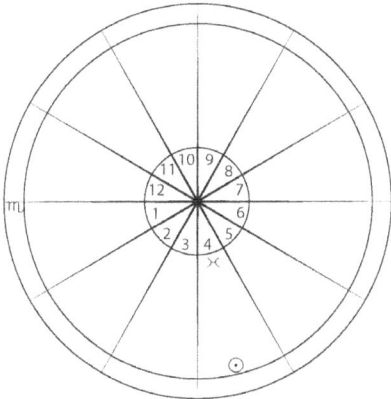

It is not unusual for this child to seem stubborn or firm about things that are of interest. His/her room is his/her sanctuary and if it is shared, then one spot must belong to this youngster. Then your child will have a sense of belonging.

With an investigative nature, your young fish will ask "why?" many times. The sooner s/he learns to look things up or to do some sort of research, the easier it will be on you.

You will discover that this child is quite intuitive and will say things off the wall that are right on. Pay attention to this child and you will learn.

Your youngster has good instincts as a rule, and you can count on the truth coming from his/her lips. But do take care that there is an attitude of justice mixed with revenge from time to time and you may wish to dissuade this type of attitude. Teach tolerance and temperament.

A need to get even is sometimes apparent. When I was young, my father taught me, "The best revenge is no revenge. It keeps them looking over their shoulders." He was right because if this is something you can teach this child, s/he will sail through disappointments.

PISCES
Fourth House - Sagittarius Rising

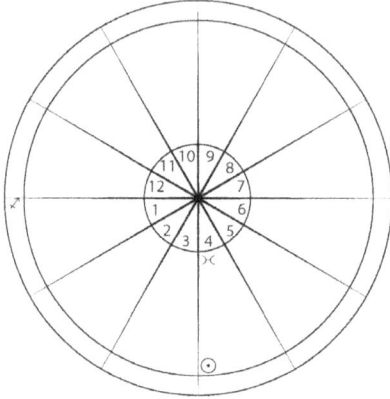

It is a good idea to take your little one outdoors camping or fishing if possible. Teach him/her to set up a tent and survival techniques. This is a child who thrives in nature and is a good survivor!

Your young Pisces will tell you that s/he is lucky, and you can believe it. Good fortune seems to follow this child wherever s/he goes. Pay attention.

If your little one feels inclined to do something new or out of the ordinary, be certain to make him/her aware of any pitfalls you may see, but then wish him/her "bon chance" and let him/her go on to the new adventure. The outcome will not always be successful, but more times than not, it will be.

If his/her hips get sore or his/her legs get tired, you can be sure that this child is not happy with his/her approach to life and needs more space.

PISCES - *12:15 a.m. to 2:45 a.m.*
Third House - Sagittarius Rising

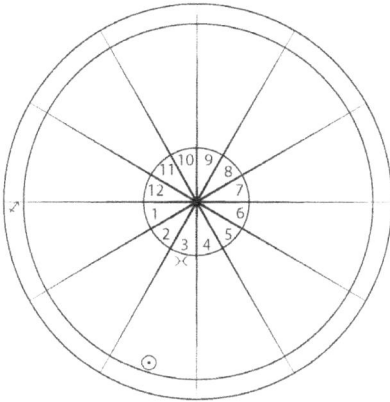

You have an interested scholar on your hands with this child. Interest in Botany and the environment will be at the forefront and you can be sure that your little one wants a pet.

A child I know wants a pet very badly, so her parents replaced a live animal with stuffed animals. Although she is temporarily satisfied, she still talks about the "doggy" she is going to have in the future. When that time comes, she will cleave to this pet as though she had a new brother or sister. The pet will be a good substitute for a best friend. This is what happens to this child with Sagittarius Rising and the sun in the third house. Sometimes s/he will want a horse. Depends on where you live!

You will also find that you have a good student. It is possible that your little one makes up a new language that only s/he and one or two others know. This will delight your child and you will find that codes are of a special interest to him/her.

PISCES - *2:45 a.m. to 3:00 a.m.*
Third House - Capricorn Rising

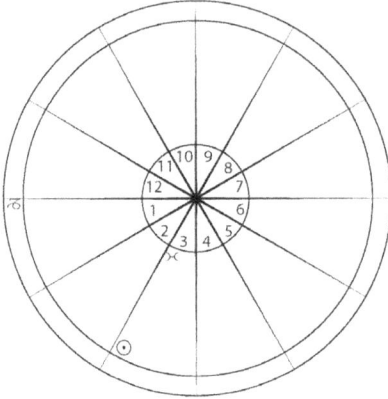

Your little one likely would like siblings or at least one. S/He will feel responsible for another child, even an older one. It is likely that your child assumes the position of parent when a sibling has a problem. Even if younger, your child may feel more responsible and protective toward his/her sibling(s). At about the age of 8 or 9 you may find that your very mature child tells you that s/he can be home alone and does not need a supervisor or baby-sitter. S/He means it! Your fearless child feels very responsible and mature and feels (or believes) that being in charge is his/her natural right.

Some responsibility is good but don't be afraid to let this little one continue to be a child.

A good student, you will find that science is an interesting subject for your little one and you can get him/her a telescope as a present.

PISCES - *3:00 a.m. to 4:45 a.m.*
Second House - Capricorn Rising

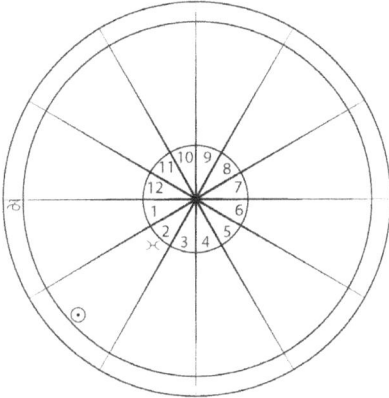

You will find your child to be very responsible and good with money. However, don't get any cheap items for him/her because quality counts and means a lot. You will find that your child is a bit of a snob when it comes to "things." Your Pisces wants the best and will work to earn enough to get the top of the line article rather than settle for second best. It will be difficult to always comply with your child; however, teaching him/her to earn those "things" that s/he deems necessary will give the items value, something important to this child.

You may also find that your little one finds money in his/her pocket when it is important. Also, your child may have a generous streak and be happy to share his/her booty. When I was a child, I always loved to walk home with my brother. He would always find that he had money in his pocket, and we would stop by the candy store on the way home and get some candy for our long trek home. (No, we didn't walk miles, just a few blocks.)

Your child has pride and it matters to him/her what others think, even when s/he says it does not matter . . . it does! Reputation is important to your child.

PISCES - *4:45 a.m. to 5:00 a.m.*
Second House - Aquarius Rising

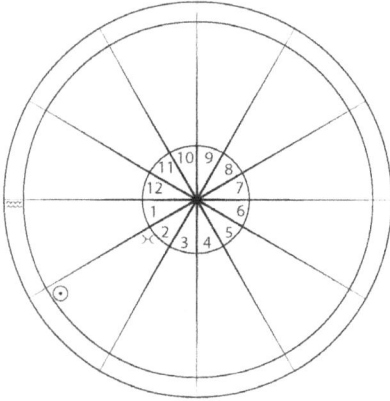

Your child may have what you consider off-beat values. The things that s/he values may not coincide with your definition of what is of worth. Try to understand and ask your little one what is most important and what is important to him/her and go from there. If you try to interject some of your own hopes and wishes, you will find they are rejected. Your child likes to do his/her own thing and treasure those things which are unique or unusual. Those bugs may not mean much to you but your little one may find them fascinating.

Your child wants to be seen as important and wants others to find him/her unique. Teach him/her early on to not be late for events and to show consideration for the people who are waiting on him/her. Eventually, people will think your child selfish if s/he keeps others waiting for him/her and is inconsiderate about time. A watch is a good asset for your Pisces child so that s/he can show consideration and good breeding. It seems as though the small consideration of being on time will be an asset to your child as time goes on. If s/he learns early to be considerate of other people, it will go a long way later in life.

PART FOUR

YOUR CARDINAL SIGN CHILD

Your Cardinal Sign Child is often a self-starter and quite independent.

The time of your child's birth gives additional understanding into his/her needs and what area of your child's life is important to him/her.

It is a good idea to remember to deduct one hour for daylight-savings-time (i.e. if your child was born at 8:41 PDT, subtract one hour and use 7:41).

If the time is close to the hour, it is possible that the definition prior to or following the one given will apply. Also, if your child is born in a very northerly area or in a very southern hemisphere, the same may apply.

ARIES

Aries children are lovely and usually cheerful. They have ready smiles and are eager to please. There seems to be no angst with this child.

Your Aries child may seem aggressive at times. This behavior is learned from others when s/he doesn't understand something. S/He best learns to divert this behavior by learning to be assertive instead.

Your child is very forthcoming and has foresight.

Your Aries child is like a nymph. Very innocent and still learning about life.

One time, while I was learning Astrology, I began doing charts for everyone who worked with me. I asked them to please read the descriptions and tell me if they were close. One Aries man walked over to my desk after receiving his horoscope and threw the papers on my desk. "I am not arrogant," he yelled at me.

These children have good athletic skills and are especially good in track and field, basketball and swimming.

Short-term projects are usually successful with your child. However, if you give an assignment that takes too long or is too complicated, your Aries child will become bored and abandon the project. When setting goals, it is good to give smaller goals that lead to the destination. This way, there is achievement along the way. The little successes lead to the ultimate finish and your child feels a sense of accomplishment.

Your child has an artistic side. Be certain to have pen and paper on hand so that drawing is included in daily activities. There are times when the only explanation may be on paper and not verbal.

Be sure to check their eyes early. Should your Aries child get headaches or earaches, there is something hurting his/her feelings

You may find your Aries to be very self-reliant and independent. Don't worry, s/he still needs you, in spite of this spirit of "I can do it myself!" In spite of the fact that your affection may be rejected, your little one needs lots of love and also needs positive attention. Eventually, once s/he trusts you, your love and affection will be returned!

Red, orange, and yellow are great colors for your Aries!

ARIES - *12:00 a.m. to 1:00 a.m.*
Fourth House - Capricorn Rising

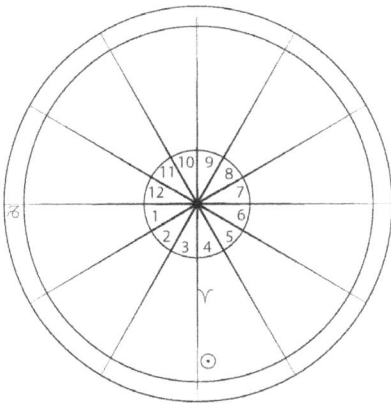

Although s/he is a born leader, you will find that the limelight doesn't always suit him/her. Instead, you may find your child enjoys letting the fame go to someone else, who (according to your child) "deserves it more." Instead, your Aries enjoys being the boss! S/He will start at home, thank you. After that, it's the conqueror who will emerge and help you to rule the household (at first) and then all s/he surveys. These qualities are inborn and with a jutting jaw, s/he will push forward.

You will enjoy watching this wonderful child elevating someone else and staying out of the spotlight. S/He will let you know that another's star is acclaim for him/her.

Although s/he may be a little bossy, you will find that your Aries child is a good little helper in everything. Once you tell him/her the "right" way to do something, be sure you are not mistaken because you can be quoted should you decide that something should be changed.

You have an entrepreneur on your hands and your child will always be thinking up great ideas! Teach him/her to put these ideas down on paper and to figure out how to accomplish them.

Your child may appear darker, compared to siblings or peers and you will notice that s/he has strong bones and a jutting jaw. These are normal attributes and even out eventually.

If your little one seems morose or depressed, it is a good idea to teach him/her how to journal and put down some of those feelings on paper. Later, you can invite him/her to revisit what has been written and to begin to write down solutions. Your little one will have a good foundation for his/her future self and will grow with more confidence.

ARIES - *11:30 p.m. (previous night) to 1:00 a.m.*
Fourth House - Sagittarius Rising

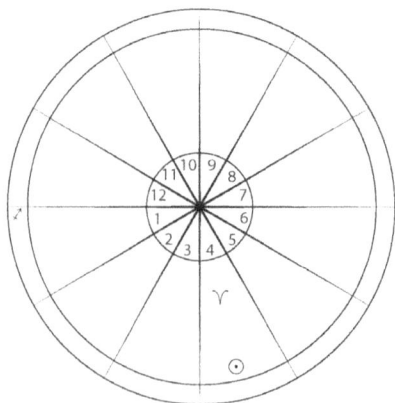

A true adventurer, your Aries child is often exploring first his/her environment and then every other place s/he goes. S/He loves to find treasures. Not necessarily those things of value, such as jewelry, but more like those things that provoke memory. You can share history and make memories with this child. Times outdoors are precious, and you will be able to share experiences with him/her.

If you try to hide "things" from him/her, be sure they will be found. Your child is an explorer who already knows every inch of his/her environment and every reasonable hiding place. S/He is not as much nosy as s/he is curious and adventurous.

Read to this child. Old classics, such as The Jungle Book by Rudyard Kipling are especially entertaining. You can also read travel books and stories about life in other places to happily broaden his/her horizons! One day, you can visit these places together!

ARIES - *1:00 a.m. to 1:30 a.m.*
Third House - Sagittarius Rising

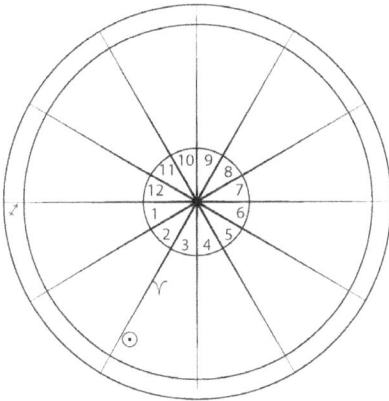

The soul of an adventurer is in this child. S/He has a great deal of curiosity and may ask you many questions. A good student, your child's curiosity is very great, and you may find him/her paying close attention to how you achieve some of your goals. Your little one's questions are sincere, and s/he should be taken seriously!

It is a good idea to have a pet for this child. It is a responsibility s/he will take seriously.

Your child loves to have siblings but could tend to be a little selfish. Although innately generous, sharing is a quality that still needs to be taught. The idea is that s/he is protective of things but once shown that nothing will deprive him/her of his/her knowledge or things, you will find a more giving and sharing nature.

Artistic talent could be found early in this child.

ARIES *1:30 a.m. to 3:30 a.m.*
Third House - Capricorn Rising

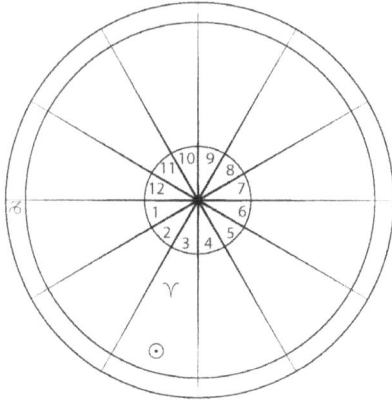

Being the "parent" is your little one's burden. This child loves to have other brothers and sisters. That way s/he has someone to parent! You will find your little one is very responsible and enjoys taking charge of other brothers and sisters. Too much authority given to this child may lead him/her to bully his/her charges. However, some authority is good for him/her and s/he can learn early on to be helpful.

An excellent student, you want to allow your child that an education is the key to his/her success in life. Whatever career or job choice, it matters not, as long as the job is one well done and one in which s/he can take pride.

You may also enjoy storytelling with this child. Ask him/her to tell or relate his/her own story and see what a talented writer s/he will eventually become!

Wherever your child goes or whatever career choices s/he makes, know that your little one will never be mediocre and will always rise to the top. You will see this trait on the playground. A good director and leader, your little one will work hard to elevate others rather than him/herself. Consequently, s/he will have many who will do as s/he says.

ARIES
Second House - Capricorn Rising

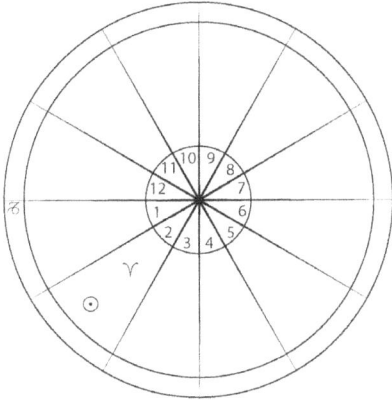

Although this doesn't happen often, your child is an entrepreneur in every sense of the word. S/He can handle your money well and will also have an affinity for antiques and other memorabilia.

A child of beauty and discipline, you may find your Aries a starter in many things. You will be asked a lot of questions that may require you to look up the answers. Teach him/her how to do the research!

Those things that belong to him/her are treasures which will in one way, or another be honored for either their history or their value. There are some treasures which are of value only because of their history. So, if you clean his/her room, be sure you know what to keep and what to toss. It is possible that you may be asked later, "where is my . . ." An answer is demanded, and you may see a little behind hanging over the top of a trash can. It is best to clean up and toss out together!

ARIES - *3:30 a.m. to 4:45 a.m.*
Second House - Aquarius Rising

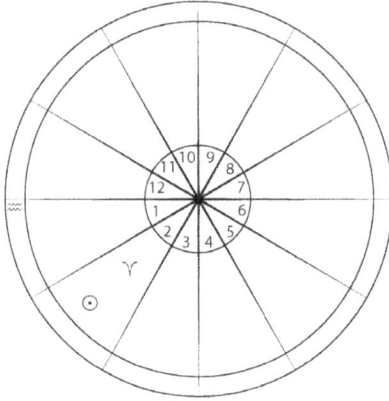

How lovely is this fair child! With wonderment in his/her eyes, you will be happily pleased at how well s/he cares for you and your "things!" These are treasures to your child and curiosity will lead to many questions from him/her.

If you should tell your little one to not touch this or that, s/he will feel compelled to leave everything behind, including his/her curiosity. If you teach him/her how to treat certain items, you will have a happy and cautious child. Your things will be treasures and valued to him/her. The same goes for people. It is good to teach your little one early on how to be kind and respectful and to value and treasure those special people in his/her life.

Let your child know that something is treasured and cannot be replaced or that it is something that should be shared and there are more out there. The differentiation is important early in your child's life. If your little one is confused, s/he will seem to be very selfish and will lead others to believe that it is "me first" and then everyone else.

ARIES - *4:45 a.m. to 5:00 a.m.*
Second House - Pisces Rising

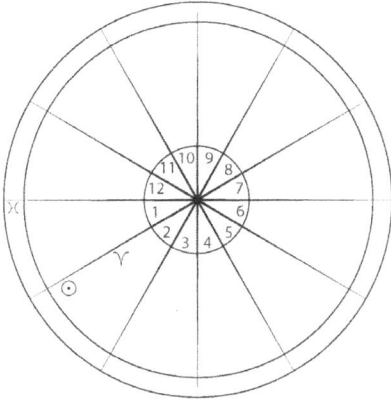

Your dreamy child will have a different type of value system from what may be expected. S/He will value thoughts, ideas and ideals. You may find a strong sense of intuition and a defender of others' causes. S/He will fight tooth and nail for justice for the underdog and does not always understand "survival of the fittest!" In his/her eyes, it is supposed to be survival for the one who deserves it the most, which may not always be your opinion.

Teach this child how to differentiate without prejudice. It is hard on you but helpful to your little one's backbone!!

Possessions that are important to your child are not necessarily tangible unless they are heirlooms. Cherished pieces from the past are meaningful to your child and stories of ancestors are of interest, as well. Certain photographs or old albums will be treasured by your sentimental child. A need to know history is sparked by items from the past as well as treasured pieces.

ARIES - *5:00 a.m. to 6:00 a.m.*
First House - Pisces Rising

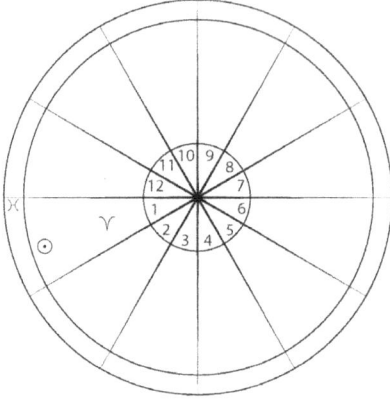

So caring and innocent is your child of beauty! There is kindness everywhere in this child and you will benefit by paying attention to his/her thoughts and ideas. You may even want to journal some of the things s/he says. Nuggets of wisdom come from the mouth of this babe. You can marvel at his/her insight.

This child loves to laugh. So, do introduce your beautiful Aries to humor and keep joy in your home for him/her to experience. Sing to this little one and soon s/he will sing with you!

S/He also needs to cry. If your little one is acting out in need of a reprimand, you may want to hold him/her and tell them it is alright to cry if needs be.

Know your motives before you make a request or demand of your sensitive child. This child is intuitive enough to know your motivation and why you really have the expectations you have.

ARIES - *6:30 a.m. to 7:00 a.m.*
First House - Aries Rising

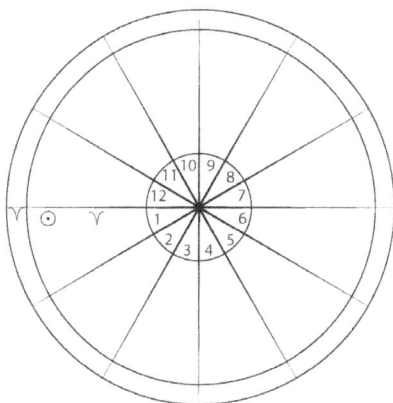

The term "bouncing off the walls" might be applied to your active Aries. S/He has so much energy and almost no where to put it. Many outdoor activities will suit this child and you can even encourage runs in the park to burn off some of that energy.

You may also want to involve him/her in sports at an early age, as s/he is quite competitive! Organized sports will help your little one channel his/her energy and put it in an acceptable place.

This child is usually quite healthy and is hard to keep down, even if s/he has a cold. The best thing to teach him/her is preventative measures to avoid illness.

If your child gets earaches or other facial and head injuries, s/he is unhappy. Find out what the problem is so that it can be rectified. A headache means that s/he is not doing things that make him/her happy!

ARIES - *7:00 a.m. to 7:30 a.m.*
Twelfth House - Aries Rising

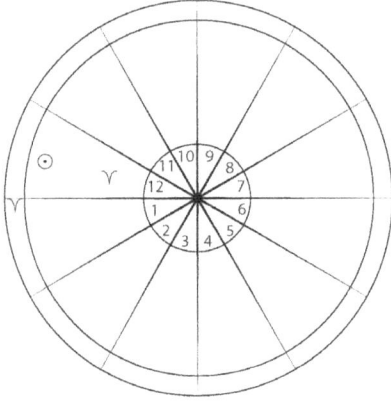

If your Aries seems to be "stuck" it is up to you to move him/her along. Sometimes your child may be so in his/her head, that reality is lost to imagination. Give this child a pencil and paper and let him/her draw some of the solutions s/he may have to problems. Later, s/he can learn to journal by putting thoughts and ideas down on paper. It will help your child to understand his/her problems and eventually help him/her to become a solver of problems for others.

There is a lot of pent up energy in your child and it is a good idea to get him/her outside for recreation and letting off steam. If they do not do this, these children could blow up. Taking a boat ride can be especially enjoyable for this child, as is any other type of nature activity.

A natural intuition is normal for your child and s/he only wants to be heard and acknowledged. If your child says, "I think this will happen . . ." and then it occurs, a good idea is to acknowledge with a statement of, "you were right!". Confirmation goes a long way.

ARIES - *7:30 a.m. to 8:00 a.m.*
Twelfth House - Taurus Rising

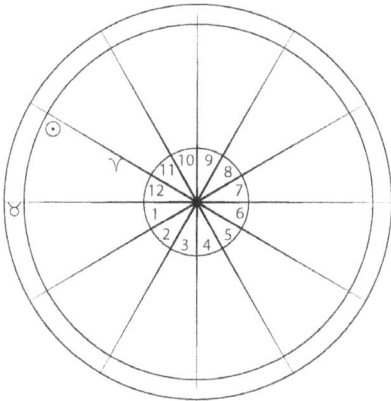

There may be times when the phrase "wishful thinking" applies to your child. It is because you will hear about dreams (or desires) for a horse or some other unattainable thing. Do not fret, instead, you can teach your little one to make dreams a reality. This is something they understand quite well.

Your child has the ability to manifest and consequently if s/he choose something that is distasteful to you, it is a good idea to redirect his/her objectives. You may from time to time find that your little one is a bit stubborn. A lesson in tolerance is important during the early years so that s/he won't come off as too opinionated when stressed in later life.

S/He has so much energy and with dogged determination can do anything s/he sets his/her mind to do. It is at that point that you will want to discuss all those "things" that are in his/her mind. You don't want to sabotage a new thought or idea, simply learn more. The more you listen, the more you will be trusted. If you think something is a bad idea voice your opinion, but with good reason. Show good reason for your objections so that s/he can learn to look at all sides before putting something into action.

ARIES - *8:00 a.m. to 9:00 a.m.*
Eleventh House - Taurus Rising

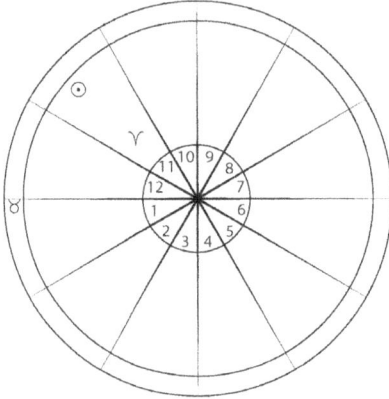

Turn jealousy into inventiveness. It is possible that your little one will find friends who have "more" than you have. Explain that s/he has as much in love and a full life as anyone else has. Also, it is important to learn what s/he values more than it is to know what is "valuable."

The friends your child makes can be for life. However, should a friendship break off, it is possible that it breaks off forever. Your child is friendly and likable, but if another finds his/her stubbornness a problem, there could be a bigger problem of a lost friendship. Flexibility is a lesson learned here, and it is up to you to show your little Aries how to be tolerant of others' foibles and how to be more adaptable to others' ways of life.

Hopes and wishes for your child could be tangible. You may find that s/he hopes one day to possess something of value that will bring prestige. One child I knew wanted Mommy and Daddy to have expensive things so that s/he could be a part of it. Eventually, not satisfied with it not belonging to him/her, s/he began to make demands for the things s/he did want.

ARIES - *9:00 a.m. to 10 a.m.*
Eleventh House - Gemini Rising

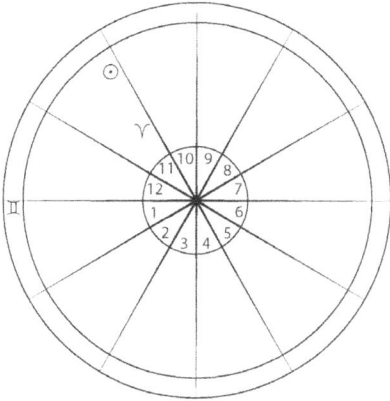

From birth, you can introduce this child to other children. Your baby's gentle and generous nature will welcome others into his/her life.

Your Aries child can enjoy being alone, wants to know all the rules, and wants to be alone (with a friend, if possible) to do his/her thing. It is not your place to participate into his/her activities. After you have taught him/her something, s/he will want to share it with a peer, not a figure of authority!

Remember that you are the parent and authority figure. Do not try to be this child's friend. Children his/her own age will be the friends. You will be the adult!

You will find your child loves glee. Enjoys running and playing. Enjoys childhood. If there is a way to carry this characteristic into adulthood, your Aries child will find a way to do so. A child always lives inside this little sprite!

ARIES - *10 a.m. to 10:45 a.m.*
Tenth House - Gemini Rising

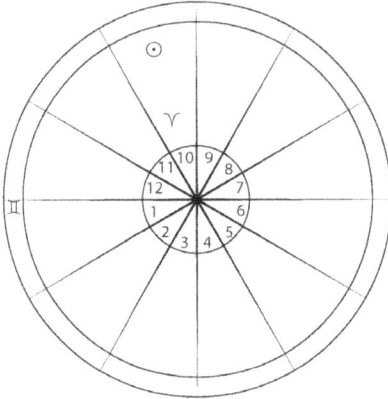

Your lovely and innocent child will be more comfortable being someone else (like in play-acting) than him/herself. S/He will make discoveries and tackle life with a smile and a strong desire to please.

Games like make-believe or charades will be fun past-times for him/her. The challenge of being someone else and making you believe it is delightful to this child. S/He responds well to praise but mostly can be encouraged to write his/her own script and act it out.

This child knows how to take charge and how to get things rolling so s/he may start early building his/her empire! As your child is very versatile, you will find that s/he changes his/her mind often before settling on one think. Do not be frustrated, rather enjoy how well-rounded your little one is and can be.

ARIES - *10:45 a.m. to 12:45 p.m.*
Tenth House - Cancer Rising

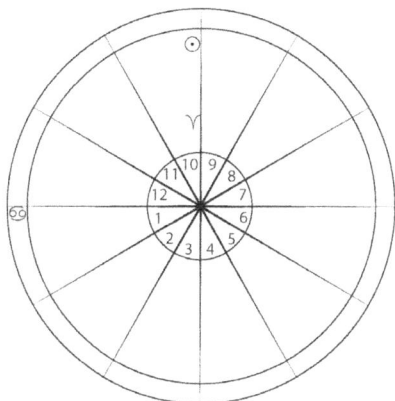

Your Aries child can rule the roost. There is no controlling this strong-willed child. These very characteristics will be good later in life when s/he runs for office and wins or when s/he starts his/her own company. In the meantime, raising this child, who feels it is necessary to raise you is not the easiest task.

One way that you can conquer this impetuousness is to give your child an area where s/he is in charge. You can get a pet, or you can have a project. Don't help unless asked. Your child will learn excellent skills from this, and you will be able to teach without any controversy. When this little one feels in control, everything is good with the world. You will be thanked in later life. By giving your little one his/her own space where s/he can be boss, you can claim the rest of life and be the parent to this little one who needs a lot of guidance.

A true entrepreneur, you may find many projects started before your little one settles on something of interest to him/her. Goaded by the need to succeed, you will find that your little genius is always thinking of the next project.

Your child is easily bored and must learn how to stay with one thing. Therefore, it is in your best interest (or it can be costly) that you help your child determine what the primary goal (success) is and how it is best achieved.

A whiz in the kitchen, it will never be too soon to teach your Aries how to cook. If the kitchen doesn't seem like the right place, get to a barbeque and teach your Aries how to grill.

Remember that this child will want to be in charge and also be known as the "best of the best." This is almost more challenging for a parent than it is for a child.

Acceptance and control are key to this child.

ARIES - *12:45 p.m. - 1:00 p.m.*
Tenth House - Leo Rising

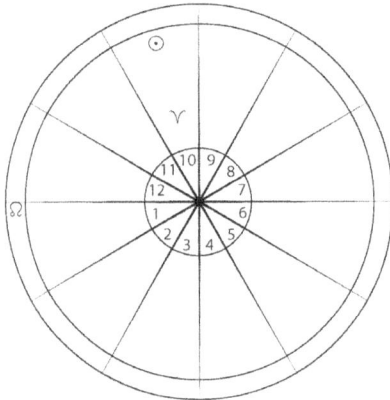

It will be hard to keep your child off the stage or to keep him/her from performing for you and your friends. Although initially shy, you will find that your Aries child is bolder with each performance and quite entertaining!

Perhaps too much encouragement might make his/her heart race, but eventually you will find a willing performer.

Any kind of lessons are good for your child who is a good student. A true leader in every sense of the word, your child is also a constant student and loves to learn new things.

Even if your child is at the top of the class, s/he does not want to stop learning. It's in his/her genes and the more knowledge, the more power.

Tenacious and strong, your Aries will follow through to the end to make everything come out the way s/he planned in the beginning. This is not a child to be underestimated. S/He will succeed!

ARIES
Ninth House - Cancer Rising

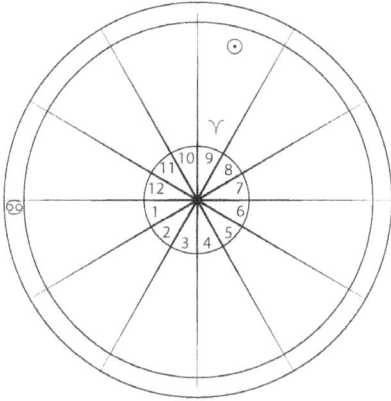

Your child is quite sensitive and very aware of the feelings of those around him/her. You will discover that this sensitive and innocent child is tuned in to the affairs of others and is kind and understanding.

A philosophical child, words of wisdom are many times uttered and can be quite profound. Listen carefully to your sweet child. You can be sure this little one has good judgment in his/her veins.

A true scholar, your little one will appreciate knowing more about world history and travel. You may want to encourage your little one to learn languages, as you will find that foreigners are often welcomed to your home by him/her. "Mi casa, su casa!" is a philosophy of this little one. S/He expects the same hospitality when visiting others. S/He will make him/herself quite at home anywhere.

ARIES - *1:00 p.m. to 3:00 p.m.*
Ninth House - Leo Rising

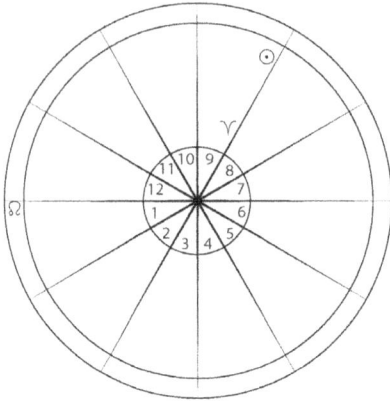

An amazing scholar, your child has great wisdom. You can introduce classical books and philosophies (other than your own) to this child and marvel at how well these ideas and ideals are grasped, although not necessarily adopted. But your little one loves to learn more and has great wisdom, seeing through other thoughts and ideas.

You have a child who can be a good student and is anxious to expand his/her horizons. Therefore, it is up to you to encourage more learning. A trip to a museum is very educational and informative, but you may find that the art or dinosaurs are most interesting.

Horses hold a fascination for this child, as do other large animals. A large pet, such as a large dog, is a cherished friend to your child.

ARIES
Ninth House - Virgo Rising

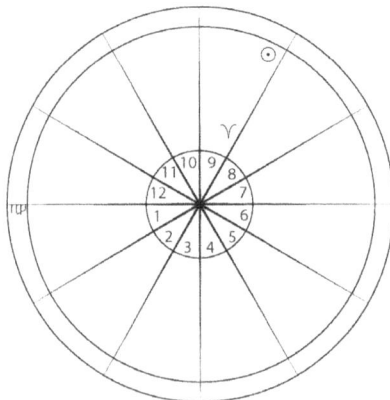

Your Aries child wants to know all the details but may not want to do the research. It is up to you. If you wish to teach this child a particular lesson and can prove its validity, then it may be easier for you to do the research.

Eventually, though, s/he is going to have to find the answers without you.

Eventually, you will find a child who wants to be professional in whatever s/he chooses to do. You can influence this innocent or let him/her fend without you. In either case, you will be proud to see your little one rise in ranks and in the respect of others.

It is going to be entertaining watching this picky little free spirit grow. On one hand s/he will scream for freedom and on the other hand you will find a willing learner.

Philosophical in spirit, you may find this turn to religious studies. At the least, your child will be curious about religions and philosophies in order to find his/her path. It is good to encourage this and not to force your own beliefs on your child.

ARIES - *3:00 p.m. to 3:30 p.m.*
Eighth House - Leo Rising

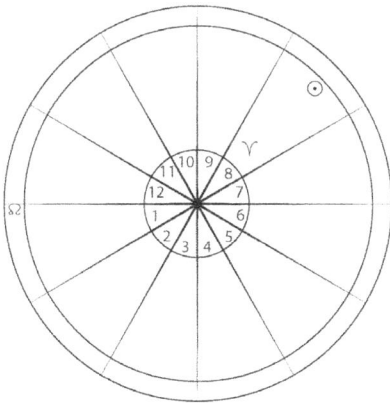

S/He will find those people who seem to have the most prestige to impress and who have the most money to use. Your Aries child is quite charming and is it easy for him/her to convince others to come to his/her way of thinking.

A student of the occult, you child may surprise you with unusual knowledge. You can be sure that your learned little one has found ways to educate him/herself.

Your Aries child enjoys learning new things and especially learning from other people. There are times when s/he will learn from another's experience and other times when you find him/her quoting from lessons at school or from a special class. In either case, learning new things is always pleasurable for your child and especially interesting to him/her are ways to make the learning profitable.

Your child is usually the recipient of prizes and other benefits. S/He will take this in stride and expect that scholarship or to win a contest that has meaning to him/her. If you don't dote on these things and create an air of "luck," your Aries child will take things in stride and not have disappointments. With no expectations, there can be no disappointments.

ARIES - *3:30 p.m. to 4:45 p.m.*
Eighth House - Virgo Rising

Your child likes order. It is inherent in him/her to have things in a certain place. S/He thinks things out before attacking them and is often considered to be a perfectionist.

Even in an athletic mode, your little one will want to know the benefits to his/her health and to his/her body.

Your Virgo-rising Aries performs with precision and knows why s/he is doing whatever is at hand.

S/He may have a fascination with death so you may want to take the time to explain as well as you can about dead people, but the best thing is to let him/her do his/her own research. You can take this child to a funeral and not be concerned about his/her behavior. S/He should be quite respectful at times of people's mourning and also understanding.

ARIES - *4:45 p.m. to 6:00 p.m.*
Seventh House - Virgo Rising

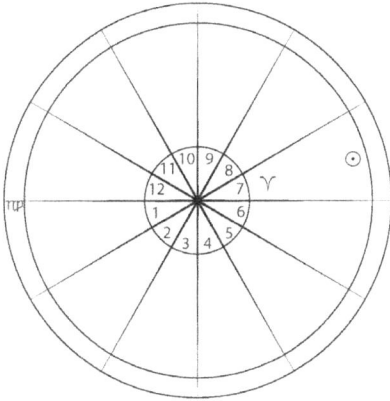

Discriminating and sometimes quite particular, your little Ram is eager to make friends. At the same time, s/he can pick other people apart with his/her criticism. It is hard to teach this child acceptance until s/he learns that no one, including your child, is perfect. Once that lesson is learned, life will be much easier on him/her.

Later in life, when s/he brings home a boy/girlfriend, you will hear, "S/He is perfect." Since nobody is perfect, you can teach your child early in life that a person's imperfections are part of what makes that person perfect in his/her life.

You will find that your child is often looking for a partner but may have a problem from time to time finding someone who will fit the criteria for perfection in partnership. Teach your child that a perfect partner is not necessarily a clone of him/herself but rather a compliment to him/herself, and that is what will make a good partnership.

ARIES - *6:00 p.m. to 7:15 p.m.*
Seventh House - Libra Rising

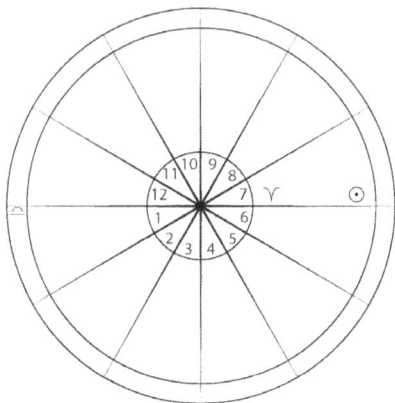

The need for partnership is very strong in this child. Initially, you can be selected as the perfect partner. Then in later years s/he will pattern his/her perfect partner after you! You will also find that whatever you consider the "ideal" mate, s/he will follow your thinking. Even if you have a contentious relationship with this lovely child, don't be surprised if s/he finds friends and eventual mates who are much like you in desires and personality.

Your child should be quite artistic and inspired by his/her surroundings. You may find that even without your knowledge your little one seeks out certain colors and unusual canvases on which to express him/herself.

A need for balance and harmony keeps your child in check. S/He doesn't enjoy anger yet is willing to fight for rights and for everything to be fair! It is never "one for you and two for me," but all things need to be equal and fair or there can be rebellion.

ARIES - *7:15 p.m. to 8:30 p.m.*
Sixth House - Libra Rising

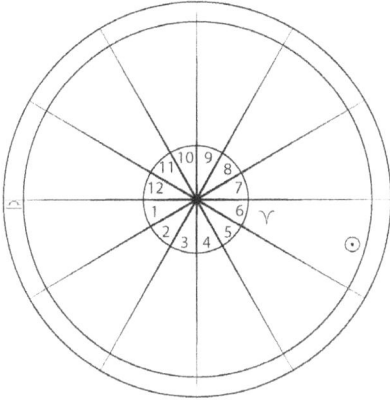

Compassionate and caring, your child wants to fix everyone. S/He is especially interested in people who have headaches (S/he can relate) and those who may have organ trouble.

Your little one may tell you that s/he wants to paint houses when s/he grows up. That is fine, too. Most importantly, your little one wants to make a contribution to the community. The details of his/her environment are quite important to this child and you will discover a talent for design and color.

Your lovely child may seem to be sickly, complaining of stomach aches. It is up to you to have this child thoroughly checked and show him/her the medical report indicating that s/he is quite healthy. If there is genuine concern about the health of your little one, ask the doctor to check the primary organs, such as liver, kidneys, pancreas and other vital organs. This is where the health is best described. If there is anything wrong with these organs, your child does not like the way life is going. If s/he has headaches, it is an ego problem.

ARIES - *8:30 p.m. to 9:30 p.m.*
Sixth House - Scorpio Rising

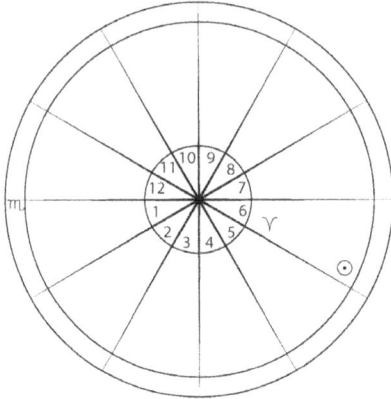

Medical Research is of interest to this interesting and interested child. A microscope is a good gift for your little investigator. Your child needs to learn how to study and to discover information.

You may find a little scientist in your midst and you can encourage all forms of research. Since your child is usually interested in health, it is good to teach exercise and healthy eating habits at an early age. One little girl I know was born a vegan and has continued to be a vegan all her life. I'm not saying you should make your child a vegan, but it is good to steer this child toward healthy habits.

You will also find that you have a hard worker. Be sure to make time for recreation so that your little one doesn't become bored or boring. "All work and no play, make Jack a dull boy."

ARIES - *9:30 p.m. to 11:00 p.m.*
Fifth House - Scorpio Rising

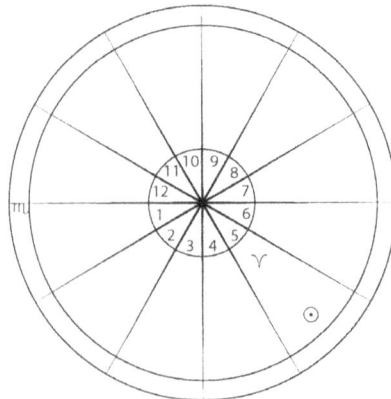

There is something very becoming about this Aries child. There is a beguiling flirtatiousness about your child. Many times, you will find yourself at a point of wanting to give in when those adorable eyes are batted at you and you are asked, "May I?" Initially, it will get your attention and you are tempted to say "yes!" However, it eventually gets old and you may accuse your little one of trying to manipulate you. This is not really so because your little one still doesn't know the true meaning. It is a matter of a game with this child who wants something and believes that this is the way to get it.

You will also find that this child is quite playful. S/He likes games and plays with great intensity. You will find a serious thinker when it is a subject that s/he finds appealing.

Playful and fun, your child will benefit from music lessons.

ARIES - *11:00 p.m. to 11:30 p.m.*
Fifth House - Sagittarius Rising

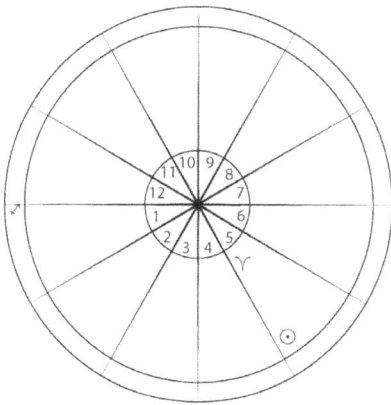

Your adventurous child likes to stand out in a crowd. In spite of the fact that you may have a shy little one on your hands, you will find that either in a quirk of some sort or in his/her dress, that s/he stands out, even while quietly standing by.

You can always ask this child to perform and s/he will happily do it for you and/or your guests and relatives. Although seemingly shy, on a stage your little one shines. You may hear him/her say, "this is the first time this has ever been done!" And for your little one, it may be. They will think of ways to be unique and different from the crowd. You will enjoy the unusualness and uniqueness of this child.

If it is something you do, s/he wants to do it. Share your experiences and time with this little one and you will have a lovely helper.

CANCER

You won't be surprised if your Moon child is sometimes moody. It goes with the territory. It seems that the Cancer child often moves with the phases of the moon. This is not anything that is your fault, it is the nature of your little one. Because your Cancer child is inbred with a sense of humor, find things that are unusual and/or bizarre during these moody times and point them out to him/her. This will snap them out of their sometimes morose moods.

Cancer children are often soft looking. They are lovely and soft.

Some of the most successful people I know are Cancers. In spite of the fact that they are considered homebodies, Cancerians just need to know that there is a home. As long as your Cancer child has a home where s/he can return, s/he will oftentimes be absent. They are explorers. They want to experience and see all and everyone around. They make comparisons and need to learn of their own uniqueness. Rather than "keeping up with the Jones'" they can learn to be the one for others who will keep up with them.

Conversely, you may have to drag this child out of his/ her room and out of the house. A good thing is to keep him/ her going and doing things so that s/he doesn't feel compelled to stay in all the time or be agoraphobic. If there are genuine activities outside the home and you direct your little one to find these activities, you will find a joyous child who likes new adventures.

Cancer children need to learn the basics early. Their foundations and security are important to them. You can teach your Cancer children to fix their own meals, etc. so that they feel secure if ever alone. If your Cancer is unhappy, s/he will tend to over-eat. When you see this happening, it is not a good idea to put him/her on a diet but find out the problem so that the desire to stuff it down goes away.

Your Cancer child is intuitive and is great at detection. Telling this child a fib is not a good idea. When the truth comes out, expect to lose your head. The worse thing is to lose the trust of this little one. When there is trust and an honest relationship, the contentment and strength of character are ever-present. However, when lied to, this child will turn his/her back on you, not trust or believe you and be more independent in a very unsatisfactory way. You will not be allowed into this child's inner life, which can be devastating. It's not that this child holds a grudge, but they will hold the memory and continue to be angry, first with him/herself for being fooled and then at you. Your honesty, no matter how ugly, is always the best way to go.

When the Moon is full or it is a New Moon, your Cancer may have a change of mood or attitude. During this two-day period, give your little one a diversion. In spite of the fact that people say it makes no sense, your Cancer child does respond to these phases of the Moon. Go outside together and howl at the moon if you need to. Let your little one know that you get it that s/he is undergoing a "mood-swing" and that you are there to help bring back sanity. Then do something crazy. It will be very useful when your child becomes an adult.

S/He will always fight for the underdog and has a sympathetic shoulder to cry on. You won't often see a die-hard capitalist, rather a generous person who enjoys what is normal!

Pastel colors are usually most suitable for these gentle souls.

CANCER - *11:45 p.m. (Prior day) to 1:00 a.m.* Fourth House - Aries Rising

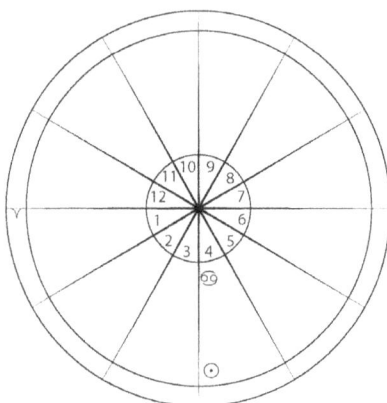

It will be hard to keep this child down. S/He is always ready for a new adventure and will leave home as soon as possible to get where s/he is going.

Sometimes considered aggressive, your daring child is characteristically curious and ready for the next adventure. With both feet on the ground, your child has a sense of adventure and mixed with his/her curiosity can at times make you feel as if you are being put on the spot. Honest answers are the cornerstone of your relationship with this child. If s/he is ready to ask the question, s/he is ready for the answer.

You will notice an entrepreneurial spirit in this child, and it is refreshing. If your little one has a curiosity or interest in something you know nothing about, investigate with him/her and learn together. You will learn something, and your child will appreciate your cooperation and participation.

CANCER
Third House - Aries Rising

It seems to be uncanny how aware your little one is. S/He may seem to not be paying attention; however, s/he holds on to your every word. You may have a child who speaks quite early or one who waits until whole sentences fly out of his/her mouth. Gary was almost four when he started to talk. By then, he formed complete ideas and sentences. When asked why it took him so long to speak, he replied, "I had nothing to say!" He was the third child and had an older brother and sister to do all the talking for him.

Once in school, you have a bright student in your life. It is good to praise accomplishments of your child. Your Cancer child will do only as well as you expect him/her to do. Therefore, it is not okay for him/her to be mediocre. Usually, your bright child can accomplish many things and is quite versatile; however, s/he needs no prompting to fulfill obligations. Feeling appreciated for a job well done is always good, though.

CANCER - *1:00 a.m. to 2:30 a.m.*
Third House - Taurus Rising

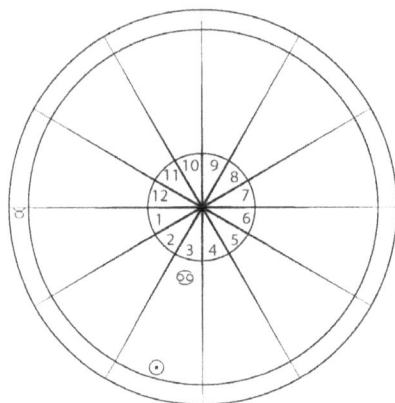

Your child appreciates nice things and protects his/her own possessions. Books and tangible mental stimulants are important to your child and a favorite toy or blanket should always be on hand.

You may find this child to be quite vocal about things, especially about those thoughts and ideas that s/he considers his/her own.

It may be hard to imagine a Cancer child as stubborn, but this is one of the exceptions. The other exception is when Scorpio is rising, but that's still different. Your Cancer child wants to be heard and sometimes silence is the method or means. If you encourage him/her to speak, s/he has won and will only speak when given a platform where s/he can be heard by everyone. You child wants to get a point across and will do his/her very best to do so.

Journals and books are great gifts you're your lovely child.

CANCER - *2:30 a.m. to 3:45 a.m.*
Second House - Taurus Rising

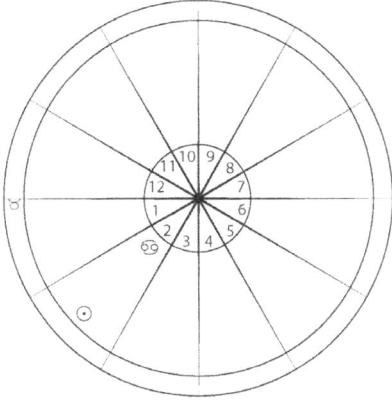

Tangibles are important to this child. Something cuddly or warm is very enhancing to this beautiful child.

It may take time to get your child to trust you, but eventually your persistence will win out. All s/he needs is love. Your child needs to be held and reassured all the time.

Silently, your child will look on with questioning eyes, asking, "where's mine?" Your little Cancer is not jealous but does feel left out when matters are such that they feel left out. It is up to you to allow your child to feel valued and important.

CANCER
Second House - Gemini Rising

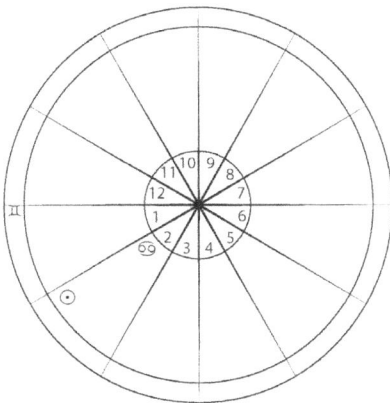

You have a bold entrepreneur on your hands. You will find this child to be hard working and quite orderly. It is important to him/her that there is organization in his/her life. Chaos leads to confusion for this child and s/he will always look and feel lost.

Possessions need to be in a place where they are accessible and can easily be found. If they are hidden in a box or closet or drawer, they may never see the light of day. Although your child may miss these things, s/he may not mention this to you, feeling that whatever it is, it isn't important, or you would have given it prominence. This could relate to a toy or some other treasure.

Your child is vulnerable and if someone comes along with a "good" deal, it will be easy for him/her to succumb to temptation. You may want to be there to comfort your little one if someone has duped him/her, but also allow the facts of the situation to settle in so that it doesn't happen again.

Teach your child how to investigate rainbows and their pots of gold!

CANCER - *3:45 a.m. to 4:15 a.m.*
First House - Gemini Rising

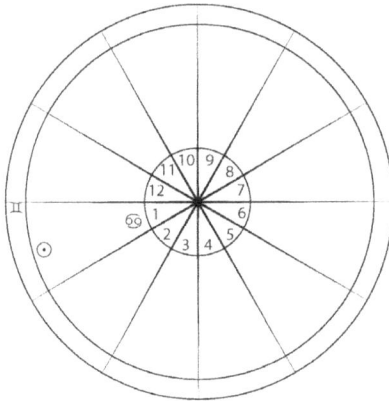

Your talkative child may initially seem shy and retiring, however, give him/her a subject that s/he can latch onto and you will discover a good student (of that subject) and also a good teacher of the same.

Your child is very versatile and cuddly. This means that one moment s/he may need some holding and once satisfied, it is on to the next thing. Do not be offended by this but know that you have satisfied a need.

On to the next is often the motto of this child.

The same goes for things s/he is doing, such as a project or playtime. As soon as your child is bored or finished with the project, s/he will pick up and move on. This may frustrate you when you want to see something done, but the most important thing you can do at times like these is to re-interest your child in the job at hand. Sometimes a certain reward is merited and other times, you can inspire a sense of accomplishment. In either case, it is good to teach this child to finish one thing before going on to the next.

CANCER - *4:15 a.m. to 6:00 a.m.*
First House - Cancer Rising

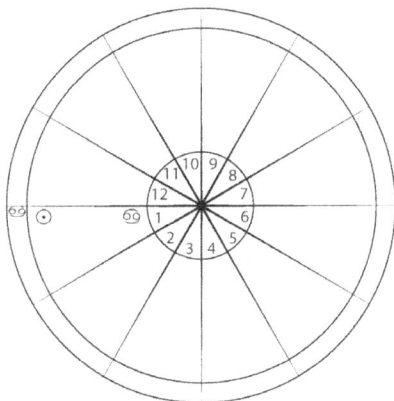

Hard working and an entrepreneur! Your Cancer child is likable and affectionate. This child is a real go-getter and is so delightful. Hard work is not hard, as long as this child knows there is a reward at the end of the day.

Should you decide to have this child do something for you, be sure to reward him/her. The benefits of doing the work make it all worthwhile. You will also notice that this lovely child works with a smile on his/her face.

S/He also loves a challenge. If you should want to challenge this child to do something extra, then go ahead, and you will be pleased at a job well done! You will also notice that this child does not grumble when doing something for you. As hard working as s/he is, you will find that whatever you need for yourself is done cheerfully.

CANCER - *6:00 a.m. to 6:45 a.m.*
Twelfth House - Cancer Rising

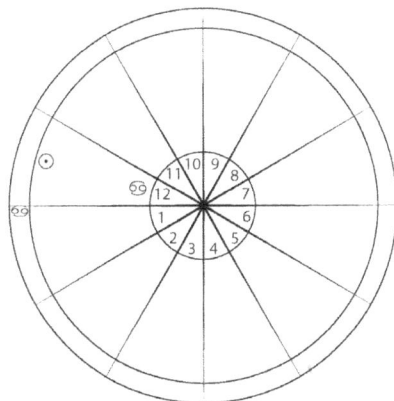

Your very serious child has a lot going on in that little head of his/hers.

Like an elephant, s/he never forgets! If you have a grievance about something that was done by a person in your life, and you were hurt by that thing, your child will remember the offense to his/

her dying day! That person will be shunned by your child, even if you have forgiven him/her long ago.

On his father's deathbed, David was told to take care of his mother and sister now that he would be the "man" in the family. David held that responsibility all his life, believing that it was always his responsibility to take care of them.

Your child is very impressionable so be certain that what you say is first valid, and secondly, not open to change. Don't make promises in anger or they could come back to bite you in the back. Remember that your child is totally loyal to you and to your emotional self. Come from a position of strength and be the boss. Your little one needs to be taught and led to right and wrong.

CANCER - *6:45 a.m. to 7:45 a.m.*
Twelfth House - Leo Rising

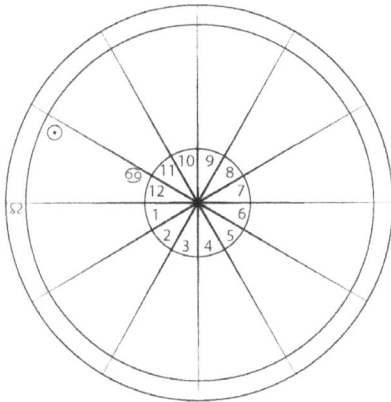

"I want to have fun, but I'm afraid," may be a statement you hear from your sensitive child.

At times you may have a wild child on your hands and, at other times, one who is afraid of his/her own shadow. It is up to you to let him/her know what acceptable behavior is, and your child will act accordingly.

There are times when you can feel a determination from your child and a need for success. A good student, your little one can be encouraged to study what interests him/her the most. You can be a great teacher to your child and allow the mirth to enter into his/her life while in the process.

Your child enjoys laughing and any occasion where that can be encouraged is a good time. Although practical jokes are great or fun, you can teach your little one that laughter does not always have to come at the expense of another's pain!

CANCER - *7:45 a.m. to 9:00 a.m.*
Eleventh House - Leo Rising

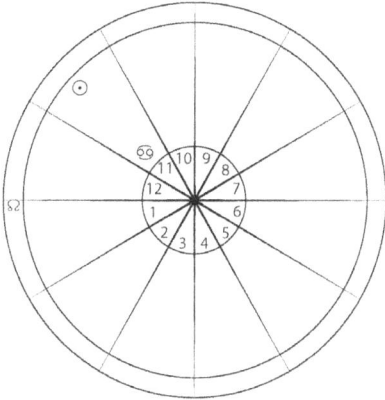

Your very friendly child will find many followers. A wonderful student and great entertainer, your child will attract young and old alike. You will find this affable child loves to love, loves emotion, and often displays affection, unless told otherwise.

This child is very cuddly and loving and enjoys your physical attention. There are times when s/he will pull away, but only because s/he doesn't want others to witness his/her needs or because s/he is sated.

You can teach your child appropriateness. When the right time to touch and when not to touch. Your little one may know innately right from wrong but still needs to be shown or taught.

It is good to show your child affection, as s/he will respond in kind, however, a sense of propriety is also a good thing.

CANCER - *9:00 a.m. to 10:30 a.m.*
Eleventh House - Virgo Rising

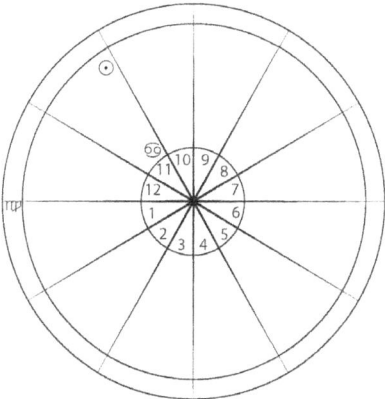

Your Cancer child has a lot of energy and needs a great deal of affection. Should s/he not receive enough affection from you, you may find that your lovable child acts out and can even destroy things in his/her path.

One little boy I knew used to hit his younger sister until

she began to scream. Then he would be punished and then cry. His grandmother picked up on the fact that he needed to be held, more than anything. Once he would begin to cry, someone would hold him, and he would be mollified.

Your intelligent child is sensitive and loving and responds well to affection. It is up to you to determine when it should be given, but mostly remember that it is important for him/her to know right from wrong and then to be given lots of loving in the meantime.

Games can be played early on and flash cards can be fun to this bright child who loves to learn new things (please don't call them lessons). Enjoy yourself with your lovable little one!

CANCER - *10:30 a.m. to 11:45 a.m.*
Tenth House - Virgo Rising

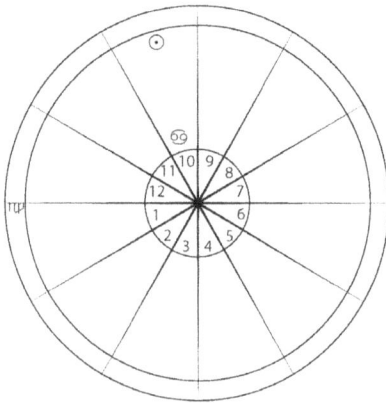

When given a task to do, you will find this child is so well organized that you may consider him/her a reincarnation of a CEO of a major corporation. Your little Cancer is so organized and orderly and yet the messiest of children. Your child may know in which pile to find something but still hasn't found someplace to file things away.

Hanging clothes is bothersome. Because "you're going to wear them again, anyway or throw them in the wash!" There is reason behind every argument so be sure to pick your challenges wisely.

If you find your child tossing things out, be sure to see what is being disposed. You may at that time teach some organization and differentiation. Sorting can be sometimes boring, but buying new things is also expensive. So, toss out those things no longer in use or necessary or recycle them (your little one will love that!) Be sure that those items being disposed are really no longer wanted.

It is sometimes painful for your Cancer child to let go of certain things (or clothes, for that matter). They can easily think of one more time it could be used!

CANCER - *11:45 a.m. to 1:00 p.m.*
Tenth House - Libra Rising

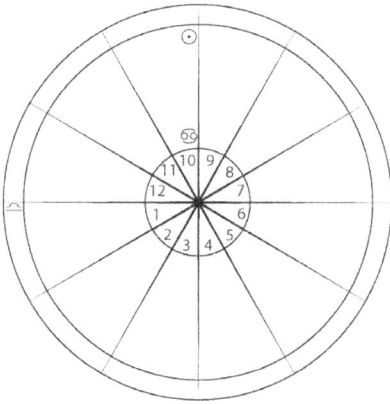

As long as it is fair to everyone, your Cancer child will take the reins. A born leader and a good organizer, your Cancer child wants everything to be fair to anyone who is involved in getting him/her ahead.

Your child is motivated by leadership. Put him/her in charge of something and watch him/her move mountains to reach a goal. It is to your advantage and a good tool for growing up when you give a certain responsibility to your little one. S/He will embrace any type of responsibility you hand him/her. After the age of six or seven, you may even give him/her the job of walking the dog or feeding the cat or any other type of task that your little one can handle.

Your child is so very sweet. This also makes him/her vulnerable. Promises made by others may not always formulate. Don't let him/her chase rainbows. Instead, work backwards from the pot of gold. It is up to you to keep your promises so that your little one doesn't become distrustful of everyone. You also want to set the example so that s/he can learn to trust and how to tell the difference.

CANCER - *1:00 p.m. to 2:30 p.m.*
Ninth House - Libra Rising

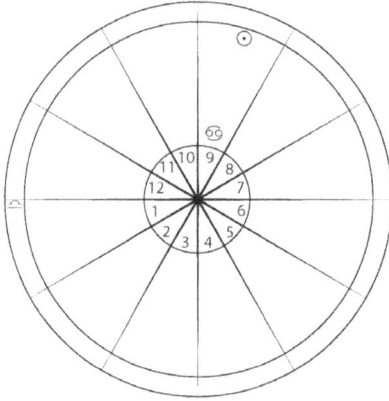

Foreigners are fascinated with your child because s/he adjusts so well to any given situation. A good communicator and a good traveler, your child is comfortable in most situations.

People enjoy the philosophical side of this wise child and you will find that s/he is also a good student and understands what s/he is being taught.

His/her artwork will show well in another country. Your child is a natural artist and in one way or another his/her eye for beauty will show itself. Introduce him/her to color and to keep him/her from coloring the walls (with artwork, of course) by giving him/her a territory to decorate. It could be a canvas or coloring book, or it could be his/her own room. In any case, you will most likely be pleased to see the creativity.

Your little one should be a good student, as his/her interests are many, and especially lean toward foreign affairs of sorts (don't forget, s/he is still little!).

CANCER - *2:30 p.m. to 4:00 p.m.*
Ninth House - Scorpio Rising

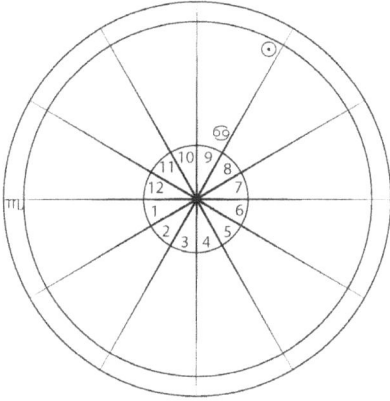

Intense, your child knows exactly what s/he wants.

You will find that once you teach your little one to do research, s/he will stop asking you so many questions. It is a good idea to say, "let's find the answer together," rather than "I don't know."

There are many questions asked of you, the biggest one is "WHY?" This can be tiresome. But when you teach your child to find the answers him/herself through research, you will have a happy and knowledgeable child. There are many sources of information to be found and sometimes the answer lies in literature, rather than from research. Teach this child discernment and you will have a happy little researcher.

CANCER - *4:00 p.m. to 5:00 p.m.*
Eighth House - Scorpio Rising

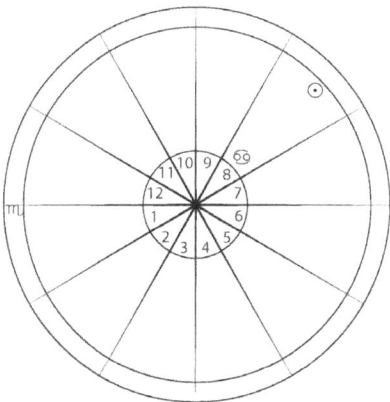

S/He may have high expectations of what s/he wants and will do almost anything to get it. Your little one needs to learn that what belongs to another stays with that other and what belongs to him/her can stay with him/her. Wanting something that belongs to another and getting it is not a good lesson for your child. You can teach your child to say, "I want one like that," rather than "I want that one!"

If you treat stubbornness as though it was determination, you may have a better opinion of your child. S/He needs to get things done, and once his/her mind is set, s/he will go right to it. It can be frustrating when you try to assist, but only find that "I can do it myself" is all you get for an answer. The fact is, this little researcher wants to learn his/her way!

Your little one can be the recipient of many gifts and prizes.

CANCER - *5:00 p.m. to 6:30 p.m.*
Eighth House - Sagittarius Rising

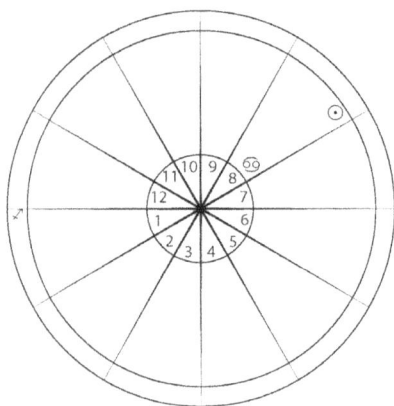

Your child may seem like the luckiest person, you know, and s/he is!! First of all, s/he has you! Secondly, s/he finds value everywhere s/he looks. Later in life, you may find that s/he is the recipient of scholarship (due to hard work) and other gifts and prizes.

S/He dresses a little different from others. You could call him/her a "trendsetter" and let it go with that. But don't be too worried if your child wants to add color to his/her wardrobe and wishes to look different from the other children. This is only because s/he wants to be an individual and to be noticed for his/her individuality!

Your intense child is goal-oriented and will look for the ways to complete tasks and to reach goals. Encourage this zeal for the future.

CANCER - *6:30 p.m. to 7:30 p.m.*
Seventh House - Sagittarius Rising

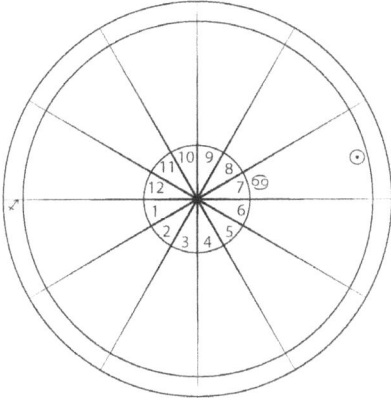

S/He may not want to be bothered with close relationships that may require his/her attention. Instead, people from other places will be more important to him/her.

The love of his/her life may not have movie-star looks but will possess character of his/her own and steal your child's heart. To your child, there is no such thing as discrimination due to looks. S/He sees beyond and into the soul.

It is the same when thinking of the "soul of the matter." Your child needs to know the root cause of things or thoughts. Your introspective child is always looking for what is right and just.

CANCER - *7:30 p.m. to 8:30 p.m.*
Seventh House - Capricorn Rising

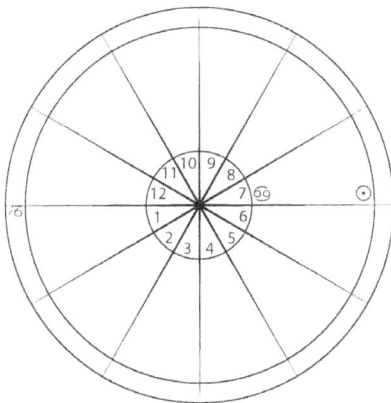

"Someone or something to call my own," is a frequent desire of your child. It could be a favorite toy or sibling. You may also find your child being a bit bossy during all of this. There is a need to be in charge and this can at times come off as bossy. And yet, your lovely child can pull it off. S/He enjoys being in charge and may start out practicing on you!

There are times when you will need to hold your child very close and very tight to assure him/her that s/he is loved. These children are in need of confirmation and approval and they may sometimes overstep in order to get your attention. When you recognize this behavior, just give some love, it helps a lot.

You can teach your child that pushing others around does not win approval but learning to make the right decision does. It will help your little one to be more understanding and joyful.

CANCER - *8:30 p.m. to 9:15 p.m.*
Sixth House - Capricorn Rising

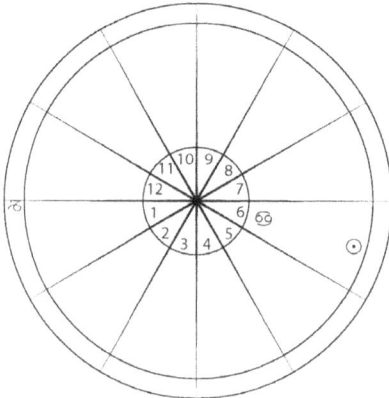

Put your little one in charge of the project and watch how quickly it gets done. Don't be surprised, however, if s/he recruits help and sits back to watch the task be finished. This type of behavior is natural to your child and the end project is what really matters.

Learning team-spirit is essential to this child and yet one of the harder lessons to learn. When growing up, being able to participate in the job, rather than bossing others around will be very helpful. Eventually you will have someone who learns to tap into his/her empathy.

If his/her knees bother him/her, something isn't working right, and your child is unhappy with his/her approach to life. Ask what s/he would change.

CANCER - *9:15 p.m. to 10:00 p.m.*
Sixth House - Aquarius Rising

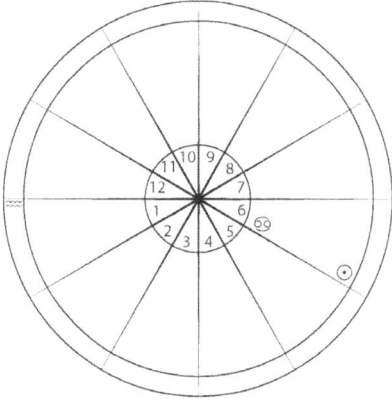

A true humanitarian, your child is the one ever ready with bandages to fix a "boo-boo" and to care for others who are in distress.

With a strong spiritual side, your curious child is always anxious to investigate other ideologies and ideals. When your little one encounters someone from a different background, that child may become his/her new "best friend" until s/he has learned all s/he can from this other person. Don't be surprised if s/he is on to the next person to learn more later. This is not a flaw in character as much as it is a learning experience. You can teach your child respect and kindness toward people rather than discarding them.

You will find that your child is a hard worker and although interested in details, it will only be the details that allow him/her to get the job done. After that, it is more about fun.

You may also find your child interested in health and healthy habits. A library of health-related missives will be pertinent to your little one.

CANCER - *10:00 p.m. to 10:45 p.m.*
Fifth House - Aquarius Rising

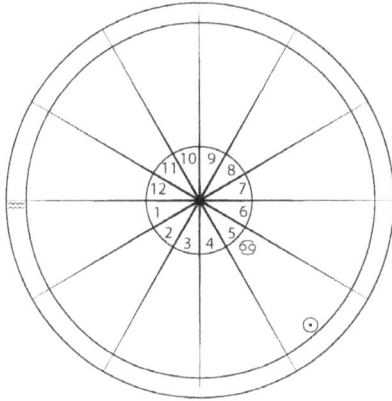

Your sweet child needs to learn to consider the feelings of others, rather than concentrating on his/her own feelings. A natural performer, it is easy to be insensitive to the emotional well-being of others, however, you child is very capable of acts of kindness and respect.

The best place to find laughter in your child is in an environment filled with love. Once your little one feels accepted, then s/he will show you a confidence you know s/he is capable of.

Usually, your little one is a good student and has a mind like a steel trap. Know that what you teach this child will remain almost the same as DNA. The lessons you teach will be significant throughout his/her life so teach with love.

CANCER - *10:45 p.m. to 11:30 p.m.*
Fifth House - Pisces Rising

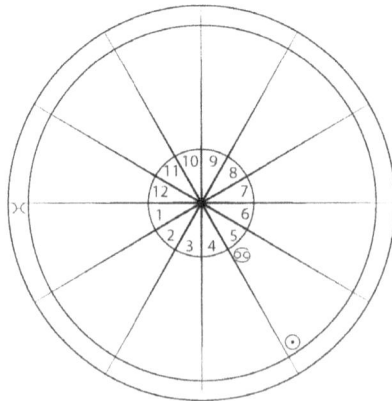

Dancing lessons are especially good for your child. (Yes, boys, too!) You will find the need for entertaining and expression important to this lovely and active child. Anything that can be done with the feet can be done by your sensitive and impressionable child.

I remember one time when my husband and I were at a football game. I mentioned that the quarterback had taken ballet lessons. Of course, my spouse didn't see it. The following year, there was an article in the paper with an interview of this quarterback. In the narrative, he told of how his future coach told him to take ballet lessons, which he did.

You will also find that you have a really good student, albeit somewhat ethereal. Even if s/he seems to be a dreamer, s/he is only thinking of all the possibilities and will shine once solutions are found.

The feet are especially important to your child and shoes and socks become a mark of pride to this child. There is identity in how s/he is shod.

CANCER - 11:30 p.m. to 11:45 p.m.
Fourth House - Pisces Rising

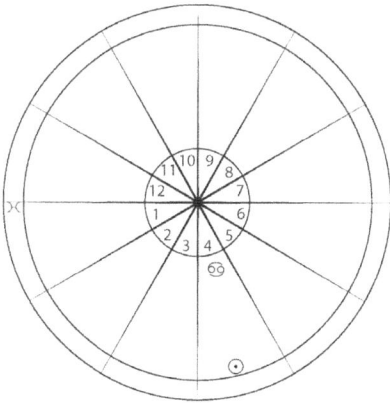

Your Cancer child is quite tuned in to everything that is going on at home, there is no pulling the wool over this one's eyes. Sensitive and lovely, you will notice that your little one loves to please you! There will be times when small gestures are just what you need, and this lovely child will be there without you even knowing it. You don't have to say anything, it just happens.

You will notice that your Cancer has an eye for design and color and may be inclined to decorate and not necessarily in your style. Give him/her a place to call his/her own so that s/he can decorate to his/her heart's content. You may also want to give some paints and paper (or canvas) to this little one at a very early age and watch how s/he puts things together.

Pastels in the wardrobe are especially pleasing and can enhance those beautiful eyes.

LIBRA

Your child's greatest asset is his/her smile. Encourage the beauty to shine through so that everyone can see the real joy in your little one's life. A lover of mirth, funny stories are always a delight for your precious child who can sometime be too serious.

Procrastination is a common trait among Libras. Teach your child to finish whatever s/he started so that in later years s/he won't keep putting things off. The best way is to turn the procrastination into anticipation. If your Libra child has something to anticipate, such as a job well done, s/he will be more inclined to go for it.

A sprite, lovely Libra wants to please you. Harmonious and sweet, this child usually presents the least trouble to parents. However, if anything is out of balance, they will scrape and fight to put things back in sync.

Your Libran loves a good debate and will take the other side even if s/he doesn't believe in it. It is a good idea to teach this child that a difference of opinion is not a personal attack. Agree to disagree. Your child will respond well to this and you will find it much easier to communicate with him/her. Teach your child to not put labels, such as "stupid," on someone who has a different thought about something. Rather, let him/her know that differences are part of the variety of life that makes it interesting. Your little one will have more appreciation for those in his/her environment.

Your Libra child enjoys a challenge, especially a mental one. S/he is good with puzzles and will spend many hours quietly putting anything together.

Libra children are very inventive. Because they enjoy things that are easy, they will find ways to invent solutions to problems. The old adage, "Necessity is the mother of invention," applies to your child. It is all right to say to your little one, "Make it work." You'll find that his/her imaginative mind will begin to create new ways to do old things.

Art and music are essential to this child's surroundings. You'll also find that s/he will want things to be in balance. If you have a lamp on one side of the sofa, a lamp that matches should be on the other side.

Color is also important to your child's environment. Your Libra child loves blues and pinks but also enjoys many colors in his/her surroundings.

Allow your child to express him/herself with paints and colors. Many stories will be told in this manner and your little one will blossom with this expression of self.

Give something in pale blue or muted colors and your Libra will look lovely!

LIBRA - *10:30 p.m. (prior day) to 12:30 a.m.*
Fourth House - Cancer Rising

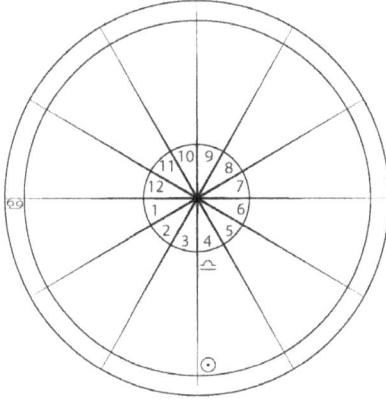

Your little one needs a lovely home. It doesn't have to be expensive or a mansion, just lovely. This is someplace to display and to have visitors and then to leave for an adventure elsewhere.

You may want to help your child decorate his/her own surroundings. You will be happy to see such creativity. Pastel colors are usually preferred by your creative and talented child.

You will also find that this child is quite affectionate. If s/he shyly rejects another person, it is up to you to learn later what his/her instincts about that person caused this type of reaction. Children are often very honest with their feelings and reactions to people and situations. If you child doesn't know, it is a good idea to learn more about your little one's instincts. They may be spot on.

Art, in all forms, can be encouraged.

LIBRA - *12:30 a.m. to 2:15 a.m.*
Third House - Cancer Rising

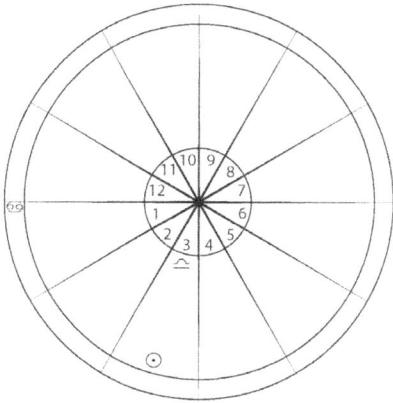

Your Libra is so attractive to so many. His/her smile is a big draw. Usually, this child loves everyone and is kind to those around him/her. People enjoy being around him/her and you will notice that your child can change the lives of people who come into contact with him/her.

Classes of all sorts are at home and you have a good student. No matter what part of your home is important to you, you will find a little clone hanging on your heels. The things at home which are important to you are also important to your child.

You can also take this child with you on short trips and introduce him/her to your friends and people with whom you work. Your child is quite sociable and enjoys meeting new people.

A good sibling, your Libra child could cherish a brother or sister. If there are not brothers or sisters around or in the offing, a pet may be a good substitute. If not, you may find that your little one brings home favorite friends to be like a sibling.

LIBRA - *2:15 a.m. to 12:45 a.m.*
Third House - Leo Rising

Your Libra child is very loyal. You will find that those who know and love your child find a true friend and a real person in this person. You can be assured that whomever s/he chooses for a friend is also loyal and friendly.

A great orator, your Libra knows how to put things into words and communicate to any and everyone who will listen. Sometimes it is not easy to keep your child from revealing family secrets so be sure to teach this little one discretion.

Your child loves to have fun and to laugh and you can enjoy the joy with him/her.

This is a child who should not be underestimated. Despite his/her "lovely" and "kind" spirit, you have a tiger on your hands. Fairness is very important to your little lion and the rights of others are always at the forefront. Your Libra child worries about his/her brethren and makes no bones about it.

Easy-going and yet seemingly stubborn at times, it is up to you to learn what the cause is and wherein lies the complaint.

This child is a wonderful sibling and loves his/her brothers and sisters!

LIBRA - *12:45 a.m. to 3:15 a.m.*
Second House - Leo Rising

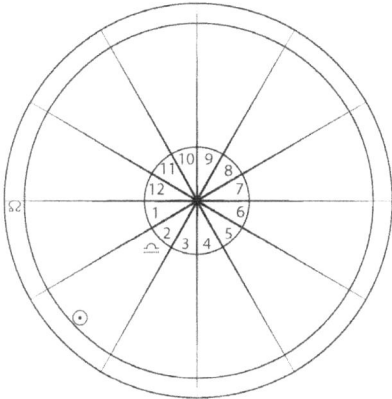

Your Libra child has a good sense of humor. S/He also has a good sense of what looks good and what doesn't.

This child often has good fashion sense and enjoys looking good. Keep some money in every pocket and teach him/her the same. This will give your little Libra a good sense of security.

You may find that your little one is a great saver and collector. Teach this child at an early age how to dispose of the unwanted and unnecessary items or you will have a home filled with disposable items, which could be easily discarded.

When you are sorting and weeding, do it together or your child could become insecure and cry, "Please don't 'frow' me away!"

LIBRA - *3:15 a.m. to 4:30 a.m.*
Second House - Virgo Rising

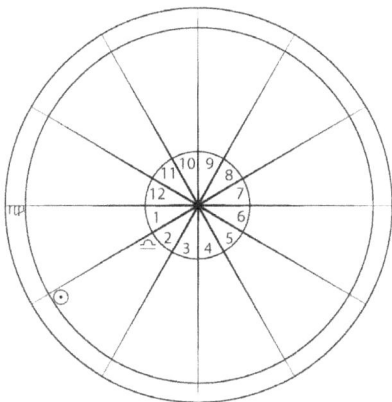

When you buy a gift for this child, be sure it is something that can be treasured and that it is also pleasing to the eye. Chances are that it will be on display. Your little one also enjoys things that have more than one use.

Money and a bank account are also good gifts for your conscientious child.

If a savings account is started early, s/he will learn the value of money and eventually learn to amass plenty.

There are times when you see that your little one prefers to go on a "spree," and shop to his/her heart's content. After that, you may want to be with this child to see what really is important among the *new* belongings and what can be discarded. You will both learn a lot with this exercise.

LIBRA - *4:30 a.m. to 5:45 a.m.*
First House - Virgo Rising

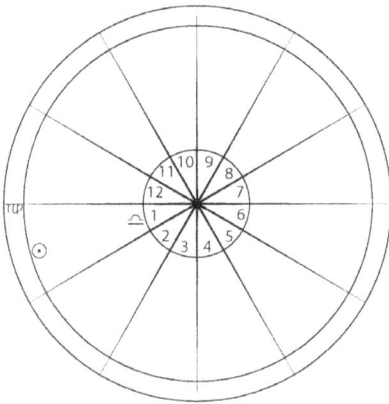

You may find quite an impetuous child. Making a decision at the drop of a hat is no stranger to this child and you can enjoy that trait, as Libra can often take a lot of time making decisions.

It is good to keep this child on his/her toes by challenging his/her wit from time to time. Do not be afraid to give him/her a puzzle to solve and watch the churning go on in that little mind. It is fun to see how your Libra solves problems.

It is possible that your child will be a jack-of-all-trades as s/he grows up because s/he is easily bored once something is accomplished. It may be difficult for you to keep up with your versatile child. Puzzles are often good distractions. Be sure you know the solution before you present a problem to this child so that there can be learning and not a greater puzzle.

LIBRA - *5:45 a.m. to 7:00 a.m.*
First House - Libra Rising

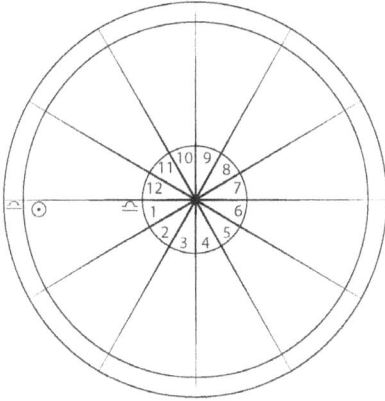

How lovely this child of beauty and sweetness! This is probably the loveliest child in the zodiac. Your little one only wants to please, and you are the first recipient of his/her kind disposition.

Filled with love and affection, your Libra will always try to make everything "nice" and "lovely." Be prepared to find little signs, such as flowers picked randomly from the general area of where you live. This child will paint pictures and do his/her best to keep the environment in balance and lovely. If s/he manages to paint or crayon the walls of your home, be assured that s/he is only trying to add art to his/her and your environment. It is still okay to give him/her a pail of suds and a sponge and allow your little one to wash the wall. Then, get out the paper and art supplies and show your "artist" where to apply his/her creativity!

Initially, your little one will be averse to hearing arguments or disagreements; however, as s/he gets older, s/he will find his/her voice and will fight to the end for peace. Your child loves harmony and will fight tooth and nail for it!

Music will be a wonderful balance for this lovely child of grace, and you will find that s/he may hum along with a familiar tune.

LIBRA - *7:00 a.m. to 8:30 a.m.*
Twelfth House - Libra Rising

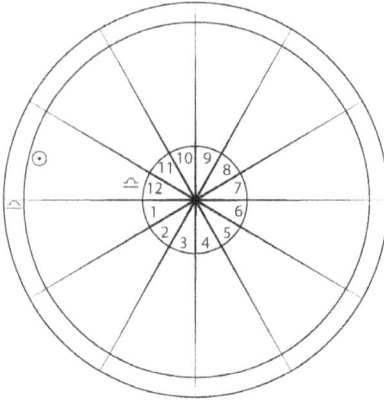

You may find a rebel in your midst. Fighting for all the right things, and yet, fighting tooth and nail to get his/her way. You will find that this child insists that you think the same way s/he thinks. S/He needs to learn that our differences are what make us human!

A talented designer and artist, you can give this child a pad and pencil early and teach him/her the basic fundamentals of drawing. You will find some wonderful designs in that notebook, as well as a talent for art. Your encouragement will help your child decide later in life what is a good route to go.

You will find, too, a quest for spirituality. Although intuition is high, and s/he may seem psychic, a need to find a higher power is also evident in this child.

LIBRA - *8:30 a.m. to 9:30 a.m.*
Twelfth House - Scorpio Rising

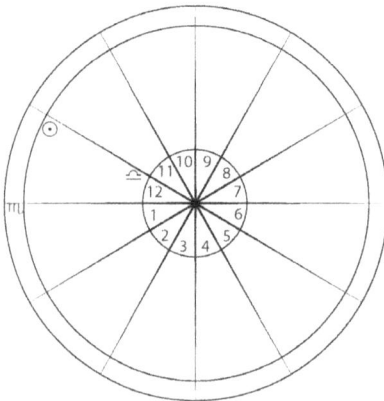

Intense and curious, your child asks a lot of questions. "Where did I come from?" is more than a question of body or location, but more a question of "Where do I fit into the picture?" There is no answer that truly unravels the mystery for your child, except that you can always tell him/

254

her that s/he came from "LOVE." This is an acceptable answer you can give your little one.

You will find an ethereal quality about your child. S/He may seem otherworldly to you at times. Not to worry, your little one is simply ruminating over a deep problem and will eventually come to a conclusion.

Money belonging to other people will be of interest to this child. Wanting to know your worth and that of those around him/her may be confusing at times, but it is part of his/her need to place values on people and things.

LIBRA - *9:30 a.m. to 11:00 a.m.*
Eleventh House - Scorpio Rising

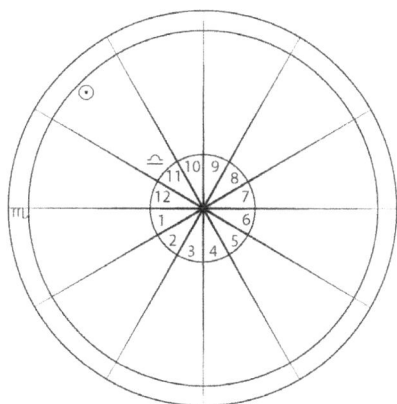

S/He walks on air. Curiosity is a key element of this lovely child's makeup and s/he will retain everything you teach him/her. You will find a loving child and a friendly child. Everyone will want to be his/her friend because there is something very alluring and sensual about your little Libra. S/He loves to *feel* what is going on and enjoys challenges.

Like an elephant, your Libra will not forget what s/he has been told (or taught) and will have an understanding of your views.

This child is physically sensitive to his/her surroundings and can "feel" the atmosphere. Do not underestimate this daring and intelligent child of grace!

LIBRA - *11:00 a.m. to 12:00 p.m. (Noon)*
Eleventh House - Sagittarius Rising

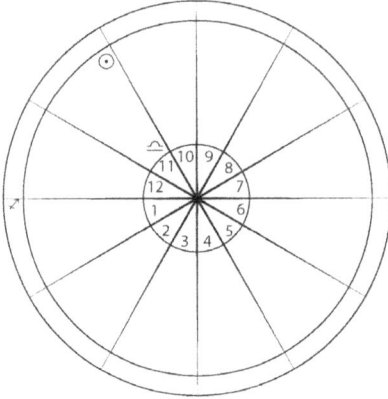

So friendly, so unusual, so curious. All these attributes in one child. And you may still find him/her to be a mystery. Your child is first and foremost a philosopher and wants everything to be fair. If it isn't fair, expect him/her to walk away whenever possible. S/He may abandon a project if someone else comes in and tries to take over.

It is good to allow your child to learn on his/her own, but there are times when you may become impatient and wish to solve problems for him/her to save him/her the pain of certain discoveries. Not to worry, your child will learn on his/her own (perhaps not the way you intended but s/he will learn).

You will also find an adventurer in your midst with this little one. Daring feats will blow you away with this friend of all in his/her environment. You can encourage your child to try new things. S/He may want to wear other than conventional clothes so that s/he will stand out from the others. Don't be alarmed, s/he is simply expressing his/her individuality.

LIBRA - *12:00 p.m. (Noon) to 12:45 p.m.*
Tenth House - Sagittarius Rising

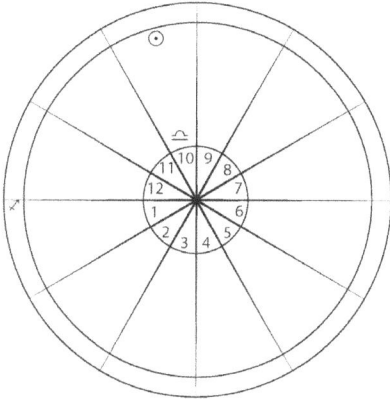

Being the boss isn't as important as having the right philosophy and those around him/her to share it. "Let's . . ." is often heard of this child because s/he prefers to do things with others and not alone. Nevertheless, s/he is often the leader of the pack.

Do not let your child be alone too often because s//he enjoys the company of others and is very sociable.

Your Libra child is a leader and manages to have followers. You will find that s/he enjoys doing good deeds for others and this is an inborn trait. Enjoy it and you can encourage it.

You will also find that your little one enjoys learning about esoteric subjects and you can encourage this. There are some things you may feel are too deep for your child; however, you may be surprised when s/he brings up the subject of something you have just learned. You may find yourself considering this child rather profound!

Education on any subject is enjoyable to your Libra and you can learn along with this wise and curious child.

LIBRA
Tenth House - Capricorn Rising

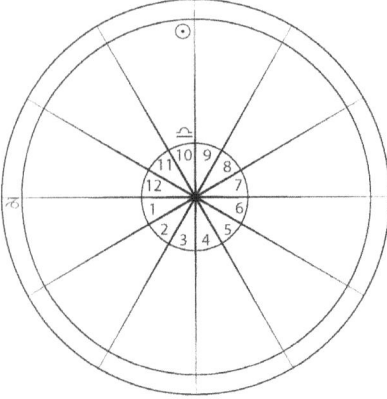

Although your Libra always wants to please, watch for an agenda. It is possible that you can be easily manipulated by this clever child. It isn't a matter of "my way or the highway," but rather, you will be assured that the idea came from you, when you really wanted something else. Should you detect this type of behavior, it is a good idea to nip it in the bud and stop this type of behavior or manipulation. When your child asks what you want up front, reverse the question and learn what s/he wants first. If your little one is trying to be diplomatic, then don't be afraid to stand your ground!

You have a leader in this child, and you want to be sure that this gift is not misdirected. Good leadership skills are learned so that you don't have a beautiful bully on your hands! The best way to avoid this is to teach your child diplomacy and tact. These characteristics are very important to this child and s/he needs to learn how to understand when someone else is asking a question and not putting him/her on the line for a "right" answer. Teaching your child how to differentiate will help him/her later in life.

LIBRA - *12:45 p.m. to 1:15 p.m.*
Ninth House - Sagittarius Rising

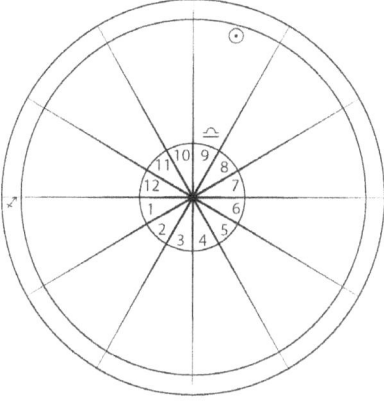

Your child has a thirst for knowledge and a need to learn more. Art is a great subject. You will also find an adventurer and traveler. You can take your child around the world and see how s/he adapts to his/her environment. It is a thrill and a learning lesson for you, as you get acquainted with an environment s/he already knows.

Your little one also understands the importance of learning and should be a good student. This is a time when you can allow your little one to choose his/her own studies, as s/he instinctively knows what s/he needs to learn.

It is hard for your child to wear a uniform. Should you place your child in a school that requires a certain dress, don't be surprised if s/he should add something to make him/herself look a bit different from the others. S/He does not wish to become lost in the crowd.

LIBRA - *1:15 p.m. to 3:15 p.m.*
Ninth House - Capricorn Rising

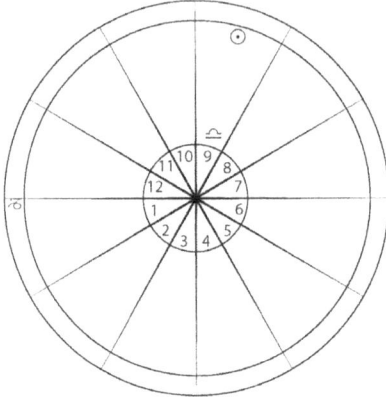

There was a song, many years ago, called, "It's A Big Wide Wonderful World," which totally describes how your child feels. One line in it: You've a kingdom power and glory ... that is how your child sees the world. The world is his/her merry-go-round and s/he is at the controls. If your child walks around like roy-alty, allow this since it is what s/he is feeling. You may want to have a "royal" day for your regal one. This would be the day when s/he gets to choose what's made for dinner, where to go shop-ping, or any other whimsical thing. This may be a monthly or weekly thing. Eventually, it will get old, but in the meantime, it is a good lesson for everyone concerned.

Your child may act out from time to time with a "My Way" attitude. Should this happen, it is a good idea to teach the order of things to him/her.

You should find that this child is a good student and it often interested in organizational things. You can help by showing your little one how to make charts and how to put things in line. This will give your little one a sense of control and s/he will have comfort in ruling his/her own world. A girl may find pleasure in a doll house and a boy in toys of military fashion.

LIBRA - *3:15 p.m. to 4:45 p.m.*
Eighth House - Aquarius Rising

A rather blasé attitude toward life and death, your child is more of a realist. Should your child feel a personal loss, it may be different, but in general, this little one has a deeper understanding of life and death. S/He is more a realist than sentimental.

You may find your little Libran is a little bit stubborn (not determined) and stands his/her ground on matters that are of importance to him/her. You may also find that s/he is in her/his own world.

Your child should be beautiful to see and quite attractive as a child and will continue to entrance people as s/he grows up. But s/he doesn't seem to be affected by those who are affected by him/her. Rather s/he goes blithely along singing and marching to his/her own drummer.

Your little one is looking for rules. Be sure they are in place so that they can be followed.

One flaw you may find is that time seems to slip away from this lovely child and keeping others waiting doesn't seem to matter. In this case, it is a good idea to teach your child to put him/herself in the shoes of the other person so that s/he can see how that person's feelings might be hurt.

2s

LIBRA
Eighth House - Pisces Rising

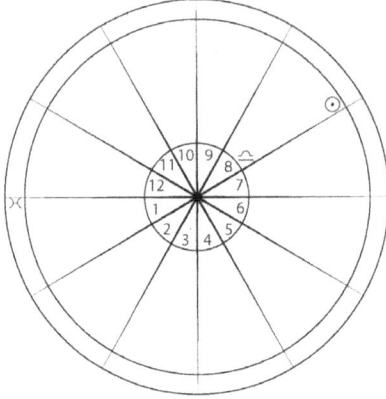

Not always good with other people's things, you may not want to entrust your best possessions with this child until later when s/he understands value. It is a challenge for your little one to understand that certain things have value, either monetarily or sentimentally.

You may find that with a sweeping gesture s/he decides to destroy everything that is on a table, breaking things you value. It is up to you to keep things that are important out of reach until some mature understanding is realized. At that time, (maybe around the age of 5) you can reason and explain. Otherwise, expect to lose valuable or irreplaceable pieces.

At the same time, you have an affectionate and loving child who only wants to please you. Any stubbornness you may detect is temporary and because s/he wants so much to have more peace than chaos, you will find your child conforming to your rules.

Be kind to your little one and you will see him/her blossom, too, into kindness. This child is filled with love to give and is a child to cherish!

LIBRA - *4:45 p.m. to 5:45 p.m.*
Seventh House - Pisces Rising

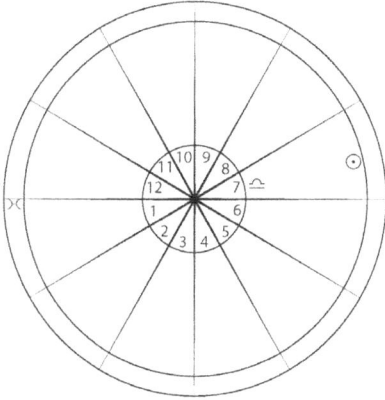

You may not always know what your child is thinking but neither does s/he. Loving and lovely, your child may be quite sensitive to noise and chaos. It is good to remember that the only acceptable chaos to this child is the one made by him/her. Otherwise, you could become frustrated trying to sort out his/her life. These children do the sorting in an even dispensing way and you will find a form of organization to what may confuse others.

Airy and dreamy, your little one may have "lofty" ideas. Even though they may seem out of the ordinary to you, in their minds these children have good reason for all of their actions.

You may find another child of great sensibilities who partners with your child. This is because your wise Libra knows what is missing in his/her makeup and will bring in the troops to counter and support his/her whims.

Always in the need of a partner, even you can be reeled in to help with a project!

LIBRA - *5:45 p.m. to 6:15 p.m.*
Seventh House - Aries Rising

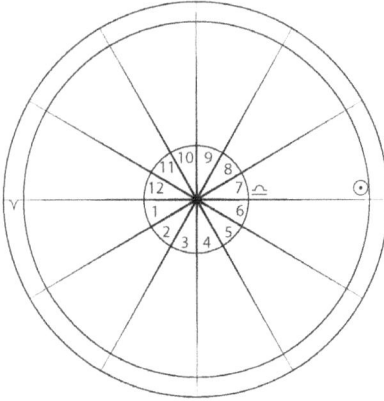

Everyone is a partner to this innovative and inventive child. If you see mock weddings or businesses pop up, don't be surprised. Nor should you discourage this behavior because your little one is practicing being the entrepreneur and partner s/he was meant to be. S/He will always be on the lookout for a partner in all things. I call them partners in crime, but they can be partners in anything!

Chores are important to your child and a sense of responsibility is also important. His/her importance in the family, as a member and active participant in all things is what makes your Libra tick. You will find that this lovely and innocent child has a lot of energy to give. Afterwards, s/he may tend to complain of exhaustion; however, this is usually after a task is finished. Then, dramatically, a big sigh will indicate that a job is done. Do remember that praise for a job well-done is appreciated and motivates one to do more and always do a good job!

LIBRA - *6:15 p.m. to 8:00 p.m.*
Sixth House - Aries Rising

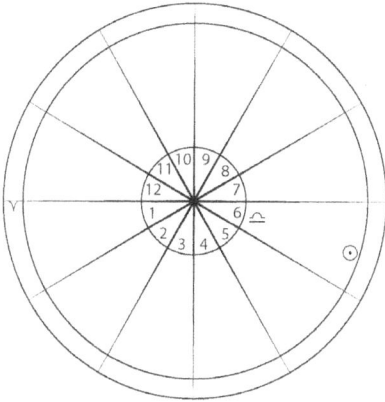

A good ear for music and an enjoyment of good sounds direct your Libra child. You can hear him/her humming a tune before s/he does anything. The song "Whistle While You Work," could have been written for a child like this.

Your child is usually joyful and very helpful. S/He loves to get down to the nitty-gritty and get things done. S/He responds to praise and is eager to please you.

You will discover that this little child is very empathetic. The little "healer" in your child will go to work immediately to "fix" anyone or thing that has a "boo boo" or "hurt".

LIBRA
Sixth House - Taurus Rising

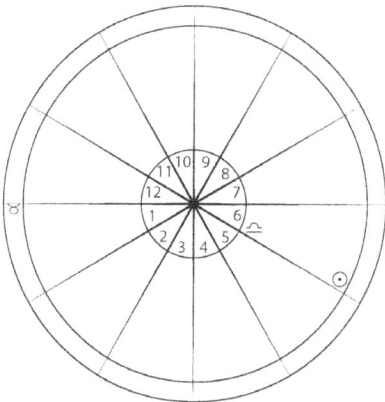

Beauty is important to your little one and the word "lovely" is a perfect adjective to adopt in conversation. "Let's go for a 'lovely' walk," is something your child will respond to and participate in with you. It is natural to see the sunny side of things for this little one.

At the same time, you may see a stubborn side to him/her. This can be more of a determination, rather than stubbornness.

265

Since your little one understands reasoning, it will be easier to explain things to him/her than to get frustrated because your little one is already frustrated when s/he doesn't understand something.

Singing is good for this child and you can prompt him/her to sing along while working to relieve boredom or any angst.

LIBRA - *8:00 p.m. to 9:30 p.m.*
Fifth House - Taurus Rising

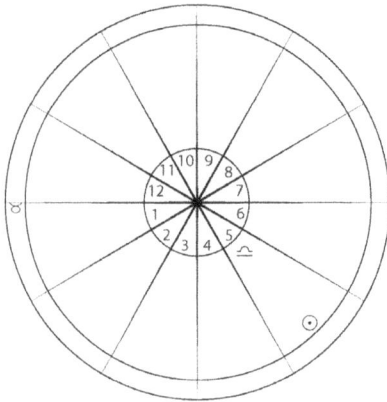

Listen to him/her sing! What a lovely voice. If not, s/he may be yelling. In either case, your child needs to be heard. It is not a bad idea to give voice lessons to this child. If you don't have a great vocalist, you will have someone who knows how to control his/her voice and modulate it so that your eardrums don't burst! It is always a good idea to teach him/her how to control his/her voice.

Your child will show a great deal of sensitivity and although seemingly bold, your little one is really quite in tune with other people's lives. S/He wants to help everyone!

Your child has a great deal of determination, and it is good to listen to his/her hopes and wishes to see what really motivates him/her. You will find a lover of other little children and some- one who cares about their feelings and well-being.

LIBRA - *9:30 p.m. to 10:00 p.m.*
Fifth House - Gemini Rising

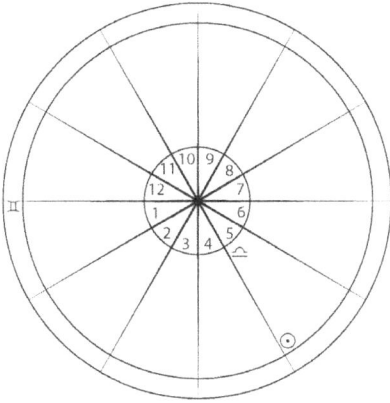

You have an orator and quite possibly a comic in your circle! Your little Libra has quite a sense of humor and loves to laugh! You may want to encourage this and prevent practical jokes by pointing out that they could harm some people. Do know, though, that your Little Libra has a need to entertain. Your laughter is encouragement. If you ignore this child, s/he will find other outlets for his/her humor. It is up to you as to which direction it takes.

You may also find your little one is quite good in debate. Although you may feel the brunt of it when they try to convince you of something, later in life, this proclivity for a good argument may come in handy.

Entertaining by playing a musical instrument (no drums) will also be appreciated by his/her audience.

LIBRA - *10:00 p.m. to 10:30 p.m.*
Fourth House - Gemini Rising

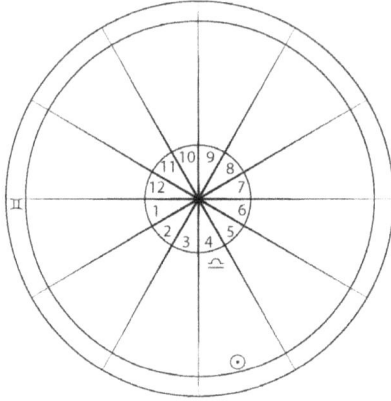

Having company and being social are really good for your child. It is good for you to entertain and you will likely find that your lovely Libra has a sense of being social at all times and is quite an interesting addition to your soirees.

Piano lessons are good for this child. In fact, you may find that you are asked for these lessons by him/her.

Your child should have lovely hands and can type quickly and play piano and do many things with his/her hands. It is possible that s/he may enjoy woodwork and other crafts.

Most of all, you want to compliment your little one's artistic ability. Lovely Libra enjoys praise and it is up to you to give it!

CAPRICORN

Your Capricorn child is very strong and quite brave, showing a lot of responsible behavior, but don't forget that this child is sensitive, too. Don't give too much responsibility to your child before s/he can handle it. Let your little one be a child with all the fun things that children do. If you are having a tough time with an only child, remember those things that made you happy when you were a child.

Your little one is disciplined and happiest when there is a plan.

Stories from the past are interesting to this little one. You can tell ancestral tales and keep your Capricorn happy. Fairy tales are not as interesting as family lore and anything about their heritage will fascinate these children.

I want to be in control. These children are like little adults from early childhood. Their faces have maturity and seeming wisdom. They are usually very accomplished at anything they set their minds to do. Your little Capricorn will want to take care of you and your needs.

In social situations, this child wants to be in control of the games. This can alienate other children who don't want to be told what to do by another child. This is a take-charge person from the onset. As an alternative, it is good to teach your child the art of delegation and the sharing of responsibility. Learning at an early age that everyone should have his own field of leadership teaches him/her the importance of first assuming responsibility for self and getting his/her job accomplished. It also teaches your little one how to trust the abilities of others. In later life, your son/daughter will thank you for the insight.

Your child has high ideals and dreams of accomplishment. They will tell you early on that they want to be a millionaire. They will say that they want to be the richest person on earth. This is because they believe that money is power and wanting to be in control in important to them. They have the sense of kings and queens, ruling their monarchs. On Halloween, simply put a crown on their heads and watch them shine. With a wand in their hands, they are magic. These symbolisms, when used, allow your child those moments of supremacy without imposing themselves on others at the wrong times. Timing is everything.

Reputation is more important than fitting in. Don't complain about your child to others. Especially don't complain in the presence of your child. Humiliation is very painful to this little one. Because these children seem so mature, it is hard to remember that they are quite sensitive and can be easily hurt.

Your little Capricorn takes everything to heart. When you tell a true story with an unhappy ending you create fear. Allow before talking about experiences that what you relate not only will be heard and taken seriously, but that you also may instill fear. Use discrimination: caution is good fear but may cause pain and illness.

Many ballet dancers are Capricorns. The discipline of this classical dance is appealing to them and they have a place where they have an opportunity to take center stage. The training helps them to be in control of self. Self-mastery is particularly essential to the rest of their growth.

Capricorns enjoy the simplicity of black and white; however, they can look maudlin. Encourage bright colors and accessorize with the black and white.

CAPRICORN - *Midnight to 2 a.m.*
Third House - Libra Rising

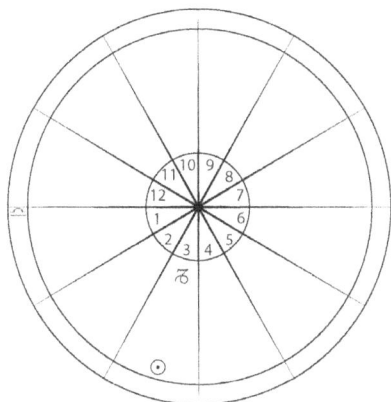

A poet. Your child is lovely and harmonic. At the same time, watch his/her brothers and sisters run when they are being bossed around. Explain to your sweet child that when s/he grows up, s/he can be the adult and boss around the little kids, but in the meantime, it is up to him/her to BE the little kid! This is a hard nut to swallow for your child, who tends to be a bit bossy or manipulative, but you are doing him/her a big favor when you take the burden of telling others what to do from him/her.

A love of siblings, you can teach certain songs from your own childhood to this lovely child and watch how s/he cares for siblings. You will find that at an early age, your little one will want to assume the responsibility for his/her siblings, such as babysitting.

Too much responsibility is over-whelming to this child and there is just so much you can pour onto your little one before s/he bursts.

Also beware of how easily you can be wrapped around this child's finger! It isn't just the puppy-dog eyes, it is that your little one has a knack for finding your weaker spot and leaning on it to get his/her way. So, pay attention, when a request is being made. Your child is so very lovely and easy to say "yes" to. Alternatives are always a good way to move some of those requests too hot to handle!

CAPRICORN - *2:00 a.m. to 3:00 a.m.*
Third House - Scorpio Rising

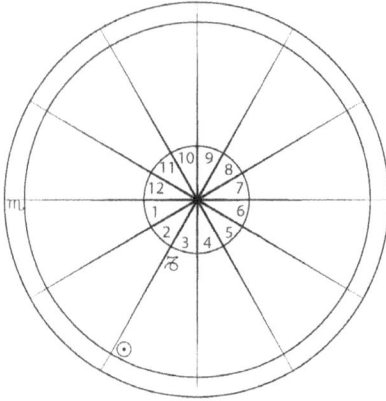

Intense and curious, you have a child who can easily frustrate you if you allow it. You can be worn down with all the questions, especially the "why can't I?" question, which is asked often.

"Because I said so," is not a good enough answer. You really have to explain such things as, "You could get hurt," or "People don't like to have a little kid in their midst asking so many questions." It can go on and on. You can be worn down and frustrated.

On the other hand, should you keep this wonderful curious child busy with some sort of research, there won't be time for all these questions, and you will have one happy camper. Start out by asking the question first. Continue with challenges so that your little one doesn't get bored but rather enjoys the journey.

A little journaling with the promise of privacy is always a good thing for this Capricorn child. You may want to start out with a scrapbook and move on to a journal. See which works best for you.

CAPRICORN - *3:00 a.m. to 4:30 a.m.*
Second House - Scorpio Rising

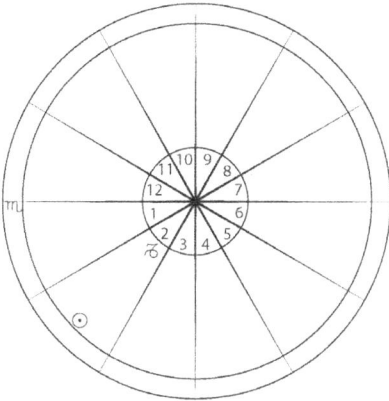

It is important to learn early on that if your child likes a certain item that may belong to someone else that he can earn one LIKE it but not one that belongs to another. There is a big difference. "We will get one like it," makes it easier for your child to understand the difference between yours and mine and that mine will be mine when I get one myself. It is part of fair play and is also a part of understanding possession. You want him/her to keep those things which belong to him/her and not someone else's possessions.

Learning to share is also a challenge for your child. It is a good lesson to teach sharing to your little one at an early age because by the time s/he grows up, it can come naturally.

Another thing your child will enjoy is the privacy of what belongs to him/her. This means that not everything needs to be shared and some things can be kept private. When learning how to differentiate between what to share and what to keep to oneself, your child will be happier and feel better about him/herself.

CAPRICORN - *4:30 a.m. to 5:30 a.m.*
Second House - Sagittarius Rising

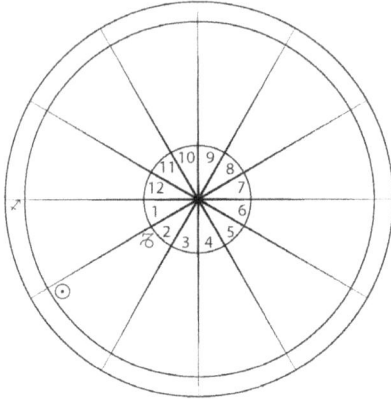

Creative with assets. Your very lucky child always bounces back on his/her feet. This is the child who finds money in his/her pocket when passing an ice cream or candy store. His/her generous nature allows that everything will be shared. Like Lemmings, his/her followers will be everywhere. You may find a few have followed him/her home as well. Be prepared for the entertainment.

S/He may be a bit bossy from time to time, it is his/her nature, however, in the long run, his/her generosity compensates. Usually, it is not a question of who has the prize, but more of let's do this. There is a sense of togetherness with this child.

Your child may go through a gangly stage as s/he learns to grow into his/her body; however, eventually those long leg will stop growing and everyone else will catch up with him/her.

CAPRICORN - *5:30 a.m. to 7:00 a.m.*
First House - Sagittarius Rising

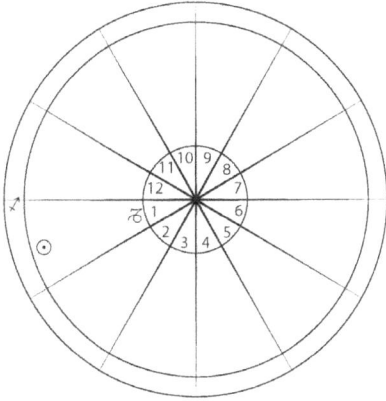

Does not want to conform! Your little Capricorn doesn't like all those rules and yet may aspire to be a politician one day because then s/he can make all the rules. It is a conundrum.

Stalwart in his/her conviction, you will find that your child enjoys justice and the right way to find it. Learn from this child because there is a lot of wisdom that comes from his/her mouth.

Your Capricorn may want to know more about his/her ancestry, and it is a good thing if you know, too. Ask your own parents to write a biography and some of their known family anecdotes and then pass them on to your child. You will bring such joy to this child.

CAPRICORN - *7:00 a.m. to 7:45 a.m.*
First House - Capricorn Rising

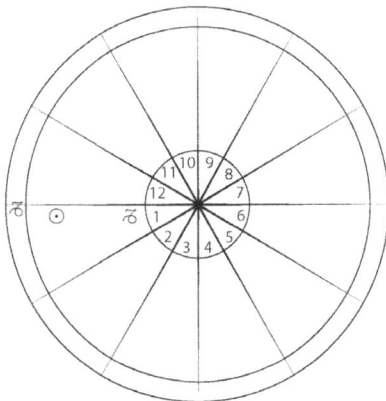

Your child wants to be in charge and in being in charge will keep everything in order. You may find this child a bit bossy from time to time and you will need to remind him/her who the boss really is.

The same thing goes for being judgmental. Your Capricorn may form opinions at an early age and others who do not conform to his/her way of thinking is "wrong." It is possible that your little one is only parroting you or it could be that s/he is influenced elsewhere. You can teach this child to keep an open mind before having an opinion. It is a good idea to teach your child how to weigh options before forming a complete idea or thought.

CAPRICORN - *7:45 a.m. to 8:45 a.m.*
Twelfth House - Capricorn Rising

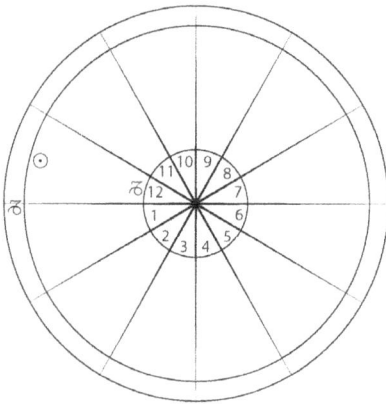

Your Capricorn child is quite proud but doesn't always know how to express it. This may mean that your little one seems insecure. There are times when s/he needs to be reassured that s/he is lovable or even likable. This child enjoys being smart and mature. You will find that s/he may tell you that s/he is very self-reliant.

There may also be times when your child just needs a hug. Don't hold back, just go ahead and hug and allow your little one to cry if necessary.

Your child is sensitive and intuitive. Listen to what s/he has to say because it may be very informative and/or interesting to you. Ask your little one to try to be as specific as possible.

Your little one may be a worrier. Help him/her to learn how to solve problems and watch them go away. Your child wants to change the world and needs tools. Lessons that don't come from schoolbooks but rather those that come from life are the better teachers for him/her.

Remember to show gratitude and praise for jobs well done.

CAPRICORN - *8:45 a.m. to 9:00 a.m.*
Twelfth House - Aquarius Rising

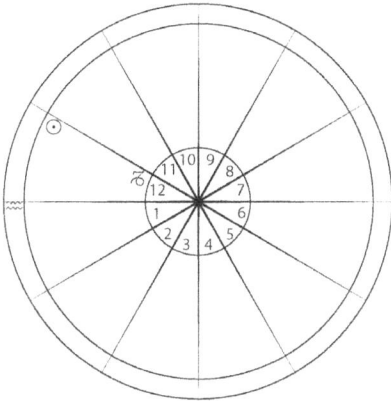

Even though s/he may ask you why there are rules, your child enjoys having them and you will find a rather obedient child. If the rules are too restrictive, you may discover that s/he will do his/her best to push to make those rules and regulations more lenient.

There is a lot of compassion in your child and it simply needs to be tapped. Once shown how to help other people, your little one will be there on the ready to help others with compassion.

Your child will often look for the "better" life and you can teach him/her early on the benefits of the life s/he has. Oriented toward "success" it is up to you to help him/her to define what is "success," such as completing a task satisfactorily. Your little one's self esteem will be elevated, and you will have a happy child.

CAPRICORN - *9:00 a.m. to 10:15 a.m.*
Eleventh House - Aquarius Rising

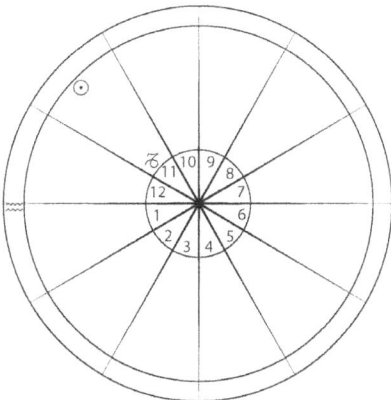

The friendliest child in his/her environment, you will find that this little one could also want to tell everyone else what to do. In many cases, your child will be successful and able to get others to do his/her bidding. However, there will be times when someone will push back. This is the one who will teach your little one the lessons that are necessary for him/her to grow up.

Teach this child the difference between lessons learned and defeat. It is not a good idea to feel defeated because other substitutes may take the place of strength, such as sugar addiction. Your little one wants to stay on top and may feel defeated at times. Those are the times when your wisdom comes to play, and it is up to you to teach your child how to be independent and strong.

If your child complains that something isn't fair, ask him/her to explain what would be fair. Even though s/he wants to and will follow the rules, your Capricorn child may want to change a few to his/her liking. Therefore, it is up to you to explain why certain rules are in place and why they were made.

CAPRICORN - *10:15 a.m. to 10:30 a.m.*
Eleventh House - Pisces Rising

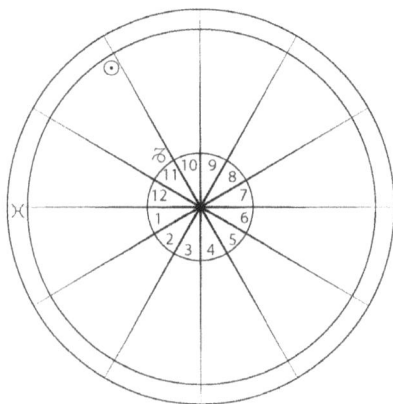

Your child needs to have a good self-image. It is good to teach him/her to find his/her strengths and to display them. A good dancer, and light on his/her feet, you can teach (or give lessons) your Capricorn how to control how s/he moves about. Not only on the dance floor will your little one be able to move about with ease but also on the soccer field or other sports location.

Your little Capricorn is very sensitive and wants to be involved in many things. Help this child to differentiate between those things that can be done and those that will help express him/herself. Eventually, your child will be more centered and able to find his/her way. You want to help your child with direction!

A friend to all, your sensitive child may be bringing home others who may seem less fortunate than s/he is. This is a good thing and compassion can be a great strength for this little one. You can encourage this behavior and help your child to learn to solve problems on his/her own.

CAPRICORN - *10:30 a.m. to 11:15 a.m.*
Tenth House - Pisces Rising

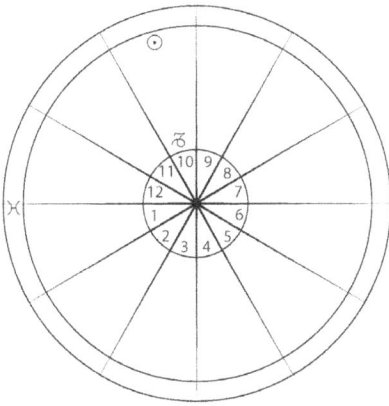

What others think is very important to this child. S/He is quite sensitive about his/her reputation and you can show him/her how to keep a good reputation with compassion and understanding. It is up to your child to learn to understand other people and their needs. S/He needs to learn that not everyone is alike and that each person has his/her own desires in life.

Your child enjoys being in charge and doesn't always feel as though s/he has a handle on it. You can point out his/her strengths, such as compassion and understanding. Your child will then gain more confidence and be able to be the best s/he can be.

You will find that your little "leader" will rule with compassion. You can point out to this child the misfortunes of others and with great sensitivity s/he will react. You may also want to teach the difference between one form of behavior and another, kindness vs. bullying, so that s/he knows the difference.

Being in charge is a lot of responsibility for this child who believes s/he can handle it. However, it is important for your child to be footloose and free of responsibility at an early age. If s/he has the reigns too often, s/he could tend to push others around because s/he is in charge and everyone should do as they're told (by your child). To avoid this, allow your child to be a participant in activities where s/he is NOT in charge. You will have a happier little one who will have greater understanding of others' feelings.

CAPRICORN - *11:15 a.m. to 12:15 p.m.*
Tenth House - Aries Rising

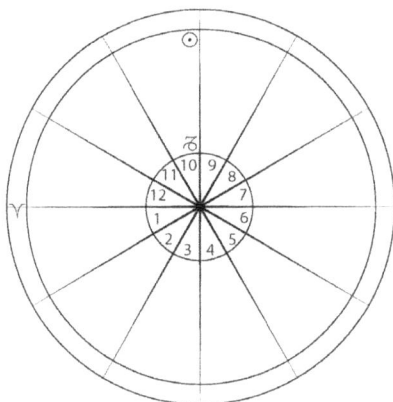

Not only does your entrepreneur want to be the boss but of his/her own company. You will see that at an early age your Capricorn wishes to be in charge. This is hard on you and on your child. S/He feels that s/he is responsible for every success or failure and will take everything to heart.

In spite of the fact that this child can grow into good leadership, the best way for him/her to become a leader is to first allow him/her to learn to obey orders and commands. That way, s/he will understand when telling someone else what to do how it feels to be on the receiving end of such orders. This will build character and save a lot of grief later in life.

Your child could become a very good athlete, and this can definitely be encouraged. The discipline it takes to be a sportsman is inherent in this child and his/her performance will show that you have a star athlete in your home.

Once at home, your little one should be treated like everyone else. The Captain of the team can stay on the play field, and the child should remain a part of the family, following family rules. As your child learns the difference, s/he will become a good leader!

CAPRICORN - *12:15 p.m. to 12:30 p.m.*
Ninth House - Aries Rising

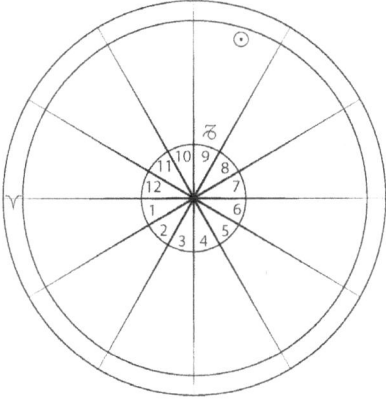

It will be hard to pin down this child. S/He may show an early interest in the military and you can teach the pros and cons of a military career. Learn the reason for this interest and you may find that the desire for travel is great and is an easy way to get there. You may also find that your child wants to find an easy way to grow and mature. All these things happen after the age of nine when your child begins to plateau in his early education.

As time goes on, you may find that your little one has the desire to become a principal of a school or wishes to have a travel agency.

Your little one will choose some interesting careers while looking toward the future. You can introduce your little one to many options and assure him/her that those choices are his/hers to make after puberty. In the meantime, it is important to play with others and learn about all the rules.

A sense of faith or religion is important to this lovely child. You will find a faithful participant in a belief system that is suitable to all of you. In fact, you may be surprised how much your child learns on his/her own and how faithful to your tenets s/he is.

CAPRICORN - *12:30 p.m. to 1:15 p.m.*
Ninth House - Taurus Rising

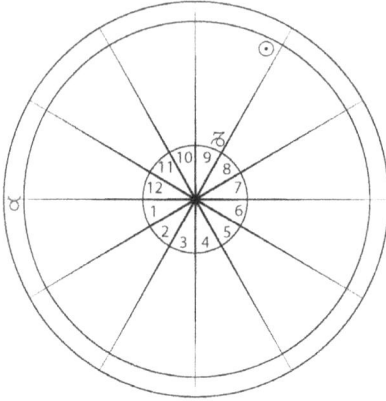

Your practical child has a strong voice. Teach him/her to use it in a practical way, either by giving him voice lessons or helping him/her develop his/her interest in foreign countries, travel and other languages.

You will find that your talented child can mimic others' voices and accents. A little sensitivity will help here so that your child doesn't hurt any feelings.

A love of sweet things may be a problem as time goes on but with a good, healthy diet, you have no worries. Health charts could be put up on a bedroom door which will indicate the benefits of a healthy diet. Then it is up to him/her.

You may also want to teach your child to sing or give lessons to him/her. Music is a wonderful outlet for your disciplined child.

CAPRICORN - *1:15 p.m. to 2:00 p.m.*
Eighth House - Taurus Rising

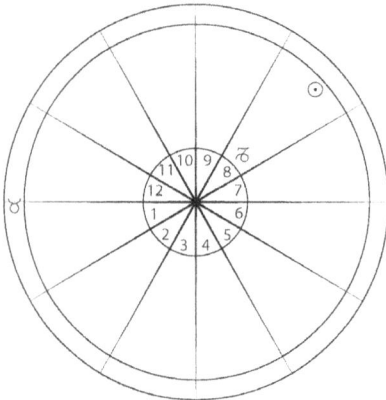

An interest in money begins at an early age. Your little one will look for rewards for his/her efforts, and it is at this time when you can teach value to this impressionable child.

Rewards, such as sweets, should be avoided, as your

little one may tend to over-indulge in those things that are unhealthy for him/her.

You may find that your child looks for ways to "earn" money or rewards. As time goes one, s/he may also be the beneficiary of awards and gifts. Your child may walk around letting you know that s/he is just lucky.

This is a child who will understand the stock market at an early age. All you have to do is show him/her once and then the rest is easy. S/He may ask people to not give him/her gifts but to give money instead so that s/he can invest. Be wise when showing your child how to ask.

CAPRICORN - *2:00 p.m. to 2:45 p.m.*
Eighth House - Gemini Rising

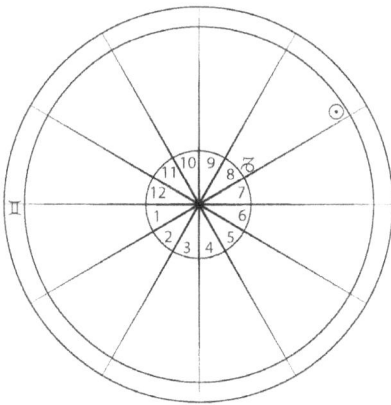

Don't be put off by the mention of death around your Capricorn child. Chances are you will be asked simply for investigative purposes and to satisfy a curiosity.

Your smiling child belies his/her true feelings. Even when unhappy, your little Capricorn will put on a happy face and fool everyone. It is a natural tendency for this child to smile and eventually make everyone around him/her happier.

Capricorn seems usually dour in most circumstances. However, your Capricorn with Gemini rising is different. Even when his/her mood is down, a brave new face and appearance will brighten any room. You will be told what a pleasure it is to have such a lovely and cheerful child in your midst.

You may also find your child using his/her arms and hands a lot to describe things, even though it may be considered an Italian thing to talk with one's hands!

CAPRICORN - *2:45 p.m. to 3:45 p.m.*
Seventh House - Gemini Rising

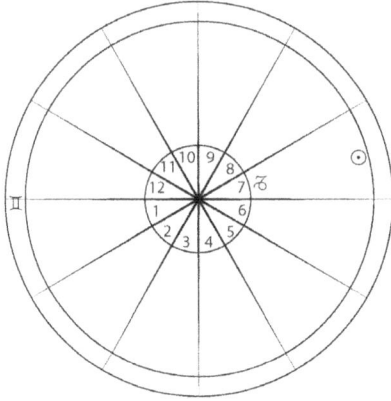

S/He may be sad on the inside, but your Capricorn will put on a brave face and smile for the camera. Although your little one may seem cheerful, it is a good thing to have heart-to-heart talks with him/her to learn if there are any concerns or "things" going on that may cause him/her distress. It may be something like world domination or a friend's injury. Whatever it is, it is up to you to listen, sympathize, and discuss the problems. Your wisdom will be appreciated later.

Your Capricorn child can be introduced to books at an early age. S/He will enjoy reading once taught. You can find yourself reading the same book to him/her over and over, and it is because your child is trying to learn how to read him/herself.

You have an intelligent and eager-to-communicate child. It is good to engage him/her in conversation.

CAPRICORN - *3:45 p.m. to 4:30 p.m.*
Seventh House - Cancer Rising

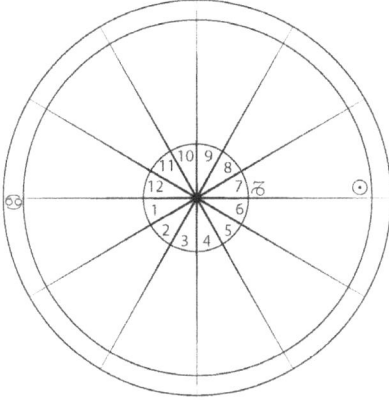

Until s/he finds the right person to do his/her bidding, you may find many new "partners" entering in and out of his/her life. You may also need to teach your little one to not be too bossy when dealing with others.

Sensitive and intuitive, you have a wonderful friend in your little Capricorn. Try to keep from confiding in this child until s/he is older and more able to understand your confidences. Should you tell your problems too soon to this child, you may be somewhat of a burden to your sensitive and understanding child. Your enemies become his/her enemies and sometimes that isn't fair. Your child needs to be able to pick and choose at will, using his/her own intuition.

CAPRICORN- *4:30 P to 6:15 p.m.*
Sixth House - Cancer Rising

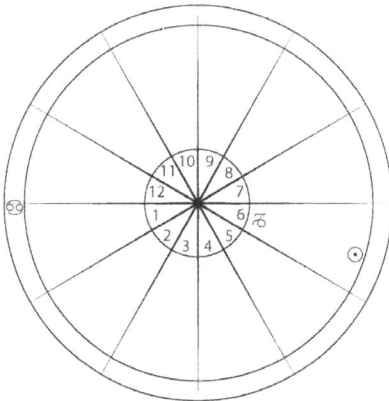

Your child wants to work for him/herself. At an early age, this entrepreneur will appreciate help getting his/her business off the ground. Encouragement is the most important help you can give. You may also want to teach your child how to investigate his/her desired ambition and learn of others who were successful.

You will find a wonderful kitchen apprentice in this child who loves food. It is good to teach nourishing dishes to your child, as s/he may have a sweet tooth. Teach him/her about spices and which ones bring out the most flavor. Perhaps you can learn together!

Your child has a capacity for making others feel better. This may give him/her an element of power and pride and it is well-deserved. This healing gift is greatly appreciated by those who are the recipients. It could be a touch, a hot compress or it could be a soothing word. Whatever the remedy, your child is usually intuitive about it and able to help others feel a sense of well-being.

CAPRICORN - *6:15 p.m. to 7:15 p.m.*
Sixth House - Leo Rising

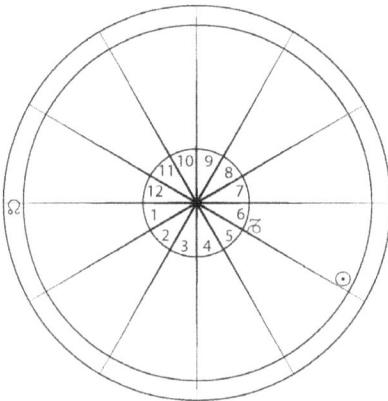

Give jobs to this child that allow mirth. This strong Capricorn wants to work and work hard. Sometimes s/he believes him/herself to be a super-hero. Work that allows your child to shine and be recognized for a job well done is good for your Capricorn's ego and also performance.

The more praise s/he receives, the better the job. You will be pleased with how much hidden talent your little one has.

You will also find that your child is a good student and you can teach him/her almost anything.

Most important, as much help as you get from this little one, remember that s/he is still a child! This child needs love, praise, and appreciation. Your child is loyal to you always and needs to feel a sense of appreciation and loyalty back!

CAPRICORN - *7:15 p.m. to 8:45 p.m.*
Fifth House - Leo Rising

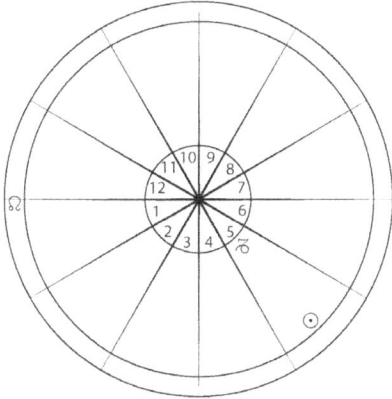

Although your Capricorn wants attention, s/he also wants positive feedback. Do him/her a favor and don't say that his/her performance was good if it wasn't. Although the truth may hurt, constructive criticism goes a long way. You can say things like, "Have you ever thought of doing it this way?" Give alternatives and advice when criticizing this child and you will be appreciated and respected for your opinion.

If you are too critical, your child can bend a deaf ear to you. Don't forget to praise him/her to let your child know his/her actions are appreciated. Your constructive criticism is most respected, and it is important that you don't review without offering comments of suggestion and alternative. Two things happen, one is that your child knows you were paying attention, which is important; and two, your child knows that you care enough to offer suggestions to make his/her performance better. This does not mean that your little one needs to perform on a stage, it means any performance, such as a school activity or test taken. You have an intelligent child who needs at times to be steered in the right direction. You, the person most respected, should be the one to do so.

You also have a wonderful entertainer, who needs appreciation and applause.

CAPRICORN - *8:45 p.m. to 9:30 p.m.*
Fifth House - Virgo Rising

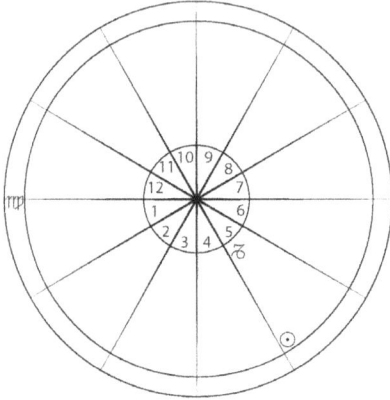

Your little Capricorn feels responsible and is quite good with other children. You can see this when you watch him/her interact with toys, giving them titles and vocabulary. Eventually, these characteristics will continue with other children who are younger.

If your child wants to be the entertainer, s/he must be the star. Teach this little one that for him/her it is better to be the producer or the director.

Practical, almost to a fault, this child is very good behind-the-scenes. Teach him/her how to keep lists and arrange things and events. As a "producer" rather than a performer, your child will excel. Performances, such as music recitals are always good for your proud Capricorn, and s/he is quite studious, but his/her biggest pleasure will be when s/he works from behind the scenes and sets everyone else in gear.

Appreciation from those who have been made "stars" is a good thing for your Capricorn child.

CAPRICORN - *9:30 p.m. to 11:30 p.m.*
Fourth House - Virgo Rising

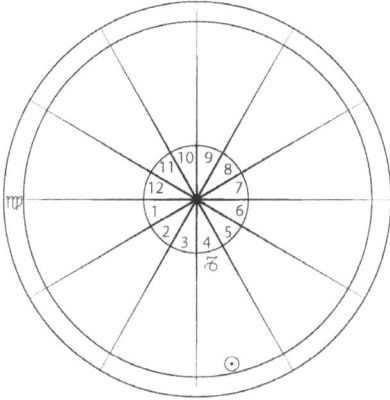

Down to earth and practical. Your little one always wants to be on the go. This Capricorn child is quite intelligent and wants you to recognize him/her.

A real homebody, there are times when it will be difficult to get your little one to move from one spot. If your little Goat happens to have a room to him/herself, you may find that all of life's necessities are there for him/her. Except to come out and eat, this Capricorn child may never want to leave the environment s/he has made for him/herself.

Once your Capricorn sees other worlds to conquer, it will be different. His/her room will be headquarters for future plans, but your explorative Capricorn will want to see more of the world around him/her. As long as s/he knows there is a home someplace, s/he doesn't need to be there anymore.

CAPRICORN - *11:30 p.m. to Midnight*
Fourth House - Libra Rising

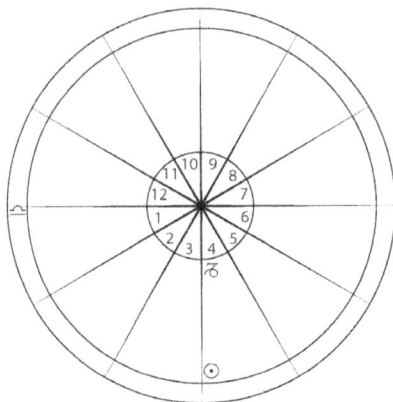

A lovely home is important to your proud child. S/He is usually kind and sweet but don't be surprised if you have been manipulated by this clever angel. S/He will keep you on your toes. Listen carefully and you will know what his/her true desires are. After that, it may be difficult for you to say "no." If you do not wish to cave in and do his/her bidding, the best way is to give a logical reason why. Understanding comes with knowledge and your child is more likely to agree with you when knowing your reasons for any rejection of a desired outcome.

There is no such thing as "because," to your child's understanding. "Because why?" will be the question. Have good reasons for any denial and you will have a child who understands and "gets" it.

Your child may love art and music but may not be an artist him/herself. Instead, with a good eye, s/he may enjoy the surroundings that include these basics.

SUMMARY

It is much easier to raise your child astrologically than it is to just go with the flow. In this time of no discipline, it is easy to see that you can have understanding and that discipline has a different perspective.

My own children did not like that I spoke about my concerns about them on the phone with my friends. That was my form of discipline. I never kept a promise that I did not keep.

If you met my children today, you would find that they are the kindest and most respectful people you ever met. Even as parents, they are kind to their own children. They make me very happy and they love me a lot.

There can be all kinds of activity in your home, no matter how many children you have, from one to thirteen. I know families with one and with thirteen. Each child is different. Embrace the differences and your greatest weapon, which is love!

I hope you have enjoyed *Raising Your Child Astrologically*. I hope you will have the pleasure of Raising Your Child Astrologically!

ABOUT THE AUTHOR

Maria Comfort has been an astrologer since 1970. Initially self-taught, she studied with some of the greatest and best astrologers in the world and has done the horoscopes of many famous and infamous people from around the world.

Maria raised her children astrologically and is proud to say that they grew up anyway!!

Although she takes Astrology seriously (not beginning things when the Moon is Void of Course, etc.), she also takes in other aspects.

As a Virgo, she is very thorough in everything she undertakes and completes everything she begins that is of interest to her.

She has two college degrees, one in Art and one in English Literature. She did not attend college until after she became an Astrologer and also studied Astronomy in school.

Find more great books from Empower Press & GracePoint at
www.gracepointpublishing.com

www.ingramcontent.com/pod-product-compliance
Lightning Source LLC
Chambersburg PA
CBHW072134090426
42739CB00013B/3194